PRAISE FOR

WHAT HAPPENED AT TASSAJARA

"Radiant in memory and moment, free of cliche and lit by laughter and care: here is a living history of monastic Zen practice reborn in the West. Nobody tells it better than David Chadwick, firsthand and fluent in the everyday mind of a community woven of work, word, and breath in wondrous form and emptiness." —**Steven Tipton**, author of *In and Out of Church: The Moral Arc of Spiritual Change in America*

"Even more fascinating than the first book. I love the Stories!" —**Neil Rubenking**, Principal writer, PC Mag

"David Chadwick's writing rhythms meet exactly what he has to say. These Tassajara stories illuminate the early years of Tassajara as a Zen monastery. His precision and specific detail are not only of the people and place but of an era. The weaving in of American cultural evolution is exciting, informative, and true. Only this author, I think, could have reported such a full story." —**Natalie Goldberg**, author of *Writing on Empty*

"Collecting memories of those who were there, David Chadwick brings us to Tassajara Zen Mountain Center deep in California. His voice is concrete, vivid, and imaginative with acute observations. Centering around Shunryū Suzuki Roshi, a quiet, humble, ordinary-looking, authentic, and determined leader, so many different personalities came together and created a magical meditation center, open to guests in summer with mountains, a pristine creek, a hot spring, and gourmet vegetarian food. Fascinating episodes well-narrated." —**Kazuaki Tanahashi**, Japanese calligrapher, Zen teacher; author of *Moon in a Dewdrop*

—ALSO BY—

DAVID CHADWICK

Thank You and OK! An American Zen Failure in Japan

Crooked Cucumber: The Life and Zen Teaching of Shunryu Suzuki

Zen Is Right Here: Teaching Stories and Anecdotes of Shunryu Suzuki

Zen Is Right Now: More Teaching Stories and Anecdotes of Shunryu Suzuki

A Brief History of Tassajara: from Native American Sweat Lodges to Pioneering Zen Monastery (editor)

To Find the Girl from Perth

Color Dreams for To Find the Girl from Perth

The, the Book

Tassajara Stories: A Sort of Memoir/Oral History of the First Zen Buddhist Monastery in the West—The First Year, 1967

WHAT HAPPENED AT TASSAJARA

Stories of the First Zen Buddhist Monastery in the West, 1968—1971

TASSAJARA STORIES VOLUME 2

DAVID CHADWICK

MONKFISH
BOOK PUBLISHING COMPANY
RHINEBECK, NEW YORK

Paperback ISBN 9781966608455
eBook ISBN 9781966608462

Library of Congress Cataloging-in-Publication Data

Names: Chadwick, David, 1945- author
Title: What happened at Tassajara : stories of the first Zen Buddhist monastery in the west, 1968-1971 / David Chadwick.
Description: Rhinbeck : Monkfish Book Publishing Company, 2026. | Series: Tassajara stories ; vol 2
Identifiers: LCCN 2026016587 (print) | LCCN 2026016588 (ebook) | ISBN 9781966608455 paperback | ISBN 9781966608462 ebook
Subjects: LCSH: Suzuki, Shunryū, 1904-1971 | Zen priests--United States | Zen Buddhism--United States--History | Tassajara Zen Mountain Center--United States--History | LCGFT: Biographies
Classification: LCC BQ988.U9 C47 2026 (print) | LCC BQ988.U9 (ebook) | DDC 294.3/927092--dc23/eng/20260507
LC record available at https://lccn.loc.gov/2026016587
LC ebook record available at https://lccn.loc.gov/2026016588

Book and cover design by Colin Rolfe

Monkfish Book Publishing Company
22 East Market Street, Suite 304
Rhinebeck, New York 12572
(845) 876-4861
monkfishpublishing.com

Dedicated to Katrinka McKay, my beloved wife
and mate of twenty-two good years

Look directly at mind and become Buddha.
–Bodhidharma

CONTENTS

PREFACE

The second *Tassajara Stories* book continues the saga from 1968 in Tassajara's second year as the San Francisco Zen Center's monastery founded by Shunryu Suzuki. Tassajara Zen Mountain Center was not like any Buddhist monastery that came before it. There were men and women, married and unmarried couples, and children during the summer guest season. Students came for a period of concentrated Zen practice in a remote environment before returning to practice at Sokoji, Suzuki's temple in San Francisco, or wherever they lived in the outer world.

The primary practice was zazen, Zen meditation. Before Tassajara, the most one could do was to go to Sokoji a couple of times a day to sit with others and chant a brief sutra afterwards, attend an extended Saturday schedule, and go to a couple of lectures a week. At Tassajara, there were two forty-minute zazen periods early in the dark morning, two at night and often one before lunch. We rose at the same time in our cabins and rooms, had meals together in the zendo, the meditation hall, following an ancient ceremonial way of eating called *oryoki*. We'd work together and bathe together with sexes separated in the hot springs water. There were concentrated weeks of zazen called sesshin several times a year and, unlike the sesshin in the city, they continued until bedtime.

The first book covered the story of how the Zen Center came to buy Tassajara Hot Springs, located deep in the Ventana Wilderness of the Los Padres National Forest in Monterey County, California, and continued through 1967, the first year. This book follows me, others, and the evolution of Tassajara through the last four years of Suzuki's life. As with the first book, it also includes a great deal of what had happened and was happening outside of Tassajara—through the stories of what influenced us and how we got there, stories from and about our guests, friends, and neighbors. The action takes place mainly at Tassajara, but not entirely. I include here a paragraph from the preface to the first Tassajara Stories book.

> You may notice there's a lot in these pages that didn't happen at Tassajara. That's because my life, our life at Tassajara, didn't exist in a vacuum. Just like each of us, it had no separate existence. *Shakkei* is a Japanese term referring to a garden's "borrowed scenery." It's the outlying mountains and trees and whatever else one can see from a garden. If we look at what happened at Tassajara as being the garden of the book, then the other content is the shakkei. This borrowed scenery sets Tassajara and our experience in that valley in a broad context that gives background and color to who we were and how we got there, and includes the mountains, the woods, the road, our neighbors, the city, the times, the war, the counterculture, what was happening all around us.

This second *Tassajara Stories* book can stand alone, but there is a lot of introductory and background material on the characters that is in the first book. So ideally it should be read or listened to after reading the first one.

These accounts come from decades of research, remembering, and archiving that evolved along with the books I've written and the labyrinthine cuke.com where so much of the material has been embedded in interviews, podcasts, correspondence, the SFZC's *Wind Bell* publication, and narratives. *Tassajara Stories* meshes with my prior books, especially *Crooked Cucumber,* sometimes covering the same material from another angle or with an updated, elaborated, or corrected telling. Go to cuke.com/ts for notes on all this and much more including an index, glossary, photos, sources, errata, and maps.

I hope you enjoy *Tassajara Stories* as much as I've enjoyed living it and getting these slices of that life down to share with you.

David Chadwick
Sanur, Bali
February 9, 2026

—CHAPTER ONE—

EARLY 1968

The Non Burnables

JANUARY 8

Tassajara was dark and chilly in the late afternoon when festivities began. Richard Baker had driven Shunryu Suzuki in over the rutted road, the front trunk and back seat of his VW bug packed with goodies for the occasion. Due to obligations with the Japanese American congregation at Sokoji, Suzuki hadn't been able to come for New Year's Eve happenings. That was a fairly sedate event—mochi pounding, 108 bells, zazen. At this belated New Year's party eight days later, we ate mochi too—and we drank sake, beer, cider, and plum wine—if you like the sweet stuff. After dinner we continued partaking and entertained each other with stories, poems, songs, and quasi-musical rhythmic clatter.

There was a guitar that a few of us shared, a tuba made from an unused snaking toilet pipe blown into an empty paint can, a washtub bass with heavy string stretched to a broom handle, another contribution from the laundry area—a washboard, a kazoo, some pans from the kitchen struck with large wooden stirring spoons, and a fifty-five gallon drum borrowed from the trash area with the words *Non Burnables* painted indelicately on it. That was our bass drum—and the name of the short-lived band.

We'd been at Tassajara for a year and hadn't had any parties with booze. Actually, we hadn't had any party. The time had come.

Kobun Chino said at temples and monasteries in Japan, the monks have a New Year's bash centered around making and consuming sticky, glutinous, rice mochi—and plenty of sake.

This was not a heavy drinking crowd, but a few of us took advantage of the libations to a greater extent than others. Jane Runk, not a person inclined to excess, missed a good deal of the revelry. She'd sat next to Suzuki during dinner. He kept filling her sake cup when it was empty and she dutifully imbibed her teacher's offerings. "I'm dizzy," she said as the plates were cleared. "I don't feel so good."

"Maybe you shouldn't drink so much," Suzuki said.

"But you ... you ... " she blurted out while standing up, then lurching forward against the table. Richard helped her to her room.

I sat down in her empty chair. "Kobun," I said. "How does one stop drinking when drinking with Japanese? You and Suzuki Roshi have been filling other people's sake cups every chance you got."

"We are obligated to serve you," he said. "When you don't want more, you must leave your cup full—like Suzuki Roshi's."

"Oh, thanks for the explanation," I said, reached over to Suzuki's full sake cup and downed it. He feigned disapproval. I reached for the sake bottle, refilled the cup, put it back in front of him, and bowed.

The walls of the dining room's crackling cast iron stove were showing faint spots of red, the stovepipe the same at its base. It was maxed out. That was enough to take the chill out of the air which must have descended into the thirties outside as we fell into darkness.

The entertainment was morphing from one surrealistic moment to another. Niels Holm belted out free-associated Danish poetry with a background of the assembled percussion and cacophony. "What did that mean?" I asked when he was done. "There are cows in my mother's kitchen," he answered.

For a while Suzuki moved a piece of cardboard up and down blocking and unblocking the glow of an Aladdin lamp, the strobe light of the show. It was so sweet and uncharacteristic to see him play along with a goofy scene like this. There was sporadic improvisational dancing that continued as Kobun Chino sang a traditional Japanese song about sake.

It was good to be back. The second two-month practice period would begin in mid-February. Till then we'd have more work and sleep and less zazen. Either schedule was fine with me. Bob Halpern and I resumed adding an untimed period of sitting after evening zazen, a practice that sometimes included a trip to the baths, steam room, and a dip in the frigid creek—at times a light snack before retiring. All was rolling along splendidly. Then one day Peter Schneider, the director, tapped me on the shoulder after lunch at the picnic tables. "We're going to start rotating people," he said.

City Exile FEBRUARY

Bob and I each had a room in one of the railroad flats across from Sokoji. They were called that because there was a long hall down to the kitchen with rooms on one side like a sleeping car in a train. The charge for a room was fifty dollars a month—if one could afford it. They were managed by Claude Dalenberg. How fitting. He'd lived in the communal East-West and Hyphen Houses of the Beats in that same neighborhood, an era which carried into Suzuki's early years at Sokoji. He had an informal management function back then too.

By taking this turn in the city, we were allowing other worthy students to attend the sixty-day practice period at Tassajara, a mandatory selfless gesture. I knew they also wanted to give Tassajara a break from us. But the problem was us together. Why not just send one of us to the city? We were free to return in mid-April for the spring interim. Actually, Peter had told me to be sure to get back as soon as the practice period was over to get the dining room ready for the guest season.

Bob and I knew the city would offer temptations to lure us from pure practice, so we vowed to attend every zazen. But we didn't vow *not* to do anything. We saw *Cool Hand Luke* and *The Graduate* our first night in the city, then walked around town till midnight. We didn't get drunk or stoned so that was good. Bob didn't have those urges. Thus, he was a good influence on me. I did duck into a bar and got a shot of Irish whiskey though. The next morning in zazen we were like those nodding bobble birds that dip water.

We were determined to eat pure food. We walked to the grocery store in Japantown and bought brown rice, miso, and vegetables. We gathered some mismatched bowls and ate breakfast oryoki style while sitting on zafus—not in the apartment's communal kitchen and dining area, but in my room. His was too messy. We chanted the whole long meal chant in English as that's what we chanted during breakfast at Tassajara.

To Golden Gate Park and the Haight, free Digger food for lunch, back in time for five o'clock zazen and service, then brown rice, miso soup, and bok choy for dinner. No chant for dinner as it's the medicinal meal. We saw *Bonnie and Clyde* and then decided to make an exception to our dietary regimen and got hamburgers and milkshakes. We returned to the apartment building but were too buzzed to sleep so we sat zazen. Then we went out and got some ice cream at an all-night diner. Falling over the next morning in zazen. Thus the days progressed.

A Rehearsal

Bob went to extremes to be near Suzuki. "I stick to him like a glove," he said. Bob would sit as close to Suzuki as he could. Except for Richard Baker's first zafu on the right side, seats were not assigned as they were at Tassajara. Bob would get to the zendo earlier to get the closest seat. One problem with Bob sitting in front of Suzuki was that he was just about always sleepy in zazen, more so than I was because I'd get more sleep at night. Suzuki would get up during the periods and go around with his teacher's stick correcting postures and giving those nodding two quick whacks on each shoulder—after notifying them by first resting the stick on the right side. Bob would straighten up before Suzuki got to him.

One day Bob was nodding so bad that Suzuki got up just for him. He straightened up, so Suzuki went back. That continued a few times till Suzuki just stayed right behind Bob and hit him as soon as he started nodding. Suzuki stayed there, continuing to hit him harder and harder each time he fell asleep until the period was over.

Bob asked Suzuki if what we eat is important. Suzuki, who was not eager to hear food fetish questions, said, "Yes, but it's more important how you sleep and it's best not to read before going to bed." I assumed Suzuki thought Bob must be staying up late reading, and he often did just that after we'd returned from our evening's gallivanting. Bob, however, did not think of this as a suggestion for him, but as a rule that should apply to all humankind. So he chastised me when he found me sitting up reading at night. I told him that indeed I was going to be lying down and sleeping soon, but Suzuki had told him not to read in bed, and I didn't have a bed. None of us had beds. We used sleeping bags, futons, and tatami or a pad on the floor or just on the unpadded floor. He said I didn't understand the spirit of the rule.

I found Bob in the bathroom bowing to himself in the mirror. "Is that a new practice that Roshi suggested for you?" I asked.

"I'm rehearsing the bow we do at the door with Roshi on the way out of the zendo," he said.

Fillmore Auditorium

On a day in late March, after zazen and evening service, a group of us walked to the Fillmore Auditorium to hear Albert King. I went off by myself and sat next to a wall near the front where I could better see the blues great and his backup band. I got into a zone following the notes and movements of the musicians, the audience dancing, gyrating. After a while my mind carried me back twelve months to the same place—but to a far different event.

Flowers were handed to us as we entered. Dark, long smoking incense sticks stuck in oranges filled the air with a sweet, spicy pungency. Hundreds of us sat quietly on rugs spread out across the floor or on chairs circling the rugs. The room became so quiet we could hear the rain on the roof.

Gary Snyder walked in wearing light cotton clothes, beads, rings on his fingers and ears. He sat on a rug on the stage in half lotus. After some moments of silence, he struck two wooden clappers together and began to read—and would continue to read nine sections of his evolving epic poem, *Mountains and Rivers Without End*. As he read, the Mahalila Mandalagraphers projected evolving mandalas and evocative images on the screen behind him.

His reading began, "I was a girl standing by the roadside ..." while the screen showed a girl's face that went through kaleidoscopic changes. The poem and the imagery wended on for two hours of coyote, logging truck, the Bodhi Tree, a Japanese garden, Shiva and Parvati, the hellish and the celestial.

The poster for that event flashed in my mind's eye—black with red line art surrounding a circular black-and-white photo I took to be Snyder bottle-feeding a coyote, at the core of a mandala framed by a scalloped floral pattern nestled in the belly of a fox, its paws forming mudras. The message blended into the whole with stylized lettering: "Zen Benefit, $2 donation, *Mountains and Rivers Without End*."

And now traces of the poem, the poster, and the mandalagrapher's images, swirled about, joining Albert King and those gathered at the Fillmore one year later. There was room for everything—concrete and imagined in this vast space. I rocked side to side with eyes closed.

Someone tugged on my shoulder. The show was over—but echoes of it all played on as we walked home in the rain.

*ZEN BENEFIT
GARY SNYDER : poetry
with MAHALILA MANDALAGRAPHY
MOUNTAINS AND RIVERS WITHOUT END
WED. • MAR. 15 • 8PM •
TICKETS AT DOOR $2.00 DONATION
FILLMORE AUD.
* FOR ZEN MOUNTAIN CENTER

Got Wheels

I bought a ten-year-old Volvo from a guy in the East Bay who said he was Ed Fox. "Ed the Fox," he said. "Ring a bell?" Turned out I had heard about him. He'd stowed away on a flight from Australia to L.A. and made the headlines because he'd survived.

Now that I had a car, Bob and I could be on call to drive Suzuki or his wife Mitsu wherever they wanted to go. We did a lot of errands for Yvonne Rand and Gloria Coonan in the office. Whatever was wanted, we were on call. And people could borrow it. We all put so much into making Zen Center thrive. We called ourselves slave labor. True, but we were slaves for each other.

One Monday Bob and I drove Suzuki to Mill Valley to give a talk to Bill Kwong's sitting group that met weekly at the Altamont Recreation Center. Afterwards we went to Kwong's home to have breakfast with Bill, Laura, and their three young boys. It was more like a tea ceremony than a meal though. We were served a dollop of porridge in a tiny bowl, a small bowl of miso soup, a few pickles, then a dainty cup of green tea. An austere and peaceful meal. When we left, Suzuki was amenable to a suggestion that we augment the breakfast we just consumed. So we drove to a pancake house where we drank cups of coffee and ate piles of pancakes. On the way back to Sokoji, in answer to some probing question Bob had asked, Suzuki said, "Practicing Zen is hard. It's at least as hard as quitting smoking." Bob threw his cigarette out the window and dramatically pretended to throw the pack out.

Mitsu told us she was always happy to have Bob or me drive Suzuki instead of Richard because when she'd been in the car, he drove too fast. Bob saw Richard as a rival and made sure she understood we were always ready to drop what we were doing to drive her husband—including to Tassajara. And he added, "The last time I was in a car with Richard, he drove a hundred miles an hour."

Saving the Suzukis APRIL 4

Martin Luther King, Jr. was assassinated. I was so upset. I'd become aware of and inspired by King in 1963 during my brief experience of college and some involvement with the civil rights movement the following year. I stayed in my room and looked out the window for hours. I could hear other students crying, people on the street, everywhere, talking, sharing, angry. Things were heating up three blocks away on Fillmore Street. There were crowds of angry people in the streets, storefront windows getting broken.

Bob and I got worked up worrying that a full-scale riot would ensue and that it might spread. We ran over to Sokoji, went upstairs, and found Suzuki in his office. I called Mitsu over from the kitchen. We told them what was happening and insisted they let us get them out quickly to safety.

Suzuki responded, "I think I'll take a walk down to the Fillmore and see what is happening there. I'm not afraid of Black people. They like me. They like to reach down and put a finger on my bald head." He demonstrated by placing an index finger on his head and smiling. "I think I'll go there now."

"No, no, no, no please don't! Please, please, please don't!" we begged. Finally, we ended up with a compromise. He and Mitsu would stay there at the temple and we'd go away. The commotion in the Fillmore subsided. But sadness and anger from the assassination of Dr. King would long linger in us and in the soul of America.

Religious Zeal

In the San Francisco airport, Hare Krishna devotees would offer a whole big color copy of the Bhagavad-Gita and suggest a donation. They were more popular in the Panhandle of Golden Gate Park where they dished out great free vegetarian meals on Sundays and danced around chanting. Moonies would bestow flowers at the airport, some of them bringing in as much as seventy grand a year for the Unification Church. The Soka Gakkai folks would ask passersby on Market Street if they'd like a free meal. Bob and I received such an offer one day. Bob said, "Sure." I wasn't so keen on it, but it was free food, so there we went.

Soka Gakkai were evangelical Nichiren Buddhists, Nichiren Shoshu, or the true sect of Nichiren. They were the largest sect of Buddhism in America, and unlike Zen, Vipassana, and Tibetan, attracted minorities and the poor. Their organization had been actively campaigning for world peace since World War II. And they were the only Buddhists I knew of who said all other Buddhists were heretics.

Inside there were a lot of people, mainly young, being ever so nice to us. Attractive young Japanese women sat near us and made sure we were happy with the meal which wasn't bad. Then we were asked to join them in an auditorium.

The meeting mainly consisted of everyone chanting the Gohonzon—*Namu Myoho Renge Kyo*—homage to the Lotus Sutra. It was explained to us that all we needed to do was to chant that and not only would we attain Buddhahood, but we would get whatever we wished like a new car. "Good," I said, "I'd like a new car."

So we chanted with about a hundred others. Bob got into it. After a while he was chanting feverishly. I could tell that the regulars there were pleased at what appeared to be a new convert. But when their chanting came to an end, Bob didn't stop. Lots of smiles around the room appreciating his enthusiasm. He was a man possessed. He went to the aisle and kneeled, "homage to the Lotus Sutra" forcefully erupting from him, spittle spraying as he walked on his knees reverently toward the altar. "*Namu Myoho renge kyo! Namu Myoho renge kyo! Namu Myoho renge kyo! Namu Myoho renge kyo!*"

The joy of the assembly in Bob's devotion began to wane. There were other items on the agenda. But he wouldn't stop. Eventually they gave up and four guys carried him out still chanting like a man in a trance. He kept chanting lying on the sidewalk, pedestrians looking curiously at him as they walked by. Finally, he stopped, looked up at me from the pavement, winked and said, "I'm saved."

State of Mind

As it was with many students, Bob and I wore cheap *zoris,* the traditional flat sandals. We preferred wearing ones that were short so that the toes stuck a tiny bit over the edge. Almost anything we did he would ascribe a dharmic or health related reason. The reason for the short zoris was mindfulness. As a result, we frequently had bloody toes—mainly the big one—from stubbing them on protrusions. That was especially so at Tassajara where there was so much uneven rockiness. Bob said we could know our state of mind by looking at our feet.

One day in the city on a shopping trip for several of the Zennie apartments, we drove to the Oakland Food Mill. Then we went to Telegraph Avenue to enjoy the scene with hippies and students. Bob went barefoot and shirtless, saying, "Let's go with the flow, be natural." While strutting around thus, he stepped on a piece of glass from a broken bottle of cheap wine that lay next to a reclining figure. It was a bad cut. Lots of blood. We went to a clinic where they sewed him up. I looked at his bandaged foot and asked, "What's your state of mind now, Bob?"

Monterey Temple

One morning after zazen and service, Mitsu asked if I'd drive Suzuki and Katagiri to the Monterey Zen Temple. She gave me the address and said her husband knew how to get there. Tim Burkett said he drove Suzuki there once. Suzuki told Tim he'd tell him when to get off the freeway. As they approached Monterey, Suzuki was sound asleep and Tim got nervous. Then, at about a hundred yards before an exit, Suzuki said, "This one." I had maps in the car and figured out the route as a backup plan. Suzuki did wake up before the exit though—as he had with Tim.

The Monterey Zendo was in the home of Kisan Ueno, a Soto Zen priest who few at Zen Center were aware of. He'd founded the Monterey Zen Temple in 1963. Ueno greeted us at the front door.

Addressing him as Rev. Ueno, which is what he used, I told him we'd met before at the opening of Tassajara. Once inside I realized this was a meeting of Soto Zen priests. The Bishop was there, and Maezumi, Kazumitsu Kato, and some others who I didn't recognize.

There was a Caucasian man in robes. I introduced myself and he said he was Daino Doki MacDonough Roshi. He invited me to come to Stockton to visit his Middlebar Monastery. Aha—he was John's teacher before John went to the Bishop's lair at Zenshuji in L.A. and was given the seductive Diamond Koan. He'd also been Dan Welch's first teacher.

Dan had initially met Suzuki in 1963 when MacDonough asked him to look Suzuki up while he was in San Francisco and pass on his regards. I asked Dan about MacDonough once, and he said he didn't want to talk about it. That was close to John's take on MacDonough, too. MacDonough sure looked out of place at this meeting. From what I saw of him greeting the other priests, I don't think he knew much Japanese which is what the others would be speaking. The meeting was about to begin. I said hello to Maezumi and the Bishop and went off to visit friends. I returned at four in the afternoon to gather my rides and return to Bush Street.

Driving back, Suzuki and Katagiri wouldn't talk about MacDonough either. I got the feeling they were coming from the same attitude my father had when he said, "If you can't say anything good about somebody, don't say anything."

Yvonne said something to me akin to my father's aphorism when I told her no one would dish dirt on MacDonough. "Well," she said. "ninety-nine percent of what we say about others, is about ourselves."

Secret Dragon

Bob and I would offer to help Yvonne in the office. She'd get us doing boring stuff and, after a moment, he'd take a potty break and look for more rewarding things to do, like mainly drive Suzuki somewhere or make up a reason to bother him. One day he said that he'd been upstairs helping Suzuki to get into the Sokoji attic to check out the pigeons that were cooing up there—especially during mating season. It was a large old building with a huge attic. The entrance to the attic was in the high ceiling above the long kitchen table. Bob thought the way to get there was to put a chair on the table. He said he turned to get a chair and when he turned around, Suzuki was already up there sticking his head down. Bob could not see how Suzuki got there. Suzuki said to Bob that instead of manifesting as a big dragon, he had a little dragon in his kimono that people couldn't see. "Yeah," Bob said, "he had a secret dragon that must have helped him to fly up to the ceiling."

Spring Shosan MID-APRIL

Bob and I drove down to Tassajara to attend the shosan question and answer ceremony on the last day of sesshin. We didn't have permission but decided if we made no noise, entered after everyone else, and sat in the back, no one would disrupt things by telling us to leave—and we might not even be noticed. Our plan was to exit as soon as Suzuki's closing statement was done and be on our way up the road about the time everyone was exiting the zendo. Ed Brown walked in late from the kitchen and jerked his head a little when he saw us but just raised his eyebrows and went to his seat.

Suzuki started off the ceremony by telling a story.

> A monk asked Hyakujo: "Has anything special happened in this temple?"
> Hyakujo said: "I have been sitting on this mountain."
> The monk respectfully bowed to Hyakujo. Hyakujo then gave him a big slap.

Then, he said, "This morning I talked about Nansen's *Everyday mind is dao*—and then there's something special. If you understand what's special and what's common, then come discuss this point with me."

Phillip Wilson, the shuso, head monk, said something in Japanese and asked what the meaning of it was in everyday life.

Suzuki answered, "*Kuchu issen seki?* That can be something special or something common. If you hang those ideas up though, then they're nothing but stones hanging in the air. Do you understand? What is the practice without it being hung up by itself?"

Phillip said, "Thank you very much," and started to move on when Suzuki added, "Without answer is the best answer."

I didn't understand the Japanese, but I knew what this was about, because Suzuki had a scroll of a sumi painting that he said meant stones hanging in the air, and indeed it was a painting his teacher Ian Kishizawa gave him of stones in the air. He said it meant don't create unnecessary problems by obsessing pointlessly over stuff that isn't real. Or, as he indicated to Phillip, don't get hung up on what you're thinking.

The next student asked Suzuki to say something about echo. Suzuki asked if he meant *eko*, the brief chant done by the priest at the end of a sutra, dedicating the merit to all sentient beings. No, the student didn't mean that. "Echo the phenomenon," he said. Suzuki didn't catch that and asked if he meant Eko the Chinese master. The student explained further and Suzuki, finally getting it, said that everything was the echo of your mind or your activity.

A student asked him how being in a sesshin can be practicing the Middle Way. Suzuki said that when you forget about the Middle Way, you're practicing the Middle Way.

A student said the hardest thing to do in Buddhism is not to be attached to anything and asked why is that? Suzuki said it's impossible not to attach to anything and that true non-attachment is to be free from ideas of attachment and non-attachment, that they're two sides of the same coin.

Ed Brown said that Buddhist practice was no practice and asked if there was any practice that wasn't Buddhist. Suzuki said that if it's based on a dualistic idea, it's not Buddhist practice. He said there's no alternative to sitting alone in the center of the universe, on the top of the mountain.

A student said Suzuki always asked, "Did you understand?" and inquired what he meant by that. Suzuki said he meant, "Do you accept it?" And then he added, "Good question."

A student said he was drowning in the ocean and asked if he'll wake up and find it's a dream. Suzuki asked would he rather be on dry land and the student said he didn't know. Suzuki suggested it's better to be in the ocean with great depth and difficulty than on dry land where there's not much hope and told him he'd learn to manage it.

A student said that hearing the stream and feeling it flowing within her makes tears flow from her eyes. Suzuki said that's because she's new to practice and the feeling is unusual for her and that she'd get accustomed to it.

Tim Burkett said he had no question. Suzuki said: "No question? Oh, all right. I hope you can continue your practice in that way. You should think more when you have a problem. But right now you are going on a big freeway. Very good."

A student asked how we were to understand the bodhisattva's vow to save all beings. Suzuki said it looks impossible, but we should continue our practice without thinking about possibility or impossibility, that it expresses our inmost nature.

A student said she wondered if her zazen was true zazen. Suzuki told her not to doubt her zazen, just get up in the morning and join us. Don't think about it—that is true zazen.

A student asked, "Why are we you?" He said, "Why are you me?"

"Yes, why are we you?" she asked again.

He said, "I don't know. Ask yourself."

Richard Baker was last. He pointed out that a lot of Suzuki's answers were not to do anything or to forget about it. He thought that might be OK with us but doesn't seem helpful to others, too much like the poem that says that the shadow of bamboo doesn't disturb the dust on the stairs. Suzuki said, "Yeah," and laughed. Richard added that grass doesn't always grow by itself. Suzuki said, "Uh huh," and Richard asked, "What do you think?"

Suzuki spent a while commenting on this. What I got out of it was he said of course we should take care of the grass and be disturbed by the dust but still appreciate the shadow on it. He said this is a point that many Zen masters had difficulty with. It wasn't a matter of being successful but how you work on it. He said it's a subtle point and that no one but you can work on it. Actually, he said, "No one but you cannot work on it," but I was used to him using double negatives. Dan had explained to me that, in Japanese, double negatives were still negative.

Suzuki told Richard, "As your teacher, I am trying to help you in various ways, but at the same time I know I cannot help you." He laughed. "As a disciple and teacher, this kind of effort should always be continuing. That is why I am trying pretty hard with other students. I appreciate your effort and your way of working on your own problem. This is very much true with everybody, but we should make more effort to know how to work on ourselves, how to help ourselves, how to take care of our practice. This is the most important point. So let's make more effort on this point. Each one of you are making a pretty good effort on this point, but not enough in comparison to our teachers and masters who attained perfect enlightenment."

Suzuki made a closing statement which ended with, "So I should like to be a good friend and good teacher of each one of you. Thank you very much."

A Realization

A few days after the Shosan ceremony, the practice period was over and I found myself going down Tony's Boulevard, as an old-timer had called that perilous steep road.

I looked forward to soaking in the hot springs water, to walking in the woods and up and down creek, but what did it, what filled me with pure joy, I hadn't expected—getting settled on my zafu and being still and quiet with my fellow students in the Tassajara zendo. The first few days back, I could physically feel myself winding down from two months in the city. The sensory inputs back there were composed of smoke and celluloid, wheels and cash registers, of cement and iron.

Bob Halpern was now an iron worker building high rises. It frightened me to think about it. He threw himself into it. Our vacations were over.

Back to four-and-nine days, days with a four or nine in their date. Kobun Chino called them *shikunichi,* which literally means four-nine day. Those were our mainly days off. Just one zazen in the morning followed by a briefer service and after the oryoki breakfast we were free till evening service and a special meal together in the dining room. That was every five days except at the end of the month they became further apart though not at the end of February.

I got a room in the dorm, the last one on the right. I lobbied Peter for it when I left in February. There was a tatami on the floor by the window. When I wasn't getting the dining room ready for the guest season, I did a bit of renovation. A few days later there was a walled-in frame beneath the tatami, so I could lift it and store stuff under it—like my backpack. I could sit on it and see out the window to the courtyard below with its arbor, and creek yet further down. At night I could go to sleep with the moon in my eye.

After firewatch and lights out one night, I walked down the steps of the dorm and along the path past the Pine and Stone Rooms. I stood on the bridge to the baths looking down at what I could see of the creek, still fairly full flowing from the spring rains runoff. My thoughts were full of good intentions, resolution to follow the schedule and do my duty as mindfully as I could. To drive it deeper, I recited the "Bodhisattva's Vow."

> Sentient beings are numberless, I vow to save them.
> Delusions are inexhaustible, I vow to end them.
> Dharma gates are boundless, I vow to enter them.
> The Buddha way is unsurpassable, I vow to realize it.

Walking through the opening to the hot plunge, what little visibility there had been was no more. A tinge of fear shot through me. I returned to the Vow. As I stepped into the hot water, I thought, *I will continue this vow forever.* I thought it with force, as if it were a weapon against fear, expressing *I will follow the vow. I will meet the moment with the courage of the vow.* Then, as I stepped down further and the hot sulfurous water rose to my belly, I suddenly realized, deeply, not conceptually—I will not determine—I will find out—all I can do is watch as this, whatever it is, unfolds.

Spirit Worlds

Phillip Wilson had just returned from three days hiking in the woods and was telling a bunch of us around the coffee machine how he'd become afraid while he was alone in the dark. Big fearless Phillip afraid of the dark. I asked Phillip if he was worried about wild boar or mountain lions? No, he said he could deal with them. It was the spirits of thousands of years of Indians. He could sense them and some of them were angry at white people for destroying their way of life. The Spanish had rounded up the local Indians and taken them to the Carmel Mission. Maybe they were safer in the mission. Putsy the ranger said that up to the turn of the century, Indians would be found in that wilderness hanging from trees.

Phillip had opened up so that the Indian spirits could get in and that scared him. He realized he was safe though because he was part Shawnee.

"At Eiheiji," he said, referring to the great Soto Zen temple, "we had a celebration where we would come disguised as different things. I came as an Indian. They had me get up and do an Indian dance.

"I could see the spirit world of Eiheiji. Not the Buddha world. I also saw the spirits of generations of monks in the polished floors of Eiheiji. It was a ghost world. One time I went to the *tosu*, the toilet, like at one o'clock in the morning, and I saw a big white glowing ball about a foot in diameter with hair standing up straight, like a porcupine. It was alive. I had never seen a creature like that before. They had flying squirrels. They caught them and kept them for a while and let them go. But this thing was alive and had its own light. I pinched myself. I started to walk toward it. Something said, 'Danger.' I backed up. I said to myself, if it's still here after I take a pee, I'm going to go over and introduce myself. I came back and it was gone."

Phillip said he told Kobun Chino back then about what he saw and Kobun said he'd never seen anything like that. I told Phillip I wouldn't call that glowing ball a ghost. It's more like a spirit. He said nobody had ever said that and asked what type of spirit. I said I had no idea.

"Roshi's not a white man," Phillip said. "He's not an Indian. He doesn't know the mentality that went on here and he doesn't need it. And he always put me down for doing the Indian thing. I was always bringing up the Indian question. So he'd make fun of me. I was telling him about this Indian I met and this and that. So he said, 'I am not Indian. I am Japanese.' Then he looked out at the rocks, and said, 'That's Indian.' And those rocks became red. The iron in the Tassajara rocks began to stand out. And the qualities of the rocks changed. I don't know if you can understand that, but something took place with the Indian thing.

"The whole thing started because I had a relationship with one of the Chinese girls at Zen Center—not a sexual relationship, a friendship. One of the Wong girls. She took me to an Indian Powwow. There I met some Sioux, some young bucks. You know how they get hot-blooded? Their father was the chief. He had a huge gut. One of them came up to me and said, 'Can you have yourself cut and pierced and hanged from a pole? Can you be like us? Can you be a real man?' I saw all this hot blood and I said, 'God, that hot blood's great.' But I said, 'I probably could but I prefer not to. I've already had my baptism as a Buddhist. So I feel that I am a man. And I've been through a lot of other things that make me a man. So I feel like I'm just as much a man as you are. Although I do sympathize with you, and I like to share the feeling of it with you.'"

When Phillip said he'd been through other things that made him a man, I thought of his experience as a right guard on the Stanford football team's starting line. "In the third quarter," he said, "my body would begin to complain a lot. So I became a ghost. I would move my body and it would be like I was floating in the field.

My body would be trying to stay up with me. The fourth quarter I would be floating above the game and would just know where to go. I knew where everyone was going. After the game they'd put me in the hospital, and it would take three days to recuperate. I did that every week. I kicked the shit out of everybody."

When he wasn't at Tassajara, Phillip lived with his wife J.J. above the Katagiris and across the street from Sokoji. He was close to Dainin Katagiri's wife Tomoe and their boys. He bought a toy bow and arrow for their son Yasuhiko. "Reverend Katagiri refused it," he said. "He didn't want anything to do with the Indian thing and said, 'You have to ask me if I want that gift. You don't just give it. You can't do that.'"

Phillip thought that was strange because Katagiri would get into Phillip's big red truck without asking and say he wanted to drive it.

Phillip got that truck from money he made being in *Planet of the Apes*. At Stanford, Phillip was friends with Dick Zanuck, son of film producer Darryl Zanuck. "He came into the gambling den we had going there," Phillip said, "and thought because he was so rich from a powerful family, he could take it over. He was like a semi-gangster. His father was too. Anyway, I told him if he didn't like it, he could get out. He liked that because nobody stood up to him. Zanuck invited his Stanford buddies to go to Palm Springs with him for the weekend. Then he got in a fight. They attacked him and I came in. I saved his life and got all cut up. So there was some bonding going on there."

As Phillip told that story, I got an image of the Hulk from the old comic book bursting out of Bruce Banner in an unstoppable rage.

Through his relationship with Zanuck, Phillip got a role as Sergeant of the Apes in the movie *Planet of the Apes* which had just hit the theaters in March 1968. Phillip was built like a gorilla to begin with, and he said that he actually became an ape when he was all made up for his role. He had that side, but he often talked in sweet childlike tones. He was telling me all this while we were sipping green tea from delicate little Japanese teacups.

Phillip was on a roll. "A friend of mine who's Indian," he said, "took me out along Old Woman Road near Joshua Tree National Park. We went up a dry creek bed for about five miles and came to this big wash. He had brought along his wife and a .22. He was shooting his .22 and stuff. He and his wife were arguing. Finally we got to this stone. Up in the center of it was a part of the rock sticking out, like a serpent going back and forth.

"He said, 'Phillip, I get some very strange vibes from that. What do you think about it?' I said I didn't feel anything. He said to get closer. That was my undoing. I climbed up on the rock, on the ledge where the serpent thing was. This was about ten feet off the ground. I said, 'This has a funny carving in it.' I put my hand on it, and it began to vibrate. I turned around. My friend was in a heated argument with his wife. This thing kept vibrating. Then the whole rock broke open. It was like looking through a television set into another land. It looked just like this land only a little different. Behind I could see mountains and terrain and I was in a gully with rocks all the way around. I could see back. It was a little green, but still desert. This Indian walked over the knoll. He came about twenty feet away from my television screen and squatted down on his haunches. We talked telepathically. This guy said, 'I am a relative of yours from a long time ago. I've come here to give you some of my magic.' He proceeded to give me his magic. I don't know what it was. It was some kind of power thing. This must have gone on for about five minutes. I don't know. It was timeless. And all the while this rock was going *voo-voo-voo*. When he went back over the knoll, I took my hand away and the *voo-voo*ing stopped. And they were still arguing. I asked them, 'Did you guys see anything?' They said, 'What?' I was drained of energy. I just went over on the other side of the rock and sat down in the shade. I'd been used up. Going back to the car was like, the party's over."

I asked Phillip if he ever had any experiences along those lines with Suzuki. He said, "No, all these phenomena I've gotten through the Indian side." He paused. "Except at my shuso ceremony," which had taken place just a month before.

"The only time I experienced that power in Zen was when I picked up the staff for the shuso ceremony. In Richard's shuso ceremony he answered every question and I thought, I can't do that. Richard was clear. But I could do it. The staff transformed me."

Deer Like Us

Back in the dining room filled with chattering guests, many of whom I remembered from the prior year, the Watsonville Domino Club and the Monterey Rough Riders had come and gone, and the summer was cruising along smoothly. I loved the schedule with the mid-morning and longer afternoon breaks which were good for getting to projects in the shop or venturing downstream and upstream.

A couple of students working in the dining room had stopped in the courtyard while bringing over stacks of plates. They put them down on the table under the arbor and were looking toward the hillside. I walked over and peered across to see what they were looking at. "Wow," I said, "deer on that steep hillside." I wouldn't have thought deer could even go there. I didn't think I could even get to that spot and if so I was sure I'd slip straight down to the creek. Kobun was walking by on the path and I motioned for him to join us. We stood there quietly just watching the deer defy gravity. The deer noticed us and scampered away. Kobun said, "Your life is just like that."

D9 Be Mine

Eldon Pura was always welcome. He was an Italian American farmer and electrician in Greenfield. He'd first come as a day guest in '67 and spent a good deal of that visit helping with some electrical work. Turned out he knew how to handle heavy equipment. He came back and did some excavating. He brought a huge D9 bulldozer on a trailer—the biggest, longest thing I'd seen come into Tassajara. He said he had to go back and forth a few times to get around the switchbacks on the road. With it he made what some called a dam in the creek out at Grasshopper Flats. It wasn't really a dam because it didn't go all the way across. Eldon called it a berm. The creek bed was wide there. The berm went far out from the bank, over a hundred feet. We could drive a truck on top of it and dump rocks over the side. The purpose of the berm was to divert the creek over to the other side and stop erosion of the bank on the side we used. We had little enough flat land as it was.

I went out and watched him operating that fine machine and improvised a little tune with a chorus that went, "D9 be mine" a bunch of times.

Eldon had the nicest disposition. He would bring a gallon of his homemade wine to lunch outdoors with us in the summer and be reminded that we didn't drink alcohol. He just couldn't keep that in mind, especially since students had gone to visit him in Greenfield, drunk his wine, and helped him make it—stomping barefoot on the grapes.

The Impresario

Bill Graham, the great entrepreneur of rock music for the Bay Area, had reservations for two nights. How exciting. He'd opened the Fillmore and Winterland auditoriums in San Francisco where the big-name bands had been playing. In March of 1968, he'd opened Fillmore East in Manhattan. He came in as an overnight guest at the urging of friends who told him he needed to take it easy for a few days. In the dining room I thanked him for his support with our fundraisers, reminded him how he'd let me in to his shows for free when I was out front passing out fliers for the Zenefit or some fundraiser for the Zen Center.

Graham wasn't out of place with us but for a guy used to making and breaking deals all day every day, Tassajara's isolation from the rest of the hustle-bustle type world was a challenge for him. Our one phone line was like a tiny straw for over a hundred people, and he was used to a giant pipe just for him. He made it through dinner and the next day's breakfast fine, but he was frustrated that we had no TV so he couldn't watch a San Francisco Giants baseball game. He drove up to Chews Ridge to listen to it on the radio and didn't return.

Fly Strips

Summertime that year we had legions of flies. Meat and fish were served to the guests and remnants ended up in the compost. There was chicken and horse manure for the gardens. It took time for us to learn not to breed flies through carelessness. Compost and manure had to be well-covered with some combination of dirt, tarps, and screening. I ordered a dozen fly traps, quart jars with tops that allowed flies to enter but not leave. There weren't any poisons or chemicals used. I put something like chicken scraps in them and set them out near the garden and compost but not near where people would be congregating because those traps were gross looking and foul smelling. In a few days they'd be full of dead flies which I'd bury as a gift to a tree. We also used fly strips in the kitchen which were sticky. They'd attract and fill up with flies and were gross. Sometimes a dead or wounded fly would fall off one, so we learned not to hang them over food prep areas.

One day, I walked into the kitchen and there were a few yellow strips hanging down from the ceiling. They were hard, rectangular, plastic, and clean looking. I asked what they were and learned they were Shell Fly Strips. It wasn't long before almost all the flies in the kitchen had died. I found that alarming and said those strips should be removed immediately. Why? Because they created an environment that's lethal to something as big as a fly. You want to work in an environment like that? What's it gonna do to you—and the food? The answer I got from the nameless person in charge that day was that if the Shell company put them out, they must be OK. We can trust them. If I had any hair, I'd have started pulling it out. I ranted about it in the kitchen. I ranted about it to staff. No one wanted to take sides.

Fortunately, Sterling Bunnell came to visit. I took him to the kitchen. "Oh, them," he said. He identified the active ingredient as dichlorvos and said it was the same as what was used in purple strips earlier in the century. Called it a neurotoxin. He said back then it was blamed for an increase in leukemia. He explained how it mimics just what cancer does. Said it would take years to determine just how dangerous they were, but he wouldn't hang out near them. I went around quoting him. One morning not long after that, they weren't there anymore. No one knew who removed them—except the culprit.

Arroyo Seco

A group of us walked to the Arroyo Seco River on a day off. My fellow travelers were Niels Holm, Tim Buckley, Tim Aston, and Jerry Fuller. We brought bag lunches, left at sunrise after a quick munch of gruel and soybeans on the deck outside the kitchen. We walked downstream all the way to the Arroyo Seco—what a trip—it's shorter than the trail to go that way but takes just as long—swimming and wading through pools, jumping rocks.

At the Arroyo Seco River we rested and ate our bag lunches on a bank under the Horse Bridge. There was a Forest Service trash can for our paper bags and waxed paper. Stopping only to leap off boulders into deep pools, we walked and swam all the way up the Arroyo Seco through a stretch so narrow I could touch the granite walls on both sides at the same time. We came to a pool in a smooth rounded area with high walls hollowed out by millennia of gushing flow with a waterfall cascading down from a dozen feet above. There was a nice wide sheet of white water that crashed down on the heads of those below. Niels used a rope hanging on the side of the falls to get to the top and jumped back in. The rest of us followed. Up top was a totally different scene, wide open without the canyon walls, no large boulders. But we had no time to explore further.

We returned the way we came—up the Arroyo Seco to just beyond the Horse Bridge where Willow Creek pours in. The sky was already getting dark when we started heading up creek to where Tassajara Creek joins with it coming from the right side. Then up Tassajara Creek. There was a waxing moon but most of its light was shielded by the trees and the steep rise on each side of the creek. It got so dark we could hardly see anything.

Tim Buckley told about being at a get-together at Gary Snyder's place in Nevada City where Snyder got everyone running in the woods in the dark, not colliding with trees by grace of subtle sensing. So we did the same—ran onward on the smooth creek stones sometimes leaping, zigzagging, arriving back at Tassajara during evening zazen. Tiptoed past the zendo to soak in the hot plunge till the firewatch with her clackers came in to turn off the kerosene lamps and kick us out. The next day none of us could understand how we'd run back like that with no one falling.

Bill Lambert

Driving into Tassajara we'd pass through Jamesburg, population not many and hard to say because it's all spread out. I always wondered where does Jamesburg begin or end? We'd drive by a few homes and pass between a barn and ranch house that belonged to Bill and Marion Lambert. Lamberts' was our informal way station. We'd pull up near his house, walk by a row of doghouses with chained hunting dogs barking at our approach, and enter by the back door. Bill would usually be sitting at the large dining table, Marion often standing behind the stove, sometimes stirring boar meat stew. Marion was sweet and thoughtful. Bill was sour and ornery but engaging—and generous after some insults.

Bill Gordon Lambert was the son of local rancher William B. Lambert, who was the son of William H. Lambert, who with his brother Thomas was a whaler from Martha's Vineyard in Massachusetts. Bill G., our Bill, said they used to land in Big Sur to get supplies and timber and finally sold their ship and stayed there.

The Lambert fortunes were on the decline with Bill and Marion. Lambert Ranch was 5,000 acres, but he didn't seem to have many cattle, was mainly leasing land out and selling it off piece-by-piece.

He made some money taking people boar hunting. He and his sons and other young guys who hung out around there would help the sheriff with searches for people lost in the woods. They'd talk cavalierly about finding bodies, like about one body that was so decomposed that the head came off and rolled down into a ravine where they had to go find it. They'd brag about their boar conquests such as leaping onto the back of one with only a knife to cut the beast's throat. I'd see skinned boar or deer hanging up in the barn. Later, I'd join in on eating them.

Marion operated the Jamesburg branch of the county library, and the Jamesburg post office, both of which were in their house. Sometimes Bill sold firewood. There was a lot of oak on his ranch. I went out with him once to get some for his own use. He drove up a side road in his pickup and cut down a small green tree. He told me he only has to use dry wood to start the fire once in the fall, and it's green wood from then on. He pointed to a little creek gurgling by and said, "It's running now but it'll go dry by August. All the creeks round here used to run year-round till they started testing the atomic bomb." He pronounced the first letter of the word atomic like the "a" in baby, with emphasis on the first syllable.

Lambert would sell hay. One customer was actress Kim Novak in the Carmel Highlands. He and his son Rod did tractor and backhoe work. In 1949, Bill bulldozed the shell of the burned Tassajara lodge into the basement. I told him we'd dug up a bunch of the large rectangular sandstone blocks to make the area into a garden. Some were used for the foundation of the in-progress kitchen. He said there were plenty more, that we'd just skimmed off the top.

Bill was bitter about government restrictions on how he could use his land. There were livestock restrictions. They wouldn't let him put in a trailer park. He said that when there's a socialist takeover of America, it will be led by the U.S. Forest Service. And the more he drank the more vocal he'd get about that, and crude, as in,

"I'd like to run a red-hot poker up the asshole of every goddamn Forest Service bureaucrat!"

Fire lookout Fred Tuttle said that Lambert was just mad at himself for throwing away his life on alcohol. Sometimes Bill would go on a heavy binge, drink so much he couldn't even sit at the kitchen table. Marion might get fed up and join him. One time on my way out, I found them both in bed. Bill told me to go to the grocery store in the village, by which he meant Carmel Valley Village, and get them two quarts of vodka and two gallons of red wine, a carton of Camels, and some snacks. Put it on his tab. Store owner sighed, said Bill was much and long overdue but that he'd get on jags like this every couple of years and then pay it all back—so OK.

One day Bill said he'd seen a mountain lion with cubs on the road. He ran back to get his rifle, but the felines were gone when he returned. He complained that he hadn't had mountain lion stew in a long time. I was happy he didn't get his wish.

Bill always had horses. The way he'd break a horse in was to deny it food and water for a while.

I heard many stories about Lambert and didn't know what was true or not. I heard that in the 1940s he lost his ranch to a neighbor rancher, Esselen Indian Fred Nason, in a card game and that later Nason let him win it back. Was told by a bartender at the Stirrup Cup in the village that Lambert was introduced to a Hollywood producer there years back and that Lambert spat on the man's shoes saying, "What you have to say to that?"

"I say, I'll buy you a drink," was the reply.

Robert Beck—we bought Tassajara from the Becks—said that I reminded him of Lambert.

"Why? Because I drink all your booze?"

I guess so because Robert then told how when he and Anna first bought Tassajara, they heard Lambert was suspicious of them city folks taking that place over. For some years, the Lamberts had owned Church Creek Ranch. Bill said they called it "The Caves Ranch" and that before that it was just called "The Caves." Bill grew up riding a horse over to Tassajara, so he felt entitled to go there anytime he wished.

The Becks invited him and Marion for dinner. As soon as they arrived, Lambert asked if there was any alcohol. Robert brought out a box with twelve partially empty bottles—remnants of various kinds of booze they'd brought from San Francisco. In the course of the evening Lambert not only drank it all up but another box full just like it. When the Lamberts left, Bill said, "I think you're gonna be alright."

When Bill got in the jeep that night to go home, he started backing up on the Tassajara road in the dark. He didn't turn around. Kept backing up. As they headed up the road in reverse, Marion called out, "I'm afraid he's going to do it, but I have to go with him."

Robert said that after that, when people would ask Bill what the new people at Tassajara were like, Bill would say, "Goddamn good."

The sheriff deputized Bill so he could deal quickly with problems in the woods. Once Robert called Bill to say there were some out-of-control guys who were drunk and shooting guns carelessly on the property and that they weren't responding positively to requests that they not do so. In record time, Bill slid into Tassajara, went up to the rowdy guys, and said, "Put up the hardware boys." Robert said the guys wilted in Bill's presence and Bill escorted them out.

Bill told me that Tassajara and all the land within the Los Padres National Forest in Monterey County was surveyed incorrectly. He said that the surveyors mainly stayed at the Caves Ranch when his family lived there, got drunk, and guessed. Some of them went to prison for fraudulent surveying. He said that as long as we were strong, the Forest Service would leave us alone, but that back in the '40s when some nearby rancher was broke, they took his best land and traded it for a steep mountainside showing that's what he owned according to the survey.

There would have been plenty of booze for the surveyors, especially during Prohibition, because old man Lambert was making top-grade whiskey there. Revenuers raided the place, found a still, and booze at the Lambert home in Jamesburg as well. Bill's father had to pay a $200 fine. Bill said, "We sold moonshine whiskey to the finest people in Salinas—judges, padres, church-going people. We got $20 a gallon for it, because it was so pure. The ranch flourished then. It was a sad day when they repealed Prohibition."

We didn't pour any booze for Bill, but he liked us. He'd call us bald-headed hippies, said the lot of us were a bunch of educated idiots but we were straight shooters who didn't put on airs.

Charles McCabe

San Francisco Chronicle columnist Charles McCabe came to Tassajara a few times when the Becks owned it. He was a hard-drinking Irishman from Hell's Kitchen in New York City and booze was a frequent guest in his insightful and satirical columns. He wrote one back in the Becks' day on Tassajara with a title referring to the baths—"Stand Still and Get Healthy." When he asked the Becks what else he could write about, Robert called Bill Lambert, who came in, and McCabe wrote an article called, "The Last of the Great White Hunters." It was verbatim right out of Bill's mouth as they drank and drank the Becks' booze together. McCabe said he'd be stupid to change anything Lambert said.

McCabe was coming to dinner. He had reservations to stay a night. I greeted him outside the office and told him many of us read his "Fearless Spectator" columns whenever a *Chronicle* was left behind by a guest or brought in from a town trip. He said he wanted to try Tassajara out under new ownership. But he'd just found out in the office we didn't have a bar. He looked out of place with his city clothes and hat, the pallor of his face. He seemed uncomfortable slouching in a redwood chair out in front of the office in the shade. I'm sure he was eager to get back to his regular haunt, the Gino and Carlo Bar in North Beach. He soaked in the men's plunge and left a few hours after arrival.

Gold Jaguar

Writer Herb Gold arrived in a Jaguar sedan. He'd been publishing books, short stories, and articles since the mid-'40s. He sat with students in the courtyard and talked about the literary scene in France after the war. His Jaguar had some car trouble, so he generously gave it to Zen Center and got a ride out. It was traded in for a six-ton Dodge flatbed. Paul Discoe built sides for it. Right away we were using it to bring in heavy loads of lumber, cement, manure for the garden, and 55-gallon drums of gasoline and kerosene.

Two weeks later there was an article by Gold in the *San Francisco Chronicle* travel section on the best places to take a date in the Bay Area. It included Tassajara. When Gold returned to Tassajara, he told me he was worried he wouldn't be allowed back in because of the article. He said that he received a disapproving letter about it from Zen Center secretary Yvonne Rand. I told him that the last I checked, he wasn't on our enemies list and was confident Tassajara would survive such tabloid treatment—and thanked him for the truck.

Maggie Kress

Maggie Kress was not normally bashful, but when it was her turn to ask Suzuki a question in a shosan ceremony, she seemed somewhat shy, perhaps even lacking in self-esteem as she walked toward him. She knelt, hesitated, and said with a tone of apology, "Roshi, what if I don't care about getting enlightened, can I still practice?" Suzuki responded, "Just stay honest and open the way you are right now."

Maggie came from New York City and had been "hanging out with a bunch of dope smoking hippies in Bolinas." She found out there was zazen on Monday mornings with Bill Kwong's group in Mill Valley not far away. She'd long been interested in Buddhism and meditation, so she went, showing up after zazen was over. She opened the front door of the Altamont Recreation Club where Bill's group met. She went inside and listened from behind a folding screen to someone speaking. She took a peek. She'd had a picture in her mind of a bunch of hippies sitting around a fireplace with incense and lots of color and instead there were people sitting straight in rows. "It was all very formal and beautiful to me. I sat and listened to Suzuki Roshi give a lecture. I couldn't see him, but I was caught right away. There was something very powerful about him even that way."

With no prior experience sitting, Maggie impulsively signed up for a weeklong sesshin at Sokoji. The day before it was to start, she checked into "some horrible old wino hotel and I was scared and thought I was going to die." That fear followed her to the sesshin and expressed itself in dread she wouldn't be up to the challenge.

In zazen, she felt like she was going to be sick. During a break she asked Silas Hoadley if she could sit in the gaitan, outside the zendo. He said no and asked why she wanted special attention. She cowered at that, sat down on her zafu, and vomited in the zendo all over herself and the cushions. A few hours later, she was sitting in a Sokoji pew downstairs next to the aisle, waiting for a lecture by Katagiri. As he walked by on his way to the front, he handed her something and said, "Here, Tums for the tummy—don't be sick."

Her first interaction with Suzuki came when she was carrying a vase to put on the altar. Suzuki looked her in the eye and said, "Don't drop it." She told Silas that she took that to mean to not let her attention drop. Silas said that's a good way to take that but also, she may have been carrying it with one hand, and Japanese, especially monks, carry anything precious with two hands.

When Maggie first arrived at Tassajara, she was animated, energetic, talkative, and striking with her long bleached-blond hair. She hadn't been there long when she was taught how to hit the mokugyo for service. She felt uptight, worried she'd screw it up, lose the rhythm. Richard's seat on the altar was right next to the mokugyo. As service was starting and Suzuki was approaching the altar to offer incense, Richard leaned over to Maggie who was sitting rigidly upright with a concerned look on her face and whispered, "I love your hair. Who did it? Sassoon?" That was just the right thing to say to make her relax.

She said she grew up in a home that was like a museum. She was afraid to touch anything, felt like she was living in an extension of the Metropolitan Museum of Art, which was just across the street. She said her family wasn't rich anymore. I said that's what rich people tend to say. "No, we're not," she insisted. "My uncle made the money and my father lost it."

I asked, "What sort of business was that?"

"Dime stores," she said. "Kress Five and Dime. They called them department stores."

Maggie talked about Europe and a private Catholic girls' school she attended in Italy. She said the nuns made them take baths with a sheet hiding their bodies. But then she'd sleep with her best friend there, her first love.

Maggie and I were talking in the courtyard when she saw a woman walk by on the road above. "Oh my gosh!" she said. "That's Millie Johnstone!" I asked who that was and she said Millie was an East Coast socialite whose husband was head of Bethlehem Steel. Millie was an older, sophisticated woman involved with Eido Shimano's Zen Studies Society in New York. During the day she'd do tea ceremony for students. Maggie was a guest for tea ceremony with Millie. It was her first tea ceremony and she found it to be "an exquisite meditative dance while seated." Then in a whispered voice she added, "Millie had a pet wolf who killed her infant son. She wrote a book about it."

One day Maggie found a baby bird that had fallen from its nest. She wanted to help it so she beat up some egg yolk, squeezed the yellow liquid into its mouth, and it keeled over dead. She asked Suzuki in a lecture, "Why, when you try to help, does it often just cause more trouble?" He answered that if you see a cat playing with a mouse and try to stop it, that the mouse will tell you to stop interfering with its karma. She thought that must be an old Japanese story.

Maggie said she loved Suzuki's lectures. I asked how she could love them when she told me she would fall asleep almost immediately. She said he'd say, "Maybe when you're asleep you can understand what I'm saying better than when you're awake."

One day, Maggie and Niels went out in the flatbed to get a load of chicken manure for the garden. It was a hot day. They were both hard-headed and got into an argument about how to load it and then how to unload it. It was gooey and their clothes and arms got decorated with a splattering of that goo. As they shoveled it out, Niels started making fun of how Maggie handled the shovel. She got pissed and shoveled some onto his feet. He returned the favor. Soon they were plastered with chicken shit all over. Maggie said, "After that, everything smelled and tasted like chicken shit for a few days." Also after that, they could often be found hanging out together.

Brother David

David Steindl-Rast, "Brother David," as we called him, was a Benedictine monk who practiced Zen with Eido Shimano in New York and sat sesshins with Hakuun Yasutani and Soen Nakagawa. He got the excellent job of being the dishwasher. The dish shack is a great place to be if you enjoy interaction with others. He did. He was a friendly, calming presence. From him we learned about the *Rule of Saint Benedict*, created in the sixth century, which laid out a middle-way path for monks—strict, but not self-abusively so. Their motto was *pax*, peace. David said the *Rule* starts with an admonition to obey, and explained that to obey means to listen, to pay attention. Like in Zen, they considered every activity to be an opportunity for practice. Like us, they aimed to work in relative silence, with exceptions as in Richard's example of "Pass the hammer." The word prayer for Christian monastics is often used to stand for meditation. At Mount Saviour Monastery, David practiced meditation for decades. He said that the abbot there spoke of "falling into heaven."

Mount Saviour had a farm as well. David told me that there were two things he learned to watch out for which would apply to us—animals and business. He said at Mt. Saviour they ran into unexpected complications and responsibilities with farm animals. They created a bakery that got quite popular and before they knew it, the monks were spending an inordinate amount of time making bread, balancing the books, and driving a delivery truck around.

In June, two priests came for a night from New Camaldoli Hermitage in Big Sur. They were Benedictines as well. They joined us for zazen. Brother David walked with them to the Horse Pasture. There they celebrated the sacrament of the Eucharist in a mass with Tassajara bread and an oryoki bowl for a chalice.

I asked Brother David if he believed in a personal god, and he said he could see god, including a personal aspect. His view of god, he said, was not theistic but panentheistic, god and nature as one. In his understanding of Christianity, mind and body are one—like Buddhism. He said that faith is the nose on the head of doubt.

David said when he first sat at Sokoji, Suzuki was going around the zendo with his nyoi. He bowed behind David. David wore a hood. Suzuki said in a firm voice, "Take this off!" and he whacked David. Someone told Suzuki that David was a Benedictine brother, that what he was wearing was called a scapular and is his sacred vestment much as the kesa is the sacred outer robe of the Zen monk. When Suzuki met David, he indicated the scapular and said, "Oh, excuse me. I didn't know this was your okesa." And he laughed.

Maud Oakes JUNE

Maud Oakes was an artist, writer, and ethnologist who specialized in studying the Navajo and a tribe of Mayan descendants in Guatemala. She attempted to fill the gap in what she saw as Americans' ignorance of their Indian heritage. In summer 1968, she sat at a table overlooking the creek on the dining room deck chatting with Shunryu Suzuki and Richard Baker. Two men hovered near them, one with a camera, one with a boom microphone. They were making a film about Tassajara for KQED, the San Francisco PBS station.

> **Richard:** "If you chose the inner world, not just dreams, but the whole inner experience, then the

outer world would become like the inner world. It would become much more real."
Suzuki: "Actually, there is no inside or outside."
Richard: "Yeah, that's how I feel about it."
Oakes: "But now when you meditate, you go inside, don't you?"
Suzuki: "Not the inside, not outside. Just open."

Maud Oakes had been a guest at Tassajara when the Becks owned it. She came our first year and again now in our second. She commented on how impressed she was with all that we accomplished. She was particularly fascinated with the stonework being done in building the new kitchen, how they'd fit the stones, then take them out and cement them in.

Oakes: "Then I noticed that girl chipping the rock."
Suzuki: "Oh, yes. She's very good."
Oakes: "That's a lot of work for a girl."
Suzuki: "Yes, excellent."

The name of that girl, that woman, was Audrey Walter. Suzuki explained she was making the corner stones. He'd been closely following the stonework, especially Audrey's.

Oakes said she'd always loved stones, that when she was a girl, she'd pick them up wherever she'd go and put them in her bedroom closet till it got so full her mother told her that had to stop. Richard added that when he came back from a stint in the Merchant Marine, he was pleased to find that his Harvard roommates had made sure his big box of prize rocks was not thrown out. He turned toward Suzuki and said, "You're the only person I know it can be said of positively that you have rocks in your head."

Suzuki: "As you know, I like stones very much, especially big ones. Someone came to me the other day with a small box and a magnifying glass and said, 'Look at these stones.' So I looked at them one by one. But to my great astonishment, those small stones were exactly the same as big ones! They were as interesting as big ones, the shapes were different, and some had very good shapes. You could make a beautiful garden with those stones. I was very pleased. I thought, this is what the universe consists of and how everything is going. So, if you cannot accomplish something great, you can work on a very small thing, on a very small scale, and the meaning is not any different at all. This is the nature of our practice and teaching."

On a Boulder

Peter Schneider and Brother David Steindl-Rast were sitting on the flat surface of a boulder overlooking the creek. A KQED TV camera was running as they spoke and laughed.

> **Peter:** "What I wanted to ask you was whether or not you plan to go to heaven?"
> **David:** "For heaven's sake, yes."
> **Peter:** "Yes, and what does that mean to you?"
> **David:** "In Christian terms, it means ultimate union with God. And in Buddhist terms it means union with ultimate reality, nirvana."
> **Peter:** "Of course, some Buddhists believe nirvana is some sort of state after death. But Roshi doesn't. He believes that nirvana is right here and now."
> **David:** "Well, in a very real sense, the Christian who lives in union with God is also in heaven here and now, and his death is relatively insignificant. How do you think this place is going to develop? I see two elements here. On the one hand is the strictly monastic element. It's a real monastery with celibate monks and so forth. On the other hand you have married couples living here and folks with children and so forth."

I was sitting nearby listening and thought, *That's a loose use of the term "monks." The only monks here are him, Suzuki, and Kobun. There is celibacy among single men and women, but it was temporary and not compulsory.*

> **David:** "Do you think that one of these two trends will eventually take over?"
> **Peter:** "I don't know. I think that many people who are religious would prefer neither living in a totally secular life out in the world, nor living one that is totally monastic. I think of a community of families with a school and their own ways of raising food—but one that is not isolated."
> **David:** "In other words, a Buddhist *kibbutz*. In the Christian sense, too, monasticism has been defined as a nostalgia for the early Christian community. For exactly that—families, sharing everything, and living a more religious life than society at large. Do you think, then, that this is a sort of pattern for a new development of Buddhism in this country? And do you think that there are some possibilities of cooperating with other monastic traditions like the Benedictine tradition right near here?"
> **Peter:** "I've been here a year, and that would be like asking a freshman in college if he thinks the university can change the world. But when you look at the slight difference between our two different communities, and our different ways, and then there are people who are killing for my country right or wrong around the world, they're almost exactly alike."
> **David:** "In this sense, then, monasticism would really have a very important mission in the world, because there are monks both in the East and the West and just by the way that they speak the same

> language of meditation and spiritual practice, there is a bridge already existing and all we need to do is use it for peace and for communication."
> **Peter:** "Yes, I think that we're all getting together, and I think that as you come East, I may also return West."

I wondered if viewers of the film would understand that by East, Peter meant Asia, and by West the Occident.

> **David:** "I hope so. It means a lot to me. Of course, our life as Benedictines is completely impregnated with ritual too. But you get used to it. And here for me is something new. The meals, for instance, are highly ritualized, or the bath with the ritual bows and all that carries over to other parts of daily life, and it makes me more aware of what's going on. It increases your awareness."

Peter Schneider and Brother David

> **Peter:** "After people eat our way for some time, they become so much more aware. They begin to realize how their teeth meet and how they swallow. It's very silent, but you can hear it all, you know. And if you stop eating and close your eyes and listen to the rest of the people eating, it's like an enormous field of all different kinds of bugs going numnumnumnumnumnum [laughter]."
> **David:** "I guess even if you don't do that, it's very beautiful to have the three bowls and every day different things in the three bowls."

Broken Nyoi

I was walking from the shop by the upper garden when I heard a loud, angry voice and sounds of something hard hitting something else coming from below. I walked over to the olive tree by Paul and Ruthie's cabin, stood at the top of the steps, and realized it was Suzuki's voice hoarsely yelling, "Do you understand?!" That striking sound kept repeating. I heard, "Yes, sensei! Yes, sensei!" Then I knew it was Phillip Wilson being hit over and over as Suzuki continued to yell at him and Phillip continued going, "Yes, sensei! Yes, sensei!"

I visited Phillip in his cabin later and asked what was that about? "Rev. Suzuki was angry with me for getting into arguments with Richard. He broke his nyoi on me." The nyoi is the teacher's staff, short with a slight curve. "He went and got another one and I begged him, 'Please don't break another nyoi on me!' Not that it hurt but I just didn't want him to break another one."

I thought it wasn't only about Phillip and Richard arguing. Suzuki had heard a lot of complaints about Phillip's behavior when Suzuki wasn't there. When Suzuki was at Tassajara, Phillip was like an obedient puppy dog, following the complete schedule and working with Suzuki in an impressive way. Around Suzuki, Phillip harmonized into Suzuki's zone. This was all Suzuki saw of him. No wonder he wanted to send him to the East Coast to be a priest for the well-bred women's group. But I didn't think that would have worked out. For as soon as Suzuki was driven out, Phillip would be in his room with earphones listening to music on his battery-operated record player. Phillip kept beer in there, too.

Suzuki brought the broken nyoi to Paul Discoe and said, "I want you to put this back together, but don't do it too well. Some important teachers from Japan will be here soon and I want them to see the broken part. I want them to know that we have tough practice in this country too."

Roshi Vibes

Les Kaye was a student at the Los Altos Haiku Zendo and a career IBM employee in the punch card division. Unlike most Zen students, Les could afford to take his family to Tassajara and stay as guests. They were there for a few days in July 1968. Peter asked Les if Tassajara could borrow his nice comfy car to help drive some Zen dignitaries in from Jamesburg. There were more than would fit in the Land Cruiser.

Later that day the said Zen dignitaries arrived—Hakuun Yasutani and Soen Nakagawa, Yasutani's student Robert Aitken of the Diamond Sangha in Hawaii, Soen's disciple Eido Shimano who was teaching in New York City, and Taizan Maezumi from L.A. Also accompanying them were Eido's student Loly Rosset, Yasutani's Zen priest son, Flora Courtois (the author of *An Experience of Enlightenment*, which Yasutani had asked her to write), and Charles Gooding, president of the L.A. Bosatsukai of former Nyogen Senzaki students.

A focal point of the visit was to honor Nyogen Senzaki, who'd come to America in 1905 with his teacher, Soen Shaku. Shaku had been invited to San Francisco to teach Zen and did so for nine months, setting up the first zendo in America. D.T. Suzuki was his translator and Sokei-an Sasaki, who founded the First Zen Institute in 1930 in New York City, was his disciple.

Before he departed, Shaku took his disciple, Nyogen Senzaki, to Golden Gate Park and told him, "Just face the great city and see whether it conquers you or you conquer it." Shaku then walked off leaving Senzaki on his own.

Senzaki did menial jobs and hung out in the city library. In time, he lectured and started the Floating Zendo which for some time was in Japantown just down Bush Street from where Sokoji was established in 1935. In 1922, he floated to L.A. He spent the war years in Wyoming at an internment camp. After the war he returned to L.A. and continued his Floating Zendo. He died in 1958. Senzaki avoided titles, fame, and wealth. He is known for his teaching, "Put no head above your head," and his last words which he taped for his funeral were, "Remember the Dharma! Remember the Dharma! Remember the Dharma!"

Senzaki established a relationship with Soen Nakagawa as a result of reading his poetry. Senzaki was Robert Aitken's first teacher. Maezumi attended his lectures and zazen in L.A. The only person I knew in the San Francisco Zen Center who'd sat and studied with Senzaki was Claude Dalenberg, who revered him.

Among this group of visiting Zen dignitaries, only Maezumi had been to Tassajara before. The others were curious to see this new Zen monastery, especially because they had students who wanted to go there. Teachers weren't generally eager to see their students practice elsewhere even for a short while. They might not come back.

Yasutani and Soen were called "roshi" and we were all excited to have them there. The other priests were called "sensei" and we assumed they'd be roshis someday. To us the title roshi conferred the zenith of what could be accomplished in human form. Loly Rosset laughed when I said, "Hey guys, let's go over there and get some roshi vibes."

Yasutani was eighty-four and had been leading sesshins in the States for six years. A number of Tassajara students had done sesshin with him, among them Bob Halpern, Jeff Broadbent, Claude Dalenberg who'd sat a few in Kamakura, and Brother David Steindl-Rast.

Yasutani was from a Soto lineage but founded Sanbyo Kyodan, an independent organization, in 1954, to promote a lay-oriented combination of Soto and Rinzai Zen that he learned from his master, Daiun Sogaku Harada.

In his talk at Tassajara, he said that Soto's founder, Dogen, studied koans for fifteen years with Esai, the founder of Japanese Rinzai, before going to China where he attained great enlightenment practicing shikantaza, just sitting. Yasutani said Dogen's koan study was essential to his awakening. Using an analogy from Shakyamuni Buddha, he said that an archer hits the bullseye after a hundred tries due to his effort with the first ninety-nine. He said that belief in reincarnation is a requirement of Buddhism, and that Buddha was born enlightened. Quite a contrast to Shunryu Suzuki who didn't say we had to believe anything in particular.

Richard Baker said this was an excellent opportunity to ask these great teachers a question. Les Kaye's hand went up. He asked what the best way was to establish Zen in America. Yasutani then Soen responded in dramatic fashion, urging us to practice with great determination, to attain enlightenment, and to establish meditation centers. Then it was Suzuki's turn. "I have nothing to say," he said, getting up and going out the side door, a unique exit. Everyone roared in delight, and the session was suddenly over.

At Soen's urging, there was to be an impromptu sunset ceremony about four miles up the road to just below where it levels off at Black Butte summit. Senzaki had designated Soen as the teacher to carry on his work in America. Soen, who was now sixty-one, had conducted Senzaki's funeral in L.A. in 1958 and was traveling with a portion of the ashes which he'd been keeping at his temple, Ryutakuji, in Shizuoka prefecture near Suzuki's Rinsoin. He'd set the ashes on the Tassajara altar for the visit and brought a pinch for scattering at our moon viewing.

Loly, Brother David, and I rode in the back of a pickup going up Tassajara road. Bumping along with us was Eido. Naturally, I took advantage of the situation to ask Eido penetrating dharma questions. A response to one was, "There are only two types of people—those who know and those who don't know." Cut and dry, unlike what I was used to. He seemed very sure of himself.

We pulled in next to other vehicles at the last turnout before the road flattens and walked out to where one could supposedly look down at the valley wherein nestled Tassajara. It was dark so I couldn't tell. As the sun disappeared behind mountains to the west, the top of the full moon appeared from the east and Soen intoned the opening of the Heart Sutra: *Maka Hannya Haramita Shingyo-o-o*. Together we chanted while watching the whole bright orb appear. He led us into another recitation of the Heart Sutra then to some other familiar chants all the while leading us in clapping to the rhythm of the words. Then he called out, "May we all exist in unity!" and we followed him clapping and calling out "May we all exist in unity!" until he suggested we form our own moon. So we joined hands and danced around in a circle. At this point he started improvising shouts at the moon and others followed. He called out, "This is true hippie dance! May Tassajara help all sentient beings to achieve peace!"

Creek Sneak

We got back to Tassajara at bedtime. I had no interest in going to bed and went to the baths. The kerosene lamps had been extinguished but there was plenty of light from the full moon. I was enjoying the indoor open-faced plunge when the silhouette of another late-night bather appeared and descended the steps. It was Soen. He was talkative, playful. I showed him how to leap into the plunge from the handrail. Went to the steam room where he chanted in the pitch dark. Every spring as the creek subsided, we'd build a little dam with creek rocks outside the steam rooms so that there'd be plenty of cool creek water to dip into after the hot plunge and steam room. There was a large old sycamore which was half rooted in the creek. I showed Soen how we could duck down and come back up inside a hollow in the roots and trunk. Slivers of moonlight danced in. He loved it.

He was like an excited kid, so I suggested we go down creek. No need to get dressed. As long as we stayed in the creek, we could pass naked behind and below the Tassajara cabins. Hopped rocks, waded through pools, and once beyond civilization walked barefoot on paths and crossed the creek twice to arrive at the Narrows' smooth granite contours magnificent in the moonlight. There we meditated, chanted, and jumped off the side into the deep pool. We walked down creek further to the place where sheer granite walls bank a pool. We floated looking up at the moon and stars. Standing in hip high water Soen clapped his hands which produced bouncing echoes. I joined in making loud popping sounds by cupping my hands and clapping them hard before a puckered mouth. This delighted Soen who tried in vain to do the same.

The next morning, Soen gave a talk in the zendo in which he told about getting a student to help him find a used bar of soap so he wouldn't have to open the paper-wrapped one in his room. "When I was young, I thought Americans were fortunate to take drink from paper cup and throw it away," he said. "Now I think it is a shame."

In the course of his talk, Soen got worked up, rose from his seat, and strutted some across the altar platform as he spoke. He mentioned our evening together in the creek and bade me to stand and demonstrate that popping sound, an exposure I didn't cherish and which brought on mild but amused scolding later in the day from Richard. During that lecture there were earthquake tremors that shook the zendo and rattled the kerosene glass lamps mounted along the walls. Soen took that as a sign of the significance of our gathering.

As we stood on the road, hands in *gassho*, palms together, watching our esteemed visitors pose for a final photo, Kobun pointed to Yasutani. "Good example of great Rinzai roshi," he said—even though Yasutani was renegade Soto. Then he nodded toward Suzuki. "And Suzuki Roshi is a good example of a great Soto Roshi." I asked what about Soen and he said, "Too much personality."

Loly Rosset

Hannelore Loly Rosset had been Eido Shimano's student, secretary, and adviser since soon after he arrived in New York City. Back in 1967, she told him she wanted to go to a practice period at Tassajara. He put up a sign with a quote from Dogen's Genjo Koan: "If you cannot find the truth right where you are, where else do you expect to find it?" But she definitely wanted to go to Tassajara and also to see the Zen Center in San Francisco. They didn't talk about it further, but he knew he couldn't stop her and she knew he didn't like it. She said they always knew what the other was thinking. So he suggested she come with him to L.A. where he was joining his teacher Soen Nakagawa, and Hakuun Yasutani, who were coming from a sesshin in Hawaii. Maybe then they could go check out Tassajara together. When they got to L.A., everyone else was interested and the visit of the teachers was quickly arranged.

As Loly was one of the visiting guests, she met Suzuki in his cabin with Eido and a few others. "You have a big nose," Suzuki said to her. She didn't feel insulted and "was very impressed with him because he was so simple, unneurotic, a little shy, and so unlike most people. I immediately felt good with him. I couldn't help it. There was just something about him, his ordinariness and a mixture of great clarity and intelligence and a little bit of Dennis-the-Menace humor in one of his eyes, the way the one eyebrow raised."

She'd been close with Eido's wife, as well, and never noticed anything questionable before that trip. "I was totally innocent about his thing with women." She got the first inkling when friends of his in L.A. didn't want to put them both up. "At Tassajara a few days later something happened that made it pretty clear—someone came with a flashlight."

Maybe that flashlight in the night at Tassajara she referred to had something to do with a student named Bonnie. Soon after the visit, Bonnie took a break from Tassajara to be Eido's attendant for a sesshin. When she returned, she reported that she loved the sesshin. She said Yasutani gave constant interviews which she overheard because Eido was translating. She said a student asked if keeping up with the news would make him more deluded and that Eido answered for Yasutani saying, "You're so deluded that it really doesn't matter." She also said she and Eido slept together every night.

Born Hannelore Eckert and brought up in a cultured German home, Loly had been a Hitler Youth, something she didn't advertise. Her assignments led to newspaper work in Paris where she eventually got involved with the French Underground. As France was liberated and Hitler's plans were falling apart, she reentered Germany and almost got killed by a drunk SS officer who pulled a gun on her and accused her of treason. A couple of customs agents stopped him and got her on a bus. After the war she lived in south Germany with her lesbian aunt and partner and mainly tried not to starve.

"I think, like Japanese, who went through the war," she said, "we had a different context than the Americans. I've always been philosophically-oriented. But not because of the war only—my grandfather was a professor who had become a Buddhist. He was the head of the University of Cologne which he founded with Adenauer. The Nazis put him out of business because of his international connections."

Loly had been in the center of avant-garde New York, married once to Barney Rosset, founder of *Evergreen Review*, and early owner of Grove Press where Richard worked. Rosset won important freedom of speech court cases publishing *Lady Chatterley's Lover, Tropic of Cancer,* Ginsberg's *Howl,* and much more. He also bought and distributed the most sexually explicit movie of any note to date, the Swedish art film, *I Am Curious (Yellow).*

After the visit to Tassajara, Loly went back to New York with Eido as planned. She would be busy helping to prepare for the September 15 installation of the Zen Studies Society's new zendo at which Soen presided. Suzuki didn't go, but sent a heavy Tassajara Creek stone by air freight in his stead. Soen gave Eido transmission during that visit. Up to then, his students called him Tai-san, but afterwards he was known as Eido Shimano Roshi.

Talking about those three teachers Loly said, "Suzuki Roshi was different in that he'd do something like clean. Eido-shi [*shi* meaning "teacher"] would never clean—he'd have others do that and Soen wouldn't either, not because he considered it below him but because he was always in the clouds and more into the universal than the particular. But he was adventurous. When he heard that I traveled all over the U.S. with two kids, a dog, a tent, and a boat, and that we camped in the mountains with bears, he got very excited and organized the whole zendo to go camping. That was the kind of thing he did—more dramatic. I like that too, but I felt so at ease with Suzuki Roshi. There was no need to say anything.

"I had a little altar in the living room with a window behind it revealing the city and the sky, and Soen Roshi was a great one for non-conformity. He always had new ideas to shake things up. He found a couple of huge mushrooms on his camping trip and put them to the right and left showing the inside to the Buddha. I enjoyed Soen and he made all kinds of hocus pocus and it was interesting but kind of a little bit weird—too dramatic.

"Suzuki Roshi was staying at my place while on a visit to the East Coast with Richard gathering support for the purchase of Tassajara. I was telling all about Soen and the camping and the mushrooms and I was sort of full of it and the next morning at zazen—we always did zazen in front of the Buddha—I came in and Suzuki Roshi had turned the mushrooms the other way around and I never said a word because I knew he meant don't get hung up on what he or I say. The next day I put them the other way around to show him I knew it didn't matter."

Loly wasn't used to Suzuki coughing like we were. "The poor man had been coughing like crazy," she said, "and whenever he had these attacks of coughs, I'd call Yvonne and tell her he was seriously ill and to take him to a doctor. I'd tell him to lie down and I babied him a little bit."

Loly took Suzuki to visit Millie Johnstone and Millie performed a tea ceremony for them. When it was over, Suzuki said, "That was wonderful." So Millie went through the whole tea ceremony again.

But before she could do it again, Loly fibbed that Suzuki had an appointment to keep. Once they were back on the street, Suzuki told her, "You know how to take care of me."

Loly had practiced tea ceremony for years and had all the accoutrements neatly placed on a tray in her apartment. But she didn't bother Suzuki with it. She knew he'd been a tea ceremony guest countless times, and she heard that when his wife did tea ceremony, that he'd leave the temple. When he departed Loly's apartment for the last time, he paused at her tea ceremony tray and said, "You're a great tea master."

—CHAPTER TWO—

THE SECOND HALF OF 1968

The Walters JULY

Bob Walter said his first steps on the path were at the age of eight, when he had a sense that everything was a dream. It was a deep opening that frightened him. He thought of that epiphany when he first read the Diamond Sutra. As an older child he had an out of body experience, a half-sleep, half-wake state, feeling like a ball rolling around the room. It was pleasurable but it frightened him, too, because he didn't know what was happening.

He went to Duke University on a baseball scholarship. His grades weren't good enough, but he said they had the best college baseball team in the country and the coach wanted him. He'd play semi-pro in the summers. He studied philosophy and especially liked Heidegger, Kierkegaard, and George Berkeley's mind-only approach. He had a major in sociology because he wanted to do social work but became a psychologist. His mentor was the eminent Rollo May known for his existential humanism.

Bob took LSD. He said it gave new meaning to the term fantastic. Everything was brilliant. It opened doors. He only had a couple of trips, thought it was a great key, was grateful for the experience, and decided that's enough of that.

Bob came to have doubts about psychiatry which he likened to the psychedelic DMT—looks good, he said, but doesn't help in the long run and can even worsen mental disturbances. He and May attended a week of lectures by R.D. Laing that strongly reinforced the direction Bob's thoughts were already heading. Laing's method was to do less, prescribe less, be supportive, but leave the patients alone more to transform on their own.

Bob's professional lineage traced back through May's mentor, Erich Fromm, who had published *Zen Buddhism and Psychoanalysis* with Richard De Martino. Bob valued the guidance he received but knew he had to push ever onward toward the unknown. R.D. Laing was inspiring but clearly unstable himself. Then the director of the clinic in New York where Bob worked jumped out of the window to his death.

Bob went to a workshop with Alan Watts in Connecticut. Watts said that psychotherapy is prostitution. Bob knew there was truth in that, but also that Watts was being flippant. He drove Watts back to New York and found he had another side—charming and humble. Watts actually valued psychoanalysis and, like Fromm, wrote about the synthesis of it and Zen. He also valued psychedelics.

Then Bob made a friend whom he called his first Zen teacher—Jack Kerouac. They met playing softball with artist friends in Northport on Long Island. Due to the company Bob kept, and the paint on his clothes, Kerouac thought Bob was an artist. Kerouac hated therapists. Bob said one reason for that was he'd been kicked out of the army for "inadequate personality." Bob said they had an instant connection. When Kerouac learned Bob was a psychologist, he went, "Oh, my god!"

Bob said Kerouac was a fantastic baseball player who did zany things on the field, would do flips, twirl around, and fall on his face. Bob's wife, Audrey, got along well with Kerouac and was impressed not only with his athleticism but also with his broad knowledge of literature and the literary scene. However, she wasn't interested in going out drinking with him like Bob.

"We'd go off on drinking trips," Bob said. "He called me his psychiatrist and I called him my Zen teacher. He was spontaneous, dramatic. He was also disturbed and an alcoholic. He had the ability to create great social situations. But also, he was frightened to death of people. He'd hide under his bed when someone knocked on his door. I've seen him defensive and hostile on TV, but he could be beautiful. Like Watts, get below their defenses and they can quickly change.

"Coming back from Fire Island one time, Kerouac said to me, 'You're just like Neal Cassady,' and he started to cry." Kerouac saying that to Bob gave a peek into Bob's personality at that time. Cassady was Kerouac's best friend and principal subject of his *On the Road*, a frenetic, impulsive, wild man. There were also traces of that in Bob no matter how much he matured and mellowed.

Bob said Kerouac would play with people "like Bob Halpern does." Kerouac would get drunk and into fights and then he'd disappear. Bob would have to deal with the situation. Once they were separated, and Kerouac arrested, after an altercation in a bar. He had no money because he'd give it all to his mother to dole out to him, and then he'd give what she gave him to Bob. Bob used it to bail him out. Kerouac also carried no identification. He told the police he didn't need any because he was the famous Jack Kerouac. They didn't believe him. Bob told them it was true and they finally believed.

Sometimes Kerouac would stay with Bob and Audrey and then he might bring someone home from a bar. Either sex. One night they also had other friends visiting whom Kerouac kept awake with the racket he was making getting it on with someone. In the morning, he emerged with someone whom Bob described as an old alcoholic man.

They'd listen all night to Handel's *Messiah*. Or Kerouac might call up Allen Ginsberg and have long talks with him. "Allen knew that Jack's mother was a bigot who hated Blacks and Jews. Jack handed Bob the phone and Allen said, 'Tell Jack the only thing he should do is fuck his mother.'"

Zazen Genius

Bob started talking to his patients about Zen. One of them went to the Zen Studies Society zendo in Manhattan and told Bob to stop bullshitting and start sitting. Bob talked to Audrey who eagerly went first. She arrived an hour early. Eido gave her a brief zazen instruction and she sat full lotus for an hour then joined others for the forty-minute period. Eido told Bob, "Your wife is a zazen genius. You, we're going to work on." After that the Walters became regulars at Zen Studies.

Bob and Audrey were eager to try out Tassajara after hearing Richard Baker give a talk at the Zen Studies Society in the fall of 1967. They were at Tassajara during the visit of all those Zen teachers the following summer. They'd heard Eido speak quite respectfully about Soen and Yasutani, but they'd never met either of them—until Tassajara. Just watching Soen walk, Bob was blown away. The first day Yasutani talked, Bob got emotional. All Soen said at that time was, "No tomorrow," but to Bob it was powerful.

When Bob first met Suzuki, he was disappointed. "He was just a little guy up there on the altar speaking softly." But little by little that summer, he saw what Suzuki had to offer. "He didn't make a strong impression like Soen Nakagawa Roshi. But Suzuki Roshi treated us like family. He was inclusive."

As far as that inclusive aspect, there was a student at Tassajara who'd tried to sit with Eido first, but was told on the phone not to bother to come if he couldn't sit full lotus. Bob said that Eido would show great favor to zealous sitters, attractive women, and the wealthy. Sometimes his discrimination would be appalling as when he made the only Black student sit in the kitchen.

The Walters' son and daughter were just old enough to work in the gardens. Audrey was assigned to cabin cleaning and Bob to get stones and wheelbarrow concrete for Dan Welch and Bill Shurtleff who were building walls for the new kitchen. While pushing said wheelbarrow, Bob stopped to let a guest pass on the path. "Hello Bob," the guest said. Bob looked up to see his old mentor, Rollo May. They got together for lemonade during the break. I'd served May in the dining room but didn't know anything about him except that the label on his napkin ring read "May," and that he was quiet and dignified. Bob introduced us, saying that without the guidance of May, he would be covered in cement dust, and that May was an inextricable part in the path that led him to Tassajara.

Back at the wheelbarrow, Bob mentioned Audrey was a stone sculptor, and she got the job of making the corner stones. Suzuki watched Audrey working, saw she knew what she was doing, and began to spend time with her on that and other stonework.

"For me," she said, "it was a special period of learning—sharing the love of stone, mindful hits, the slow revealing of form and the opportunity to speak with Roshi about Zen practice just by a brief reference to the work at hand. One day, he suggested we look for a river rock to cut for a lantern. I was amazed at his agility and quickness as he happily stepped from stone to stone along the creek bed, asking me what I thought here and there, then spotting without hesitation exactly the right one for the job—a long, somewhat rectangular rock. It was winched up, then dragged by sled to its work location and stood on end. I cut a four-sided opening near the top allowing space for a candle. Where was the lantern going? What should it look like? Roshi wouldn't say. He was coy. 'Just cut,' he said. When it was done, I found out it was going to be sent to New York as a gift for Eido's zendo. Never during the cutting process

was I given room for the attendant anxieties that might arise from thoughts such as where, when, for whom, or is this work adequate."

Before the Walters left to go back to the East Coast, Suzuki asked Audrey if she'd make a buddha. She said she would bring one back when they returned.

Enlightened World

Charlie Page was a prominent lawyer who advised us pro bono. Bill Wenner was a general practitioner who was seeing Zen students for free. John Phillips was the director of the prestigious Hopkins Marine Station in Pacific Grove. Charlie and Caroline, Bill and Catherine, and John and Arleen Phillips arrived for a weekend stay. They took all three Stone Rooms. I went to the kitchen and told Ed they arrived, and he said he'd bake a nine-loaf batch of mixed grain bread for them to take home on Sunday—three loaves for each couple.

Writer Peter Matthiessen and his wife, writer Deborah Love, were at Tassajara as students. A few students could eat dinner with the guests every night, and this was the Matthiessens' night. I seated them with the Phillipses, Wenners, and Pages.

Several at the table had read books by Matthiessen. I loved his *At Play in the Fields of the Lord.* He and Deborah had been practicing with Eido at New York Zen Studies and had done sesshins with Soen and Yasutani. Matthiessen was also a co-founder of the *The Paris Review.* He talked about planning for a worldwide celebration of the environment to be called Earth Day. Discussion at the table focused on the upswelling of awareness of the imperative of living lightly on the earth in a sustainable way. Everyone had been involved in some way with activity to protect the environment. John Phillips and students were doing research on the effects of pesticides and chemicals on the marine environment. Charlie Page was involved with creating nature preserves, parks, and protected open space. Bill Wenner was chief of the medical staff at the Community Hospital of the Monterey Peninsula, concerned with the disposal of medical waste. There was lively conversation about the interconnection of all beings. And there was that word "ecology" again.

Bill Wenner brought up the horrors of the Vietnam War. Every person at the table expressed their opposition to the war in one way or another. So many people against it and yet it continued. I'd first met Bill in his office when he removed a cyst from my left temple. Behind him was a row of identical books. He reached for one and gave it to me. *Vietnam: Lotus in a Sea of Fire: A Buddhist Proposal for Peace* by Thich Nhat Hanh. Thich Nhat Hanh was a Vietnamese Buddhist monk. In 1967, he'd visited Tassajara and gave a well-attended talk in the Wenners' home.

It seemed to me that almost everyone was anti-war and becoming an environmentalist and the whole world was on the way to being enlightened.

The Armstrongs

Anne Armstrong was a well-known psychic. She and her husband Jim came in as students. They were followers of and good friends with Alan Watts. A number of Suzuki's students had gone to Anne Armstrong for readings. Yvonne was one of them. She introduced the Armstrongs to Suzuki at Tassajara. Anne told Suzuki she felt a little embarrassed about seeing his students and didn't want to interfere with his spiritual work. Suzuki told her, "You take care of their psychological aspect and I'll take care of their spiritual aspect. Don't worry about it."

She didn't relate to any students at Tassajara that way, though. Jim said the Zen Center board had talked about their application to come as students and approved it on the condition that she not do any readings while at Tassajara. Jim said he'd for sure come for the fall practice period but that Anne had too many obligations.

Before they left, Jim said that Suzuki was going to go see her, but he never got around to it. I thought, but didn't say, that Suzuki had no intention of doing so, that he wasn't interested in interpretive systems—psychics, psychologists, or astrologers. Suzuki summed it up when he said that he was interested in Chinese astrology as a young man but he came to feel that it wasn't necessary to know so much about oneself.

Outside of Tassajara, Anne continued to do readings for a few people around Zen Center. I didn't hear any negative feedback, but I did hear some far-out stuff. She said that Yvonne, so known for her efforts to assuage the suffering of humans and animals, astral traveled to automobile accidents at night. The Bakers got a reading together. Anne told another couple something they related to me in confidence. They had one child but Anne said she saw another who was with them but not with them. There had been a miscarriage. Anne told them that they were in a sense raising that lost soul in their aura.

A Mechanic

Driving Suzuki to San Francisco in my old Volvo, we got to a place not far north of the turnoff for Monterey where the highway divided, curved, and went through a long grove of eucalyptus trees and large boulders. While ascending a slope in that part of the road, the car lost power. I put it in neutral right away to reduce friction and watched as we slowed more and more on our approach to the top with me muttering "I think I can, I think I can." And we could. She just barely creeped to the beginning of the decline and then we were descending and glory be there was a lone service station at the bottom which I coasted into. I turned to Suzuki who'd been nodding off and said, "Car trouble." I knew the problem wasn't gas. I was pleased to see a garage with a lift for working on cars and asked the attendant if there was a mechanic about. He took a look at bald-headed me, and Suzuki in his travel robes, grimaced, scratched his head, looked away, then back, and sighed.

"A mechanic lives up there," he said, "and he works at the station some, but he's a difficult guy. His wife just ran off because he beat her. Been in trouble with the police about that and other things. Angry guy. He got screwed up in the Korean War." The man hemmed and hawed a bit, searching for words. "Doesn't take to those people well," he said slightly nodding toward Suzuki. "And he'll probably refuse to help you. He sits up there and broods most of the time. Got a drinking problem. Maybe better off getting a tow back to Salinas."

"We'll try him," I said. "Which house?"

"First one up the hill."

At the door we could hear the TV was on. I knocked. He came right away. Through the screen door, I could see pain in his face. I told him my car had broken down and asked if he could help. I didn't have much of a Texas accent, but with some people it instinctively resurrected. And I knew not to mouth off, be direct, respectful, brief.

He asked what type of car it was. Who was this guy with me and what did he do? I said it's a '56 Volvo sedan, that he's a Zen master and I'm his student. He was quiet for a moment—then invited us in. We sat down on his couch. He didn't appear to have been drinking, but his place smelled a little rank. He offered us black instant coffee with sugar and found some Oreo cookies, which he placed in front of us. The three of us drank and ate the Oreos.

The mechanic's posture had straightened since he first eyed us, and his face was softening. The disturbance I could feel from him at first was dissipating. He sat with us somewhat awkwardly, like a kid, shy in the presence of a visiting elder. There were a few words spoken, names exchanged. Where were we going? San Francisco.

After a moment of silence, he asked Suzuki how could he be a better person. I was so touched by his sincerity. I don't recall what the answer was, but I remember us sitting there comfortably with someone most people would not at all want to sit with. It was the most ordinary of social interactions. I think there was nothing that Suzuki said to the guy in words that mattered as much as what he said with his body, his presence. I guess it could be interpreted as a version of "I'm OK, you're OK," or maybe, "I'm buddha, you're buddha."

The mechanic insisted we stay in his house while he went to look at the car. Suzuki fell asleep as soon as we were alone, and I watched an episode of *Bewitched*. He returned in less than an hour and said the Volvo was ready to go. He wouldn't take money. Said, "Pay down below."

Back at the station, the attendant said there was no charge. I asked the attendant what the problem was. He didn't know.

"What did you-all do up there?" he asked. "Put some sort of magic spell on him?"

The Vague

I was in the Tassajara library, located in a corner of the office, reading *What the Buddha Taught* by Walpola Rahula. Bob Halpern, who was living in the city, had come to Tassajara for a few days, and was helping with some stone work. On a break, he walked into the office, came up to me, and said, "What are you doing?"

"Trying to catch up with you in reading about what it is we're all so involved with."

"We're involved with ... the Vague," he said dramatically. "That's all you need to know."

There was a fellow sitting near us who looked up and tilted his head a second. I could see he assumed he hadn't correctly understood what was just said.

"Hi," I said. "You're here as a guest student for a week, right?" Guest students followed the student schedule through lunch and then were on the guest schedule. They paid a reduced rate, more reduced if they stayed in student quarters.

"Right," he said. "I'd rather be a full-time Zen student, but I'm also a college student and I've got to study in the afternoon or I'll get behind. I have a question. Could you explain something?"

"Shoot," said Bob.

"I think there's a mistake in something you chant here before a meal."

He read the first four lines.

> Buddha was born at Kapilavastu
> Enlightened at Magadha
> Taught at Varanasi
> Entered Nirvana at Kusinagara.

"You have a problem with that?" Bob asked.

"Well it says in this book on Buddha's life that he first taught at Sarnath, not at Varanasi."

"Yeah," Bob said. "But Sarnath is just outside of Varanasi."

The guy continued. He said he was studying statistics and so to him, correct data was important. "Why not say Sarnath, then?"

"Maybe it's because they're thinking of Sarnath as a suburb of Varanasi," I said.

"Nope," Bob said. "It's because of—the Vague."

Bob's victim gave up on that but had another question about something that just seemed wrong, not close. He'd been reading from the collection of transcripts of Suzuki lectures and he'd come to one where Suzuki said, and he read:

> Dogen Zenji says zazen practice is like going through the mist. If you go through the mist, your robes will be wet even though you don't notice it, your robe will be naturally wet. When you go out in a sudden shower, even though you feel your robe is wet, it doesn't get through your robe. But when you get wet in the mist, even though you don't feel it, the moisture will penetrate into your body. That is how we should practice zazen.

The guest said he disagreed, that the more rain there was, the wetter you'd get, and the further it would penetrate. He said you could walk in a mist without it getting you wet through and through. I said yeah, I'd thought the same thing but it didn't matter. It's just a poetic way of saying that if we apply ourselves diligently and continually, we will naturally, slowly, reap the benefits of our efforts without noticing it.

"Well, why not use an example, a metaphor, which isn't obviously false?" he asked.

"It's a perfect example of our master's teaching," said Bob. "We understand the deep meaning." And then, leaning in toward the fellow, "We know because we are walking in the mist of [voice deepening and stretching it out for effect] ... the Vague."

"Oh no, Bob," I said, burying my head in my hands. "Please pay no attention to him," I told the bewildered guest student.

"When we hear ... the Vague," continued Bob, "we smile and nod."

"Well I can't do that," he said. "You're letting what you hear bypass rational consideration."

"If we don't do that," said Bob, "we won't get ... the Vague."

"Wait, wait, wait," I said, before the fellow packed up and left. "It's true there's a strong tendency here to do that, to hear what the teacher says and just let it in. But it's sort of like appreciating poetry. We're not being told to firmly believe anything, just to look for the truth in it which clearly isn't literal. Suzuki Roshi does say that we can't understand Zen by thinking about it. But this is more about letting go of beliefs than blindly believing things. Of course, people do tend to blindly believe but, overall, I'd say we've got a pretty low reading on the cult meter."

"Cult meter?" he asked.

"Every group has a reading on the cult meter," I said. "It's not a fixed reading, either. If you walk around here, you'll see it fluctuate depending on who you're around. It can change in time. Groups go through periods of high readings and then, if they're lucky, they'll crash, and the cult meter reading will go down. We seek a healthy balance. To do that, we practice zazen, bring zazen into our daily lives, follow the precepts in a sensible way ... "

"And practice," Bob added, " ... the Vague."

A Wordless Time

Peter told me a young woman would be arriving and asked if I could see she got lunch and settled in. I was there when she stepped out of a car that brought her and her long hair. Right away I had a special liking for her. I asked her if she wanted food or a hot springs bath first. She said she just hitchhiked from L.A. and was famished but would love a bath. I led her to the baths and said the women's side is on the right. She was surprised we didn't have mixed bathing. Soon it was Tassajara bread, rich vegetable soup, and salad from our garden. She'd already fallen in love with the place.

She hardly said anything, but I learned her name was Dianne Goldschlag. After lunch, she and I went on a walk downstream past the Narrows where few venture. We went skinny-dipping in a pool and took a very nice nap together on a large flat rock.

In October '67, Dianne had demonstrated and been arrested in the massive protest against the Vietnam War at the human circle around the Pentagon. She was one of the holdout fasters who'd been force fed. She lived and worked at the Fellowship of Reconciliation in Nyack, New York, and was a friend of Catholic peace activist Jim Forest, who ran it. She had spent time with Vietnamese monk Thich Nhat Hanh, who was staying in Forest's apartment in Manhattan hiding out due to his visa status and outspoken opposition to the Vietnam War.

Dianne got her first inkling of Zen on her way west in Boulder, Colorado, when she heard a talk by the humorous and light-hearted Paul Reps of *Zen Flesh, Zen Bones* fame. She'd been in Los Angeles working at a college in the art department and was having a difficult time emotionally. She felt confused about how to interact with society and how to communicate with people.

She phoned Forest who told her to go to a Zen Buddhist monastery where Thich Nhat Hanh and he had visited the year before. He said to get hold of his friend Peter, there, and tell him that you're a friend of ours, that you need a place to stay for a while, that you'll work, and that you have a sleeping bag.

The night before coming to Tassajara, Dianne slept by a fruit stand in Carmel Valley. She was awakened by police with flashlights who told her to move on. She hitched a ride to Jamesburg and walked a good deal of the mountain road before getting a lift into Tassajara.

On the phone, Peter had asked her if she ever sat zazen. She said she didn't know what that was. She was having trouble talking and answering questions, just wanted a quiet place where she could work. That wouldn't have succeeded with most people, but I guess the Forest connection, Peter's kind heart, and Dianne's sincere sweet voice did it.

The schedule of early and late zazen, services, and hours of work was too much for some people, but she slid right into it. The only stumbling block for her was the way we ate with oryoki. I offered to tutor her in that ritualized monastic eating practice.

We sat on zafus in the zendo, each with our oryoki placed on the meal board in front of us. "You'll hear the *kaishaku,* the wooden clackers, and then we gassho and recite the first few lines of the meal chant. When the chanting stops we bow to our oryoki."

"I got that far this morning," Dianne said. "Then it was hard to keep up and I did everything wrong."

"No one cares. We've all been through that. Now, I'll go through it and you just watch.

"Untie the top knot of the cloth and pull back the sides, exposing a folded cloth napkin. Open it and spread it across your lap. Pick up the little wiping cloth that covers the utensils in the sleeve and set them aside. Open the covering cloth by pulling the corners out and tucking them back in to make a rectangular pad for the bowls nested in the center. Move them to the left. Place the small lacquered one to the right and then the medium one in the middle, lifting them quietly with thumbs pressed inside the rim like this. Hold the utensil sleeve against the chest and slide it open, revealing the spoon, chopsticks, and *setsu*—the thin wooden stick that looks like a tongue depressor with a cloth pad on the end. Take out the spoon and lay it in front of the bowls, with the bowl of the spoon on the right. Place the chopsticks between the spoon and the bowls. Set the setsu down last." I turned to her. "It would have been easier to take the setsu out of the narrow sleeve first because it's the widest of the three and it's in front of the other two. But no—it comes out last placed vertically. And it's not just plopped down there but brought out beyond the bowls like this and back in low for a landing between the two smallest bowls with the bare end sticking out. Now we don't do this but in Japan like at Eiheiji, the sort of mother temple, at some point they put a few grains of rice on the end of the setsu and a monk comes by at the end of the meal and collects that food for offering to the hungry spirits. But you don't need to remember that part because we don't do it."

"I'm still back at untying the knot," she said.

"Just do what the person next to you does when the food's served," I said. "You bow with them to the servers while you're chanting and you move your right palm up a little to show them that's enough. Be sure not to take more than you can eat because you clean your bowls with the setsu and the water they bring at the end of the meal. Then the servers come with buckets to collect the wash water and serve it to the garden."

"That's when you chant about ambrosia," she said.

"Yep—that's right. 'The water with which we wash these bowls tastes like ambrosia. We offer it to the various spirits to satisfy them. *Om Makurasai. Svaha.*' That's a little Sanskrit mantra at the end there. And that water goes to the garden."

"Where does the offering from the tip of that thing go?"

"The setsu—we don't do that so I don't know. Ask Kobun. Maybe they add it to the wash water. So you got all that down?"

"Untie the knot and … and … ambrosia."

"You got it!"

Peter had told Dianne she could stay a week. After that she went to Berkeley to get settled. I got a letter from her with fanciful creatures drawn in the margins. She said the silence at Tassajara, where she didn't have to use many words, had a healing effect. I had a few days off from the guest dining room coming, so I went to see her. I took her to the Berkeley Zen Center for early morning zazen. We stayed for breakfast and she met people.

Soon, I received another letter saying she was getting rides from Berkeley to San Francisco for Suzuki's lectures. She loved the feeling she got watching and listening to him and after a few lectures she could understand what he was saying and liked that too. I was most pleased when she was back in Tassajara.

Dianne quickly made friends with our noble canine, Noah. They went on a hike together in the woods, Noah running ahead at times. She was approaching a bend in the trail when Noah came back barking and blocking her path. Slowly she went ahead and saw a rattlesnake coiled in the path just around the corner. She realized she'd been walking in a daze, enamored of her surroundings, and very well might have stepped on the rattler but for Noah's warning.

Suzuki arrived. Soon he was in his garden tending to plants and stones. On a break from the dining room, Dianne offered to

Dianne Goldschlag with Noah

help him. That worked out well and soon she could often be found squatting around a stone with him. She said he'd talk to the stones. She couldn't believe what that little man could move by himself, big stones she was sure he wouldn't be able to budge. Dianne had a rhythm with him in work that I admired. She followed Suzuki's lead, saw it was clear to him where the stones should face, and how they and the surrounding plants should be in his garden.

Walking by on my way to the dining room, there they were again—Dianne and Suzuki—together in his garden having a good wordless time.

Cheese Sandwiches

Taking LSD without precautions can lead to some unexpected initiations. I am reminded of Mark Lewis, a high school student from Carmel, who went with a friend to Tassajara, an hour and a half away—for their first acid trip. Anyone who read about how to take LSD knew that one should pick a trouble-free setting, preferably a natural one, and take it when in a calm state of mind—and, I'd add, a straight, quiet guide. Mark and his friend took it en route, figuring they'd be at Tassajara before the acid came on and that all they'd encounter would be the inspiring vibes of the monastery and the nurturing warmth of the hot springs there. They were coming in late after everyone was asleep. They thought they would be in a safe and controlled setting. But they didn't count on Larry.

Larry had been in a biker gang in my hometown of Fort Worth. He had a steel plate in his head that was inserted after a motorcycle accident. He was a big, tough, sweet guy who was trying to set his life straight. He had stumbled upon Tassajara while riding his motorcycle on the challenging road. Normally, we didn't take students who just showed up and would not have let him stay without first having some Zen practice experience elsewhere, but it was the more relaxed guest season and mainly, he was a mechanic. Clarke Mason was in the kitchen and E.L. could use more experienced help in the shop. So Larry had been living at Tassajara on a temporary basis, working in the shop, trying hard to practice zazen, and to fit in with the community. He sold his motorbike to a guest saying that he'd get another one when he needed it.

Sometimes he'd get out of sorts and I'd take him to the kitchen and make him a stack of cheese sandwiches. That would calm him down.

Larry had gone to Monterey in our pickup truck to buy parts and get a lumber order. Kathy Cook needed to go to the dentist and went with him. He promised he wouldn't drink, but the urge got the best of him. On their way back to Tassajara that night, she did not like the way he smelled or his driving and thought the lumber on the rack was not loaded right, as it kept shifting. When they stopped to view the stars from the top of the mountain, she got out of the vehicle and said she'd walk the rest of the way. Larry, who had a hopeless crush on Kathy, sat in the pickup and sulked.

Meanwhile, Mark and his friend were bouncing along in Mark's VW Bug. The acid was beginning to come on earlier than they expected, and time had become elastic. They couldn't tell if they'd been driving for minutes or hours. They pulled up next to Larry on the dirt road and asked how far Tassajara was. Larry told them it was about five miles down the road. He added, "And if you see a woman up ahead walking on the road, don't stop for her."

They perceived a warning tone in Larry's voice. They drove on, and indeed came upon a woman waving her arms at them. She stuck her head in the open window and told them she'd just gotten out of the pickup they passed because the driver was drunk and she was sure he was going to go off the road. They told her they'd give her a ride but warned her they were on LSD. They continued down the road with Kathy sitting between them. Mark drove slowly due to his mind-expanded condition. They were not too stoned to have forgotten what Larry had told them and how big and scary he was. Now, he was driving behind them looking at her sitting between them. The boys discussed this and worked themselves up into a state of near panic which didn't ease Kathy's mind. On the final stretch, they sped up, leaving Larry behind.

Down at Tassajara, I was the firewatch, the person whose duty it was to walk around after bedtime, blow out the Coleman lamps on the pathways, make sure all kerosene lamps in the cabins were out, and periodically strike together two wooden clackers that announced all was well and nighty-night. I heard a vehicle approaching and could tell by the engine's whine that it wasn't the pickup truck I was expecting. I walked up toward the gate in time to see car lights pull over to the side and shut off. I heard car doors open and close and saw two shadowy figures dart into the tall grass between the road and the creek. Then Kathy was walking fast and crying. I tried to talk to her, but she went right past me.

I was just about to go check out the two in the grass when the pickup came weaving in through the open gate and screeched to an abrupt halt beside me. I was confused. Why didn't she come back with Larry? I shined my flashlight on him and saw his puffy, unshaven face with a menacing gleam in his eye. A gust of alcohol laden breath wafted into my face. He asked where Kathy and the two guys were. I said she'd gone to her room and I didn't know anything about two guys. He looked back outside the gate then abruptly went to the tool shed. While I asked things like, "What's up Larry?" he single-mindedly examined the sharpened axes. I was greatly relieved, though not for long, when he finally settled on an axe handle devoid of the blade.

"Those goddamn guys picked her up after I told them not to and I'm gonna find them and beat their goddamn brains out," he said. He then proceeded to walk toward the exact spot where they were, as I stayed close to his side and tried to dissuade him. Finally, I said they weren't up there, that they'd gone to bed, and we could all talk about it the next day. "They've gone to bed where?" he asked. I said I had no idea—probably some cabin. "Then I'm gonna go through every goddamn cabin till I find them," he said and started down the road with me hanging on to him and pleading for him to reconsider. The students could deal with him but the guests—oh lord. I finally convinced him that at least he should take a break and have some cheese sandwiches.

We went to the kitchen where I lit a lamp and made him five thick cheese sandwiches. He ate them, got sleepy, and soon I was tucking him into his sleeping bag.

Mark and his friend lay in the tall grass for hours surely hallucinating mind-expanded nightmares of violent death. After a long spell of quiet, they drove back out.

The next morning Larry was driven out—sad and ashamed.

Army Ants

Peter Schneider liked the men's plunge at the baths to be hotter than the standard 108 degrees. Sometimes not enough cold water was added and it would get too hot for most. But not for Peter. He said his favorite was 112 which was so hot that I had to enter it slowly and, once submerged, move as little as possible. Every degree mattered. There was a thermometer floating in the plunge. I'd guess the temperature upon entering and rarely missed by more than a single degree. Due to Peter's preference and a lack of opposition, the water in the men's plunge tended to be 110 which is somewhat challenging to enter. The hotter the water, the greater the effect on one's body of course.

One four-and-nine-day morning at the baths, Peter came out of the plunge too fast into the cold air and fainted, hitting the hard floor with a smack! There was a spot of blood on his head and a drop on the floor. Bill Shurtleff and I were standing nearby. Bill suddenly fainted and fell to the floor next to Peter. Within a minute they both sat up dazed. Peter said he was OK. I asked Bill what happened to him. He said he faints at the sight of blood. Wow. That really happens.

I was taken aback because he'd talked about working with Albert Schweitzer as a volunteer at Schweitzer's hospital in Africa.

He said it wasn't a problem there. And that's not all that wasn't a problem in the African jungle.

Bill said that army ants would march into the village, army ants as portrayed in film as terrifying legions devouring all in their path who couldn't escape, leaving human skeletons in their wake. Bill painted a different picture. He said that the villagers welcomed the army ants because they cleaned everything so well, eating all the lice and other pests. He said once he was sitting in his hut reading when they entered his open door, covering the floor like a creeping carpet. He slipped out a window and watched them slowly and methodically pass through.

He said that Schweitzer, who was known as an authority on Bach, would give lovely organ recitals in the evening. Unfortunately, they were only for the white people there, as Schweitzer didn't consider the natives to be sufficiently sophisticated to appreciate such fine culture.

From Bill's Diary

June 10, 1968. I go to live at Tassajara up the Carmel Valley in the Santa Lucia Mountains. Give away all my possessions (leaving my lengthy journal, poems, and Nigerian wood sculpture with a friend) and hitchhike down Coast Highway One with only a backpack, to live there as a Zen monk, under Shunryu Suzuki, Japanese Zen master. Sit five-day *tangaryo*, and have my first superb meditation Samadhi, a totally blissful, transcendent, one-pointed state. I felt like meditating all night. Soon I copy down my first recipe ever, for Gluten Bread (moist, heavy, and delicious), which starts my long serious interest in food. Start work as a stone mason. Friends include Dan Welch, Jeffrey Broadbent, Chino Sensei, Paul and Ruthie Discoe, Ed Brown.

July 20. Talk with Peter Schneider about my haughtiness.

Aug. Start sitting full lotus.

Sept. 4-10. First sesshin. Tough but beautiful.

Most Important

There was a shosan ceremony at the end of the September sesshin in which Ed Brown asked: "Docho Roshi, last winter you told me the most important thing is to find out what is the most important thing. I can't keep up with it, it's too fast. How shall I continue from here?"

Suzuki answered: "The way to find out the most important thing is to accept things as it is without comparing one to the other. That is the most important thing. It means that when you are in the kitchen, you should devote yourself completely to the kitchen work, without comparing it to some other work. That is the most important thing. So, to find out something important for you is not to find some more important thing than to do kitchen work, but to be completely involved in your position. That is the most important thing."

The Lovers

Clarke Mason enjoyed taking care of the generators and vehicles but said it was too easy for him. He'd already learned how to make bread from Ed, but he wanted to work in the kitchen which he saw as the second center of Tassajara after the zendo. He asked Ed if he could work with him. E.L. could take care of the shop. Affirmative. So he was in the kitchen for the winter-spring practice period. He worked well with Ed. Clarke said, "Ed was the first to admit his volatile temper in those days. He was a moody son of a gun. It never bothered me. It bothered him more than anybody else. He did a damn good job even though he'd get so uptight at times he couldn't talk. It never really got in the way of things."

During the interim, Clarke went to the city and stayed with Bob Halpern across the street from Sokoji. Bob was going to visit a girlfriend who was a live-in nanny for a schoolteacher named Marian Ebright and invited Clarke to tag along. Marian was a sophisticated, lively, beautiful dark-skinned Mexican American of

Yaqui Indian descent. She and Clarke each had a void in their lives. He was divorced and she was separated. He didn't go back with Bob that night. After a week with Marian without leaving the house, he let Tassajara know he'd stay out one more week.

Marian had been sitting at Sokoji and had met Phillip Wilson there. She'd had a fling with Phillip that left her "scared silly of him" in Clarke's words. I told Clarke I understood. Phillip had his sweet side and his dark side. Once when Halpern and I were stopped at a red light in Japantown, Phillip was crossing the street in front of us and I said, "Hi Phillip." He looked at me, walked over to the car, took my arm through the open window, smashed it hard down on the door, and walked on. Halpern, ever the contrarian, said, "You asked for it—the way you said hi."

Clarke had to get back to Tassajara. He and Marian didn't want to part but they would be reunited soon. Marian had signed up to be a student at Tassajara for the guest season—and that was before she'd met Clarke. She would go there as soon as school was out. Her estranged husband would take care of their three girls for the summer. Clarke met with Suzuki in the city, told Suzuki he was in love, and got permission for him and Marian to live together as a couple at Tassajara.

Clarke arrived at Tassajara on April 30, a day before the guest season started, and got right back into the swing of things. He was in charge of getting the student meals out and worked on guest meals, as well. He also continued baking bread, which called for him to get started at 3:30 in the morning. Sometimes he didn't leave the kitchen till ten at night. He got to zazen as much as he could, but the kitchen came first, and he was so focused and efficient that he experienced work as an extension of zazen in the zendo. Then, Marian arrived.

"I was in love with this incredibly passionate woman," Clarke said. "She was well educated in literature and stuff and I was fascinated with her. Our relationship quickly became volatile. She was demanding. My attention was divided to say the least."

Clarke and Marian were so into each other that a good deal of the time they seemed to have forgotten they were students at Tassajara. They were following the schedule and doing their jobs most of the time, but were way out of synch for Tassajara. One day they drove out and came back two days later. Clarke told me they'd driven the rough roads of the Ventana Wilderness down into Big Sur. He was gaga about what a wonderful time they had. There was no hint that he had any second thoughts about disappearing like that.

Toward the end of the guest season, a meeting of students was called. Suzuki wasn't there at the time. We had no idea what it would be about. No guests were allowed. Right off the bat, Peter announced in a grave tone that the meeting was about Clarke and Marian and whether practice at Tassajara could survive the whirlwind of their affair. I looked over as the two of them, sitting next to each other, snapped to attention. Many people had something critical to say about Clarke and Marian's behavior, how outrageous it was, how they had created an unavoidable distraction from the practice. No one came to their defense. It went on quite a while. They were asked to please cool it and they, in semi-shock at what was transpiring, nodded that they would.

The next day I wondered what the heck we'd just done. I was ashamed and felt like I'd been in a mob that had just lynched two young lovers for breaking some vague taboo. I winced at the thought of something I said at the meeting and vowed never again to get caught up in that sort of behavior. The whole place was depressed for a couple of days. I had the sense we all knew it had been way too heavy but we didn't discuss it. We buried it.

Clarke and Marian did calm down. When we met, we pretended all was well, nothing had happened. They left together at the end of the guest season. He moved in with her. Two weeks later they broke up. Clarke moved in with Halpern and got to know other Zen he-men who were doing iron work. Soon Clarke was working with them carrying massive loads of thick rebar on his shoulders walking on an I-beam way up in the sky.

Chester Carlson

FEBRUARY 8, 1906 – SEPTEMBER 19, 1968

The inventor of xerography, Chester Carlson, died just as the guest season was ending. We had services for him at Tassajara and Sokoji. In the *Wind Bell*, a publication of the San Francisco Zen Center, Richard Baker called Chester Carlson "a first founder of Tassajara." Carlson had donated generously toward the purchase of Tassajara, and was honored in memory and services. Years before, Carlson was an attorney who worked in the U.S. Patent Office. He found that all the available methods of making copies of documents were impractical, so he decided to come up with a better way, and started experimenting in his apartment's kitchen. The first commercial machine, the Xerox 914, went on sale in 1959.

He and his wife Dorris got interested in Buddhism after reading Philip Kapleau's *Three Pillars of Zen* when it came out in 1965. She invited Kapleau to come to Rochester to work with her meditation group. From that sprang the Rochester Zen Center. Their living room was the first zendo. Carlson was also a major donor to Eido Shimano's New York Zen Studies Society.

Richard Baker attended the funeral in Rochester with Suzuki at Mrs. Carlson's request. In a tribute to Carlson in the *Wind Bell*, Richard wrote:

> He was one of the greatest philanthropists of our time, viewing his immense fortune, earned only since the 1940s, as a public trust in which the value of the dollar was determined by the good it could do for those who needed help. He supported at levels no other individual has equaled—the peace movement, psychical research, civil rights and integration, institutions dedicated to preserving our basic freedoms, universities, Vedantism and Zen Buddhism, and important individual research of such persons as a Nobel Laureate and

a Vietnamese monk [Thich Nhat Hanh]. These accomplishments were attributes of a man everyone felt kindly towards.

On the day before he died Mr. Carlson bought a balloon on a New York corner and immediately released it to fly over the city. He told his wife, "I wanted it to be free." I find him now in every person I meet. And for all the people practicing at Zen Mountain Center, which he did so much to create, he is there too.

Bamboo Tube

The first time I saw Max, he was standing by the samovar staring at the moon with his hands in gassho. I made myself some tea, said hi to a couple of dharma pals while waiting for the tea to steep, added two teaspoons of whole powdered milk, and turned to leave. Max was still staring at the moon with hands in gassho. I said hello. He turned toward me, gasshoed, and returned to the moon.

In time, I got to know Max. He was emotional and an open book like Ed, and like Ed, he had traumatic childhood experiences. He spent a good deal of growing up time in his father's car going from one place to another.

Max had lived in one of the apartments opposite Sokoji. For a time he decided to follow the practice of some Indian yogis by not wearing any clothes. He did that until he got word that Suzuki said he couldn't live there and do that.

At Max's first dokusan, he told Suzuki what a hard time he was having.

"What's your favorite thing to do here at Tassajara," Suzuki asked.

"Masturbation," Max answered.

Later, Max puzzled over Suzuki's response. "What did he say?" "Something about a bamboo tube with holes in it." "A bamboo tube with holes in it can't hold water?" He wondered about going back and asking Suzuki for clarification, but wisely decided the subject had been exhausted.

Rope Trick

I was on the road by the shop just starting to tie a load down on our six-ton truck. The tall sides were up, and the twelve-foot bed was full of metal scrap to sell in Monterey. Decades of accumulated junk—a bed frame, an old water tank, corrugated roofing, pipes, barbed wire, car parts, and some large, totally rusted iron sheets from a strange tall metal shed across the creek at the first crossing just below the lower barn. Robert Beck said long ago it was where they slaughtered pigs, skinned and hung them, and cut them up to eat.

Niels walked up, looked at the rope in my hands. "God damn, man, what the fuck way is this?"

"It's a trucker's hitch. A guest showed me how to do it back in the spring."

"Here," he said, taking the end of the rope from my hands, "I'll show you a better way to do it, the way we made this hitch on a ship."

He undid what I'd done and looked the rope over. "Oh oh—look at this!" He held up a frayed section. I said I wasn't worried about it. He shook his head, walked into the shop, came back with a hatchet, and put the rope down on a tree stump. I protested but he commanded me to watch. He cut the rope in two with a whack! Then he cut the offending end off with another whack, peeled back the strands on both ends and braided them together three times overlapping. I asked if it shouldn't be braided more, and he shook his head no with a scowl and said that it is now at maximum strength—as good as the rest of the rope.

"OK," I said, "well help me get this truck tied down so I can get on my way."

He berated me for being in a hurry and said we'd get it tied down soon enough. "You see," he said, "it's a pulley. You can move that truck with it—anything that doesn't break the rope."

"It would break before it pulled that truck. It's just half inch. That truck must be ... how many tons, now? No way."

"Watch!"

"Can we do that later?"

"No! Now!"

I obeyed. We didn't exactly follow Japanese monastic seniority protocol. He got in the truck and repositioned it facing out of the shop so that it was sideways to the road which had a downward grade toward the creek. Took off the emergency brake. Left it in neutral. Fastened the rope to the frame of the truck under the front bumper and ran the other end of the rope around the smooth, thick trunk of a small sycamore tree nearby.

"You're going to break the rope."

"David Chadwick! (which he pronounced *Chadowick*), you don't know anything!" he called out loud enough for E.L. in the shop to turn his head. Niels ran another hitch off the first one going around a second small tree. "The second one gives it double pulling power," he said. With a mighty tug on the end of his two-pulley-system, he dug his feet in and strained and screamed for me to help, so I pulled too, and the truck then did move forward maybe a foot and then another and then another.

"You did it! I know you could do more but that's good. I thought for sure the rope was going to break."

"Me, too!"

After panting for a moment it was back to securing the load on the truck. He tied it all down with me assisting. He yelled at me strongly and impatiently. When the last hitch was tight, he walked around and checked each again, nodding with a grave look of approval. He said that stuff can shift and settle and to check to make sure it's all tight at the top at Chews Ridge, and then back down at Jamesburg where the paved road starts. "If it's loose, just tug on the hitches this way to tighten. And when you are ready to untie, just do this," and he pulled on the hitch another way so that it was instantly undone. Then he walked around the truck giving each hitch a swift tug so that all hung loose.

"Niels! Why'd you do that?!"

"Now, you show me!" he called out. At least he didn't walk off laughing.

Torture Chamber

Screams from the next room. They were at it again. Sam was Rolfing Max. Rolfing, or "structural integration," as taught by Ida Rolf at Esalen, had the reputation of being painful, invasive body work. Yet many people I knew swore by it.

Gasps from next door. Sam had gone through the full series of treatments from toes to nose and now was transmitting what he'd picked up to his malleable cabin mate, Max.

I peeked in through the half-open door. It made me cringe to watch as Sam's naked, bony, bald, sweating body sat on Max's naked, bony, bald, sweating body. Sam dug his elbow into Max's back. Max cried out. "The pain is a sign that you're uptight there," Sam said. "Breathe into it. Resistance will make it worse." But Max couldn't help but groan and cry out.

It was at times like living next door to a torture chamber.

Flung in the Ocean OCTOBER

Jeanne Campbell grabbed me to help her get the East West Printers' workshop in San Francisco ready for a surprise going away party for the Bakers. About twenty of us had come to the city from Tassajara. Yvonne Rand, Loring Palmer, and other Zennies had spent a couple of days busily cleaning, getting the place decorated with streamers, balloons, and flowers which with food, drink, and music created a festive environment. Suzuki was sending Richard to Japan to spend time at Eiheiji, study with other teachers, and have some firsthand experience of Japanese culture. One day in the spring Richard heard from others that Suzuki had mentioned Richard was going to Japan. Suzuki said he couldn't control him so he decided to throw him in the ocean.

Mel Weitsman and Calvin Wall played a recorder duet, Ken Spiker played shakuhachi, John Thompson flamenco guitar. Lou Harrison came with his classical Chinese music ensemble. There were slides of Tassajara, a rock band named Marble Farm, and a light show. Hundreds of people came. I urged Lou and his partner Bill Colvig to stay and dance with us but Lou thought we might not be quite ready for that.

Loring got me stoned. I munched on the goodies, then went up on the roof, the music at a nice level, a soothing view of the city at night. There was a large glass bottle sitting filled with a clear liquid. Five gallons probably. It had a cork top. I uncorked it and took a sniff, then fell back gasping. It was ammonia. I lay down with the most awful, deadly feeling. Memories of butterflies I'd euthanized till mother's sympathetic repulsion to such executions finally got through to me. I sincerely apologized to my victims—*please forgive me. I didn't realize what I was doing.* Dizzy, I lay on the roof recovering, breathing the nontoxic air and then after a while thinking, *good lord Richard is leaving. What will it be like without him?*

On October 29, there was a small farewell gathering with the Bakers and their closest friends on the *SS California Bear*, an attack freighter from WWII now serving as a commercial cargo ship with a passenger suite. It would depart the next day for Kobe after two weeks of postponements. We got word at Tassajara on Halloween that they were finally on their way. So Ginny, Sally, and Dicky Ducky, as I'd heard Sally call him, were now slowly, quietly, with few amenities, sliding away from us over the Pacific to a new and unpredictable life in Japan. And again, I wondered, *what will it be like without him?*

Cookie Threat

Tassajara afternoon tea breaks were a pleasant, brief mingling of the minions. Sometimes there would be fruit or a small treat. On four-and-nine days we'd have a sit-down tea with treat. One such day cookies still warm from the oven were served. Most people were happy to get the cookie and didn't care what it had in it. Students were gathering and waiting to start nibbling.

As I approached the dining room, Sam came out looking distressed. "I don't know what to do," he said with a slight whimper in his voice. "There's a cookie with sugar in it being served today. If I eat it, it will have a bad effect on my consciousness and practice. If I don't, I will not be following Suzuki Roshi's teaching to accept what is offered." I told him I would eat his cookie for him, thus relieving him of all practice obligations.

Later that day, I heard Sam berating Max for eating the cookie served him and thus lowering the overall spiritual vibration of their quarters and sabotaging their special practice relationship.

Lobbing Apples OCTOBER

There were apple trees at Church Creek Ranch with ripe apples that the caretakers said were going to go to waste. Some students went there with a truck and the Land Cruiser to do apple picking. Suzuki joined them. He was curious about the place.

It's about five miles from Tassajara to Church Creek via trail, fewer but more taxing by walking up-creek. To drive there from Tassajara, one goes about four miles up to Black Butte Summit, along it a short way, then back down a few miles to Church Creek Ranch on another steep and windy unpaved road.

Tassajara runs along a narrow canyon. Church Creek Ranch is more open with a great swath of sky overhead, the slopes rising more gently with large sandstone formations, oaks below, pines above, and a meadow. There was so much green, sunlight galore for the winter, and a farmhouse with a swimming pool.

Suzuki got out of the truck cab that day, looked around, and said, "Let's buy it."

Everyone was trying to be good Zen students and work hard in serious silence. They got the boxes out of the truck and stacked them by the trees. "Where's Roshi?" someone asked. Suddenly an apple whizzed by. Then another. They looked up and saw Suzuki in an apple tree. He threw another one. The serious atmosphere broke. They got the work done in a couple of hours and thoroughly enjoyed themselves.

Fondly Recalling

In morning tea with the officers, Suzuki mentioned his brief trip to Church Creek Ranch with a hint of nostalgia even though it had only been a few days since he was there. Claude, head monk for the practice period, knew what Suzuki had in mind—a sister temple. Claude had spent time in Japan where founding another temple in a similar setting would not be unusual. And he gave Suzuki some scriptural backup, which Suzuki referred to in a lecture.

"The other day, Claude said that Buddha said, 'If you go to the mountain and find some good place to build, like Church Creek or the Horse Pasture, after you come back to your monastery, you will tell your teacher, "Here is a good place to practice our way. Let's build a monastery there." Then many people will go. That is my way. I didn't provide any land or holy place like that. It was there, I just found it accidentally. People are very interested in that place, and that is why I have so many students.' Buddha understood in that way. He did not do anything—the teaching, too, was there before he taught it or before he discovered it."

In a lecture he gave at Tassajara, Suzuki was reading and commenting on the phantasmagoric Lotus Sutra, and when he came to "The leaders of men and their disciples with neat and lovely gardens abounding with fruits and beautiful flowers," he paused and said, "like Church Creek," and went on reading.

Austerity Chart

Sam and Max, which I suspected meant Max going along with Sam, created rules and a schedule for themselves that was superimposed over the already spartan Tassajara rules and schedule. Theirs included extra zazen and study, a strict code of silence—small talk not allowed. There were also strictures in regard to food and drink consumption.

It was practice period and, except for the four-and-nine-day relaxed schedule, we were eating three meals a day oryoki style in the zendo. The first two meals had three bowls each and dinner was only two bowls, usually of leftovers.

Calling the vittles from each ladle, paddle, or serving spoon a serving, Sam calculated how many were offered a day. They agreed on reducing the number allowable to them by one third. Seconds were off limits. After all, they were only eating to the extent necessary to sustain consciousness in order to practice the Buddha Way and strive toward enlightenment and the liberation of all sentient beings.

Hard-sitting, hardworking, mainly young people on a vegetarian diet ate enthusiastically at every meal. The guys definitely ate more than the gals. That's natural, as men need to eat more to produce the same amount of energy as women. But Sam and Max were eating less than any of the women—while sitting uprighteously and chewing each bite fifty times as Ohsawa, the founder of the macrobiotic movement, suggested. Also, following Ohsawa's belief, they minimized how much water they drank.

Sam tacked a chart to the redwood board wall of his room. On it each would write the number of servings they had accepted for each meal. After dinner one day I overheard Sam's review of how well they'd done that week. Max had fallen long. He'd had four extra servings. Sam was distraught. "How can I practice with you if you won't follow the rules we've agreed on?!" he cried. Max was apologizing, sniffing, begging for forgiveness. I feared he'd have a breakdown. The poor guy, just a couple of hours previously, I'd seen him shoveling gravel for a concrete pour.

Senior Denizen

"I was forty. How old! But it was a whole universe of twenty-year-olds."

There were just a few older women at Tassajara—two in their forties and one in her fifties. Katharine Thanas had studied at the

San Francisco Art Institute. Classmate Mary Quagliata brought her to Sokoji the first time. Katharine was embarrassed and discouraged because she couldn't sit a whole period without moving and that seemed frowned upon. The third time she came, Suzuki was making a round of the room with his stick and stopped behind her. She knew he was there, was apprehensive. He reached down and touched her shoulder, stayed a brief moment, then moved on. She felt energized, spirits lifted. "I was on the ceiling the rest of the period," she said.

Still, Katharine had a shy nature and was a little afraid of Suzuki. She didn't try to fraternize with him. But just the opposite happened. At Tassajara he chose her to be his *anja*, cabin cleaner, after Louise Pryor, who showed Katherine what the job entailed. On her first day, she entered nervously, not sure what to do. Everything was already so tidy. She saw a small piece of cake on the altar by the Buddha statue and asked what she should do with that. He told her to leave it there and put her to work in the garden. After an hour he invited her in, served her tea. She noted how he poured the hot water into the cups first and then into the teapot, swished it around, and poured it back out before using it to make the tea. She realized he was showing her how to make tea for him and his guests. Then he served her the piece of cake. She wondered if he thought she was asking for it but no, he was showing her how to serve the cake.

Katharine's cabin was next to Suzuki's. One day she felt ill. He came over with a pot of tea. That made her feel better. She hoped he'd come again but he didn't. At the shosan ceremony on the next to last day of her first practice period, Katharine presented herself before Suzuki and said, "Inside there's a yes and a no." Suzuki answered, "Follow the yes." She kept thinking about his answer. She said it was a powerful turning point for her because he'd pushed her to figure out what yes would mean to her and that was complete commitment.

Study Hall

Sam and Max were reading the same sutra and had set aside a special time to discuss it. They sat next to each other for the early morning study period in the dining room. A monitor periodically walked around the room waking those nodding and checking to make sure people were reading something Buddhist or practice-oriented. One morning, the monitor stopped at Max who had been staring blankly and urged him to return to reading. Sam leaned over and scolded the monitor, saying that Max might have just had an enlightenment experience, was being absorbed in the white light, and the monitor might be interfering with his becoming a never-returner. Max returned to reading.

The Cleaver

On a night before a four-and-nine day when the wake-up bell was an hour later, Niels and I sat up talking in the dark well after fire-watch. "I'm hungry," he said.

"Me, too. And there's only one solution to our problem."

"We become Viking pirates!" He pronounced that with a W sound for the V.

We walked over to the kitchen in the cold darkness. Once inside I felt my way to the kitchen altar where there was a kerosene lamp. "Where there's an altar, there's a match," I said, espousing one of the fundamental truths I learned through Zen practice. Found some quickly. Kept the flame low to not put a telltale bright glow in the window.

If it was Bob Halpern and me, we might cook eggs and make toast with butter and jam and sit down to eat at the kitchen table in the center of the room. We'd clean and put stuff back as we went along, wash our dishes, and leave without a trace. We didn't take food that would make the kitchen noticeably short of anything or screw up a planned meal.

Niels had a more direct approach. A large aluminum pot sat on the Wolf stovetop. Niels removed the lid. "It's gruel! Let's just eat the gruel!" he enthused. He stuck his hand in it and brought some to his mouth. "That's gross," I said and got bowls and spoons. He was into it though, acting like a starved madman, making grunting noises. I walked over to the stove but before I could dish up, Niels yelled out in surprise.

"God damn! God damn you, fucking crazy!" I turned to see what that was about. In the dark corner, sitting full lotus on the grill top was Ed Brown staring at us with a large meat cleaver in his lap. Niels yelled at him more with unrestrained cursing.

Ed continued to sit there quietly as Niels tried to engage him. I quickly re-covered the pot, put our unused bowls and spoons back in place, and grabbed Niels for our mind-blown and embarrassed retreat.

Lotus Sutra

Suzuki was lecturing on the Lotus Sutra night after night, reading from the text, which was full of hyperbolic description and lists. He would explain the meaning of terms and names of various mythical Buddhas, and so forth.

I went to him and urged him to stop, suggesting the alternative of having us read the sutra in study, and then meet with him later to discuss it. I was persistent but unsuccessful. However, it had some effect.

In his lecture that night, talking about Kandrasuryapradipa, I heard

> ... that is to say, to the disciples, he preached the law containing the Four Noble Truths, and starting from the chain of causes and effects, tending to overcome birth, decrepitude, sickness, death, sorrow, lamentation, woe, grief, despondency, and finally leading to nirvana. The first one is, as you know, the Four Noble Truths for the Theravada Buddhists or Sravakas. And the teaching of causality or interdependency of birth, old age, "sickness, death, sorrow, lamentation, woe, grief, despondency, and finally leading to nirvana" is the

> teaching of the Pratyekayana. Here, as you heard, there is no distinction between the teaching for the Sravakas and the teaching for the Pratyekas. From the viewpoint of the Lotus Sutra, which is a Mahayana teaching ...

Suddenly, he stopped reading and looked up.

"Oh, I'm sorry. Maybe it is too tedious for you."

Lots of laughter from students.

"I almost gave up already," he said. "So I can imagine how you feel. When I was young, I would go to school by train. As long as the train was going, I was sleeping, but when the train stopped, I woke up. I woke up suddenly because I had to get off. As long as my tedious lecture is going, you may sleep. If I stop my lecture, you should wake up."

Carrying the Stick

The zendo, though filled with students on their zafus, was often so quiet one could hear a person readjusting their position during zazen. At other times, there would be coughs, sneezes, nose blowing, giggles, soft sobbing, groans, and sighs of relief. I envisioned the room as a forest, beautifully still at times, then scampering, bird calls, wind through the leaves, the crack of a branch breaking. That's the kyosaku, the stick, smacking down on someone's shoulders during zazen, penetrating the silence of the forest. When someone carried the stick, they were called the *junko,* not to be confused with the junco, one of the songbirds of those woods.

Kobun said that among Buddhists, only the Japanese Zennists had such a striking tradition. We made our own kyosaku from hardwood in the shop. They were modeled after the original imports we received from Japan—about three feet long, round at the handle end, and flat on the business end. The junko did the rounds to whack someone nodding off—or a sitter who requested it. The sound would be sharp and the stick could sting. I liked it, found it invigorating, but my shoulders were wide and meaty. I pitied those with a narrower, less cushioned place to strike.

Dan taught me how to carry the kyosaku with characteristic pleasant yet serious thoroughness. An exciting and slightly scary new responsibility.

Ten minutes into the period I'd rise from my seat, walk softly to the front, put hands in gassho and slide my feet sideways to the mid-point where the kyosaku rested on a polished board with short legs on the tatami before the altar. I'd gassho, pick it up with two hands, holding it horizontally at eye height, slide sideways to stop before the abbot Suzuki, or his empty seat if he wasn't there, bow with him or without him, move back to the center of the right aisle, turn around, and position the stick vertically resting on my cupped fingers and held firmly by thumbs. One of our little dances.

What a view of the zendo! Most men shaved their heads as the Japanese priests did. The women's hair was up. After a moment of surveying those silent, almost motionless sitters facing the walls and partition, I'd move one foot forward slowly, then the next. If someone were nodding, I'd rest the broad end of the stick on their right shoulder. They'd put their hands in gassho and lean forward to the left. Then, whack! Then the other side, and then we'd bow together. People would request it—put their hands in gassho as I approached.

Some junkos struck harder than others. Sitting facing the wall, I got to where I could tell who some of the junkos were by the sound of their kyosaku landing. Maybe the hardest hitter was an older guy named Stan White, disciplining us youngsters.

When people first came to sit, they'd often not be told about the stick. Then they'd be sitting on their cushion doing zazen with us for the first time, hear those whacks, and wonder what the heck it was. When they realized that people were getting hit during meditation it could be shocking, even frightening.

The first time Ruthie Discoe sat, she burst out crying when the person next to her was hit. It could be especially weird for guests. I'd be asked in the dining room what that noise was coming out of the meditation hall. For those guests who came to join us in zazen—not what they expected. It was really no big deal to students though—after they'd acclimated to the practice.

Suzuki would, at times, walk around the zendo and hit a nodding sitter. He used his nyoi to hit each shoulder twice in rapid succession. On rare occasions, he would go around the zendo hitting everyone as an encouragement to make a greater effort. That's called *rensaku*. Suzuki might do rensaku in an emotional storm, as when he shouted in zazen one morning, "You think you're sitting zazen!? You're not sitting zazen! You're wasting your time on the cushion!" Then leaping off his cushion and striking each of us what seemed as hard as he could. Another time, he stood up from his seat on the altar platform and said fiercely, "I want students who will follow me through life and death!" Then he leaped down and whacked every one of us.

Once toward the end of a period, Niels kept looking up at the clock on the wall. Suzuki was on the floor in a flash and started hitting Niels repeatedly. Niels kept his hands in gassho, and when Suzuki stopped, leaned back and whispered he had to get up before the end of the period to hit the densho bell. Suzuki softly apologized and went back to his seat.

Usually when Suzuki walked around with his nyoi the feeling was alert, peaceful. Ed Brown said, "When Suzuki Roshi hit me, reality, everything just disappeared. And after a bit I would think, *wait a minute, wasn't there something happening here?* And then slowly, *Oh yes, here we are. There's a room here.*"

Unlike Ed, when Suzuki hit me, I'd gassho and think, *thank you Roshi*, or sometimes, *Oh come on now Roshi, you can hit harder than that.*

The worst was when I'd be carrying the kyosaku and Suzuki would gassho asking to be hit. *Oh no, please don't ask.* I knew I couldn't just tap him. It was a test. So I'd hit him as hard as I dared in the tiny spot on his shoulder that was muscle, not shoulder bone or neck. What a relief when it went OK. I was grateful I only had to hit him on one shoulder because he wore a sacrosanct kesa which covered the other.

As the best field goal kickers sometimes send the ball wide, there would be occasional unfortunate strikes with the kyosaku—to the shoulder bone rather than muscle. Or the neck. The worst was an ear. The most embarrassing—the head. The best was the rare sound of the wood cracking upon impact—for eventually the kyosaku would break, said by Kobun to be a sign of a job well done.

Niels said that as he picked up the kyosaku at the altar he'd envision the medieval church's instruments of inquisitional torture.

Kobun Chino said kyosaku means Manjushri's hand. He said it's a compassionate and encouraging offering and when we put our hands in gassho to receive it and bow deeply afterwards, we are expressing our gratitude to Manjushri for helping us to wake up to buddha mind.

Cold Feet

The first batch of robes were gray and thin for the summer. After that they were black or blue and made from heavier material. White shirt-length *jibon* or full length white underrobes were worn, as well. It made one look more fully dressed with the white V under the dark V where they came together below the neck.

The cold didn't bother me as much as many others. I'd go to the zendo wearing the same thin, gray polyester robe we'd been issued for the July heat of the first practice period. And no underwear. I found it invigorating to walk to the zendo that way—the zendo, which seemed the same temperature as outside. I'd be all compact in lotus position and before long would start feeling warm. As soon as I was back in my room, though, I'd put on warm clothes for the day.

In dokusan, Suzuki asked me how wearing so little in such cold weather worked for me. I said fine and he said, "Good. Pretty good." I think he saw that I was not doing so to prove something. He'd wear long underwear. A woman student had given him a pair years before in San Francisco and he'd been into them ever since. I didn't wear socks—unless I was doing work that necessitated boots, or if it got down into the twenties. Then my toes would start hurting. Higher than that, it didn't bother me. We weren't supposed to wear socks in the zendo, but some people needed socks and mittens, or they'd get chilblains.

Some students got kerosene heaters for their rooms. Sam and Max borrowed kerosene lamps from the dining room, so many that their neighbors in an adjoining room complained that they were all going to get asphyxiated.

I couldn't take the fumes from that much kerosene, so I got a tiny propane powered stove. I'd fill my rather small tank off one of the large propane tanks up by the shop. After a while, I couldn't take what it had done to the air in my room, either.

Actually, the zendo was usually a little warmer than the outside for two reasons. In cold weather we learned not to extinguish the glass kerosene lamps that were mounted on the zendo walls and altar at night—just turned them down to where only a tiny bit of the wick was exposed. Instead of a flame then, they had a glow. That was good for a few degrees. And secondly, once people were in the room, their bodies added some warmth—but not a lot.

There was a damp cloth mat in the entryway to the zendo. Tassajara is a dusty place and we were supposed to wipe our bare feet on it before entering. When it got cold, people would step over it. I stepped on it in freezing weather once and it crunched under my feet. It didn't get that cold often though.

After evening zazen, some students liked to go to the dining room, get a good fire going in the cast iron stove, warm up next to it, then go to their cabins and get in their sleeping bag as quickly as they could. I liked to get into my sleeping bag naked at night and enjoyed the initial ice-cold jolt knowing that it was about to warm up. I had an Arctic sleeping bag I'd ordered from L.L. Bean in Maine. So cozy.

Anagarika Govinda

Author and scholar Anagarika Govinda was a sweet Austrian man with a white beard whom we called Lama Govinda. Tassajara, deep in that narrow valley, gets darker every day as winter approaches, and we were having a mid-November cold spell when he and his wife, Li Gotami from India, arrived. They were accompanied by Iru Price of the San Francisco Arya Maitreya Mandala center, which Govinda founded for the study of Vajrayana. Govinda and Li Gotami ate in the zendo with us, served with bowls on trays, hers with a bottle of Tabasco sauce. They wore matching outfits, he a reddish-purple robe and pointed cap, with a long wide yellow scarf, a *katak*. The inner layer of his cap was yellow, too. She wore a sleeveless dress of the same color and a yellow blouse and katak.

Suzuki treated Govinda with a great deal of respect. They looked at Buddhist texts together. Govinda gave a talk and led an open discussion. He spoke softly with his Austrian accent, came across as humble, low key.

The Govindas stayed for four days resting after weeks of his American speaking tour. They welcomed visits by students who had many questions. On the third day, there was an exhibition in the dining room of their photography and art depicting a wide range of Tibetan culture and Budhism. Li Gotami stayed in the dining room all day explaining the subject of their work and answering questions.

I'd read Govinda's *The Way of the White Clouds*, about his years studying Buddhism in Tibet. He described the coldest scenes, one I recall where they'd boil water to wash their faces, pour it into a bowl, and plunge their hands into the water which already had a film of ice on top. And then he said that Tassajara was the coldest place he'd ever been. The fireplace in Stone One didn't heat the place that well. Peter Schneider asked Suzuki if he'd suggest students study with Govinda. Suzuki said, "I found Govinda.... I cannot agree, but I liked his attitude."

Got Mordang

One morning, Louise came up to Niels and me and said, "Got mordang!" Niels looked puzzled. "Got mordang!" She laughed and said, "It's what I dreamed you say for good morning in Danish! Got mordang!" And she walked off laughing and saying "Got mordang!" to everyone she passed.

Louise was Suzuki's first *jisha* and *anja,* personal attendant and cabin cleaner. Kobun explained that usually senior disciples hold those positions as they are the two who spend the most time with the abbot. Suzuki kept Louise as his jisha for over a year.

The first time Louise did zazen was the three-day tangaryo for those attending the first practice period. It was a bit of a shock for her to find out that she would be sitting not one introductory period, but practically non-stop for a seeming eternity. It was nothing new for Dan who'd gone through a much more severe tangaryo in Japan a few years prior. He could sit like the oak tree out front. Louise kept at it as if it were nothing new, sitting steady like a sapling. She told me that the words true and tree came from related roots meaning steadfast. That seemed to describe them both to me—each in their own way.

I asked Louise what it was like working so closely with Suzuki. "With Suzuki Roshi I never felt criticized," she said. "I was treated with utmost respect. I was never told I did anything wrong. Even though I felt self-doubt, I never felt that it was generated from him."

Suzuki had a cold and it was chilly outside. Louise suggested he wear a turtleneck shirt under his robes to keep warm in the zendo. As she followed him carrying incense, he stopped, turned around and said, "Do you think that the turtleneck makes me look like a hippie?" She knew if she said yes he would go back to his cabin and remove it. "No, no—you look fine," she told him, and they went on into the zendo.

All of us were trying hard to be good Zen students, but Louise noticed Suzuki didn't seem to be trying to do anything. "There was no forced mindfulness or forced slowness. He always seemed very appreciative of nature and aware of the stream and trees and what he was walking through and he seemed to enjoy it very much."

She was cleaning his bathroom and picked up a razor. There were Japanese characters on the handle. She thought of it as calligraphy and said, "Oh Roshi, is this a poem written on your razor?" Suzuki answered, "No, that's the name of the razor company."

When Anagarika Govinda arrived with his wife Li Gotami, their art was put on display in the dining room. Louise went with Suzuki to meet them in the first Stone Room. They sat together. Louise said Suzuki formally asked Govinda, "Could you please tell me what is the cause of suffering?" She forgot what Govinda said, but she was struck by Suzuki's question. "It was so humble and respectful of him."

Louise and I were at the samovar talking with Niels. He said, "You know what the difference between Tassajara and the city is?" We waited for his answer. "Tassajara doesn't have cockroaches!"

"Good point," I said.

Louise added, "I read that while you're sleeping, cockroaches will come and nibble on your eyelashes."

Bill's Diary

Nov. 1968. First experience of cold at Tassajara. It's terrible, but I try to wear as little clothing as possible. Read Huxley's *Perennial Philosophy*, Yogananda's *Autobiography of a Yogi*, and Prabhavananda's translation of *The Bhagavad Gita*.

Nov. 16. I start "No Eating Between Meals" vow.

Nov. 26. Lama Govinda visits Tassajara.

Dec. 1-7. First Rohatsu sesshin. I am defeated on the fifth day by cold. Very humbling. At this time of my life all my heroes are great spiritual figures: Milarepa, Dogen, Ramakrishna, Ramana Maharshi, Meister Eckhart. I want to devote the rest of my life to living like them, renouncing the world and practicing only meditation. But at the same time, I am bothered by the suffering in the outside world, especially hunger. I am torn between the solitary life and that of serving in the world. Which does the Bodhisattva choose?

Dec. Publish *The Tassajara Food Trip*, Xerox copy of my cookbook, heavily macrobiotic, 63 pages, with a woodblock print of the Tibetan mantra/mandala *Om Mani Padme Hum* on page 1. Send out about 100 copies. This is my second book.

Lovely Lady

It was winter interim when most people were gone. Cold as heck, the sun behind the ridges almost the whole day. Robert Beck was visiting, staying in Stone Room One.

During evening zazen, a vehicle came in. It didn't stop in front but turned and roared away past the zendo and toward the baths on our narrow dead-end dirt road only used for hauling things during the day. After zazen, Stan White was standing outside smoking a cigarette, as usual. He'd been in the office and said that a vehicle had gone out to Grasshopper Flats. I said I'd check it out. Robert walked out there with me.

At first, I couldn't find any vehicle, but then I saw a flashlight's beam and noticed there was a Volkswagen bus out in the dark at the end of Eldon's berm. A man was standing next to the VW bus. We walked out and said hi.

"Is this 101?" he asked.

"What do you mean?" I came back.

"One oh one—highway 101! Is this 101?"

"You're way in the middle of the wilderness, Los Padres National Forest. U.S. 101's an hour and a half from here."

"Ah, shit," he said. "What about that freeway there?"

"Where?"

"Right over there."

"There's no freeway here. Just a flat piece of land with some oak trees. Maybe you'd like to rest?"

"You a Motel Six?"

It kept going like that. He was totally disoriented, more than I would have thought possible. He was acting fairly normal, talking matter-of-factly, but he could not interpret his surroundings.

There were two women in the back of the bus. They were quiet. The vehicle would have to be pulled out of there. The front tires were a good way down the berm slope. Robert invited them to join him in Stone One. He added logs to the fire. We gave them blankets to wrap themselves and helped them sit in front of the fire.

The guy couldn't remember his name for a while, but then said he'd been called "Al." Soon, then, Al became more coherent. He said they'd taken belladonna. Ohhh. That made sense. I had never taken it or wanted to. As I recalled, it was in some eye drops and was poisonous. I didn't know if Al was right but he said that the amount to get you high is just short of the amount to kill you. In my experience, psychedelics don't generally cause one to see things that aren't there. One can interpret what's there as being all sorts of stuff or have visions. But belladonna makes people see realistic hallucinations. I'd met a handful of people who took it and they all reported that. They also all had bad trips. Seems it's a guaranteed bummer. I talked to one guy who said he saw an army of witches with hatchets coming at him.

All of a sudden Al jumped up. "Lee!" he yelled. "Lee's out there!"

Of course. There were two couples. The male from the other couple was "out there" and named Lee.

"Where?" Robert asked.

"On top of the mountain."

Robert, Al, and I headed up the road. The top could be a lot of places. Going around the first hairpin turn, Robert called out, "Stop! There's someone back in there!"

The little creek came down and went under the road in a culvert at that spot. About fifty feet back in the trees and darkness was a person sitting in the creek, sitting in the creek in almost freezing weather. It was so dark it was miraculous that Robert saw him. The guy's hands were in the air as if he were reaching for something. We asked him to come with us.

"Wait a minute," he said. "I've got to get some underwear."

After further talk we discovered that he thought he was in his bedroom in Berkeley looking in his dresser.

A while later Lee had dry clothes on from our goodwill. All four of them were bundled up in front of the fire. Robert and I took Lee and the women to the baths to soak in the hot sulfur water. Al wanted to keep talking to the fire. I was about to enter the plunge when I heard screaming. I zipped back to Stone One. Al was gone. But he was still screaming. I found him in Tassajara Creek. He wouldn't go back to the room with the fireplace. A skull had come out of it and threatened to take him back down where it came from.

After some more melodrama things calmed down and we led them to the large cabin with a kitchen, across from the lower garden, that had been Richard Baker's place. Al stayed up while his friends went to sleep. He talked crazy to me until it started getting light. Then, Lee got up, insisting that we were in Berkeley. I told him he was at Tassajara at the end of a long road in the woods in Monterey County. So he threw open the door, exposing the ground, trees, and the hillside rising beyond. "Oh yeah? See! This is Berkeley! Look at the snow!" There was no snow and Berkeley's average yearly snowfall is nil.

This was all having an effect on me. I was hallucinating a little myself, having to make an effort to hold on to the relative sanity I was used to. I realized how hard it would be to take care of people who were disconnected from consensus reality. It seemed to me that to do it right we'd need about eight of us rotating in shifts. No wonder so many professionals depend on their patients taking prescribed drugs.

By nine in the morning they'd eaten food brought on trays from the kitchen, drunk coffee, and come down to something approaching normalcy. Their VW bus was waiting in front of the cabin for them. They thanked us for our help. As he got behind the steering wheel, Al exclaimed what a great trip it had been, adding how much he looked forward to the next time.

—CHAPTER THREE—

1969 BEGINS

Big Snow JANUARY

Thick snow in the early morning darkness on the way to zazen—rare for Tassajara. Walking after breakfast into the morning light. Snow covering ground, roofs, branches, the bridge to the baths. I walked out to Grasshopper Flats, up the Hogback. The air was crisp, the smell clean and pure. I stood on the Hogback trail at the summit, gazing at the snow-covered mountainsides. The waterfall was cascading down from a snowdrift. Trees up the mountainsides and down to the valley floor were decked in snow. At my feet it was a foot deep. Within that frozen winter landscape, a stillness. But no silence. What is that racket? Oh, yes. I stood there entranced, listening to a symphony of cracking, snapping, falling, landing branches, and whole trees not accustomed to the weight—from miles around with echoes and reverberations throughout the white vista.

This winter-spring practice period would have no shuso. Suzuki wanted Jean Ross to be shuso, but she would be visiting with her mother and aunt in Michigan. He suggested she come for part of it, but she said she wouldn't do it unless she would be there the whole practice period. She agreed to come for the following fall. Suzuki didn't want anyone else to be before her, so we had a practice period without a head monk.

Kobun had returned to Japan. Suzuki was sick with another flu. Katagiri came in with around forty students from down creek. Sporting heavy backpacks, they waved goodbye to their rides and crossed the Arroyo Seco River at the Horse Bridge. They walked a short way to where the trail crosses the creek at a wide spot. There they soldiered on with help from a rope a few hearty members of their troupe strung across the knee high water.

We were snowed in a good deal of that winter. A couple of our daring winter hikers found that Larry and his wife Jules, the caretakers of Church Creek Ranch, had mostly run out of supplies. The Tassajara phone line was down. The Lamberts' phone in Jamesburg was used to contact the Church family. They sent a helicopter to the ranch which then hopped over with some welcome supplies for Tassajara. The hard part was getting to Lamberts' and back.

I was sent out several times to get mail, a few supplies, and to communicate with the Zen Center office. What joy I experienced when Peter came to me in study period before breakfast to tell me to get ready. The first trip Dan drove me up as far as the Land Cruiser would go with chains and four-wheel-drive. We had to stop a few times to remove fallen branches.

I headed out with heavy jacket, boots, gloves, and a large backpack containing only the outgoing mail. It was getting deep when I came across a camper stuck on the side of the road just outside of the entrance to China Camp. The fellow inside had walked into Tassajara a few days before to let us know he was up there but was OK. He offered me brandy. There was a knock on the door. It was Loring Palmer. Loring was coming in on snowshoes. He had the mail, which relieved me of that much weight. There was still plenty for me to do—and I'd bring whatever mail arrived the following day. It was comforting to run into someone I knew way up on that chilly snowy mountain. We visited for a bit, but I needed to get on my way.

I hadn't gone far before wishing I'd asked Loring to let me use his snowshoes. The snow got so deep in places that it was a struggle to keep going. I had to plod on, and even at times, crawl.

It took hours, but I didn't mind. It was so beautiful, still, clear, the air so crisp. I recalled an experience Suzuki had when he was a young monk cutting firewood in the snow with his fierce master, Gyokujun So'on. Little Shunryu paused to rest for a moment and looked out at the beautiful snowscape. So'on pulled the thin blade on his saw way back and let it go—slap!—painfully on Shunryu's unsuspecting cheek.

On my solo trudge in the snow, after descending a good deal, I ran into Esselen Indian elder Fred Nason in his pickup by the entrance to his ranch, where the national forest ended. He gave me a ride to Lamberts' where I had left my car. I'd done so during the interim at Peter's suggestion. I left the outgoing mail with Marian Lambert, Jamesburg's postmaster, and went into Monterey late afternoon and did some shopping, including buying a pair of snowshoes.

I stopped by Vic and Shayna's place in Pacific Grove, drank wine, played music, and slept on the couch. Got up early and by ten in the morning was snowshoeing back into Tassajara with as much supplies as I could stuff into my backpack. The snowshoes made me feel like I was walking with jumbo tennis rackets. Wearing them turned the hike from an ordeal into an inspiration. I even came upon a novel sight—a couple guys riding on top of the snow in a jeep fitted with what seemed to be huge inner tubes for tires.

As I walked back into Tassajara bearing the vital supplies, I was greeted by a couple of students eager to know if I'd brought tobacco. Yes, I had. They followed me to the office where I unloaded a large can of Top rolling tobacco and some Zigzag papers. Things had gotten dire in the tobacco department while we were snowed in. Stan was always happy to share his cheap Top Tobacco under normal circumstances. But when his stash got low, he got stingy. The week before I'd met a jonesing smoker coming back from the parking lot who said the ashtrays in the cars had already been gone through. To some, I'd just returned from what was a successful drug run.

The next time I hiked out, I took the Land Cruiser up as far as it would go and parked it so I could walk back to it the next day and drive the last three and a half miles instead of walk. We wouldn't normally leave a vehicle unattended up there for long because of the wrong people with guns and alcohol who might shoot up a lone car. But it was unlikely that anyone would get to that point in deep snow.

I'd gotten as far as the chains and four-wheel-drive would go. But then I thought, what the heck, and hooked the cable from the front-mounted winch around a tree and pulled the vehicle up fifty feet more, and then kept doing that—for fun—till I got to a place where there was only scrub brush. But that didn't hold—the chain just uprooted it. So, I walked from there with snowshoes.

While in town, I visited the Monterey Institute of Foreign Studies, a language school, and applied for the summer intensive in Japanese. I wanted to study the language of my teachers and of the country and culture they came from. I knew that the chants we did were in an older, classical Buddhist Japanese, and Sino-Japanese, but studying the modern language would surely be a good step toward learning more about them. There was also another reason I wanted to do this. I wanted a break from being at Tassajara and running the dining room through the whole guest season.

I knew they would be planning for the summer guest season staffing soon, so when I got back, I informed our dear director, Peter, that I'd only be able to run the dining room for the first two months, and then I'd be off to Monterey till the fall practice period. His immediate response was, "David, if you don't run the dining room for the whole summer, you'll never be able to come back to Tassajara again."

My response to that was, "Baloney."

"OK," he said. "I want to talk to Suzuki Roshi and the staff about this."

But Suzuki was in the city, so we forgot about it for the time being.

Bridge Out

Snowfall melt and heavy March rains swelled the creek to such an extent that it took away the bridge to the baths. I stood looking at the incredibly fierce flow with its thunderous sound and watched branches and whole trees being swept downstream. I could hear boulders rolling beneath the surface.

A large sycamore tree leaned over the creek next to where the bridge had been. Up in the shop, Paul and Niels were preparing boards and supports for a temporary bridge. Sam, Bob, and I brought long runs of heavy rope. From past years, there were already spikes for climbing, driven into the leaning sycamore trunk. Bob, who was fearless at heights, planned to scoot across the narrowing trunk to a spot above the baths, then drop down a short way onto the roof. He had the ends of two lengths of rope, tied them around his waist and started to climb. I grabbed him and said, "You are not going up there without safety gear."

Sam spoke. "If he is mindful, he will not fall."

I turned around to face Sam. "He will *not* go up without safety gear!"

So Bob put on gear that kept him connected to the tree. It would slow him down, but it would also be a shame to lose him due to a momentary slip in mindfulness.

It was still scary watching him crawl up and along the leaning trunk above the torrent. We lowered him down onto the roof of the bath house and he secured each of his ends of rope to the base of two steel railing posts located on each side of where the washed-out bridge had met the deck. Niels had shown him how to do it so that the ropes absolutely would hold. Soon, we had two lengths of rope stretched above the creek. Two-by-fours had been nailed together with holes near the ends for the ropes to pass through. One-by-four planks were were nailed on top and pushed toward the baths. We pulled the ropes as taut as we could on our side and used trucker's hitches to tighten them further. Thus, a walkway was created.

There were no handrail ropes yet. For that we needed something higher to hold them—a beam to be placed behind the sides of a thick wide opening in the wall at the men's plunge. We had such beams gathered from our demolitions stacked at Grasshopper Flats. The one we chose was about a four-by-ten, maybe six feet long. Heavy.

I began to carry it across the new walkway which swung to the sides somewhat and was only a couple of feet above the rushing, threatening flow. *Where's Niels?* I wondered. He could have danced across that. Bob too. He should have come back from the other side.

About halfway over, my weight had lowered the bridge-in-the-making so that the water was lapping at my feet. I carried the beam like a tightrope walker carrying a balancing pole. Then I tilted to the right and over-compensated to the left, and the end dipped a bit into the rushing water, which grabbed hold of it. I fought, tried to pull it back.

Over the roar of the fattened creek, I could hear fearful voices yelling, "Let go! Let it go!" and I realized I had to. In an instant it zoomed away from me at incredible speed, quickly disappearing into the downstream distance. I had a strong flash of loss that in retrospect seems archetypal, like losing a loved one in an emergency.

On the second attempt, the replacement beam and I both made it across. Soon there were two rope handrails with vertical lengths connected to the walkway ropes every few feet. It all held together, designed and overseen by Paul, and tightened with trucker's hitches by Niels so that it stayed well above the fray. Paul said it would be good until a decent replacement bridge was ready.

The Trippers

At an evening meeting of students, the agenda had been covered, and there we all were sitting around the dining room, enjoying the energy of being together and not wanting to go back to our cabins and to bed. Suzuki wasn't there to say, "Maybe this is already too much talk."

The tables were pushed against the walls and fifty or so of us sat on straight-backed wooden chairs loosely arranged in an oval. Someone broke the silence by saying he'd like to conduct a poll on a topic of interest to him. Peter, who was leading the meeting, said OK.

"How many people here have taken LSD?" the pollster asked. Almost all hands shot up. The room filled with laughter.

"Do mescaline or psilocybin count?" a student asked. "Yes," she was told. The student added her hand and a few others went up. More laughter.

Then the pollster asked who'd had more than one trip, and a number of hands went down. This line of questioning continued. How many have had five? More hands down. Ten? Many hands down. Fifteen? Only a few hands remained. At one hundred only one person's hand was up—Reb's. He had taken it alone to meditate.

Really? Alone? Maybe he was taking small doses, I thought. I never thought of taking acid alone as a good idea. That was years behind him now that he was focused on Zen practice, and maybe had come to the same conclusion that Kobun did, that LSD was spiritual masturbation.

Golden Gloves

Reb was an intense student, and our plumber. When Bob introduced us in 1968, Reb was sitting in Bob's room in the city in full lotus with a slightly crazed look of fierce determination. "This is Reb," Bob said. "We were best friends growing up." Bob pointed out the window to a long automobile. "That's a Cadillac hearse he drove here from Minneapolis. He came to Tassajara to visit me during the first practice period and he couldn't stay. But now he's here, here to attain *samyaksambodhi*," Bob concluded with a flourish.

"Well, that's wonderful," I said. "And what is *samyaksambodhi?*" I added.

"Complete, unsurpassed enlightenment," Bob said.

I don't remember Reb saying anything in that exchange. From the day he arrived, Reb seemed to me to be an older student. Like Bob, he sat as near Suzuki as he could in the zendo, watching him closely. Unlike Bob and me, Reb didn't screw around, didn't lose his focus. He got a job with the Bank of America. Attended every zazen and lecture, studied the sutras in his room. He went running, too—seriously—like all the way to the ocean through Golden Gate Park and back.

Bob said that Reb was a Golden Gloves champ. He did look strong. During high school days, Bob said he and Reb, both robust, walked down Minneapolis sidewalks side by side, elbows protruding, forcing all others to hug the building or step into the gutter.

Reb had a near-death experience not long after arriving. He'd gone swimming in the ocean and the current started to carry him out. He had a hard time getting back. A brush with death is an excellent encouragement to practice sincerely and, in his case, even more sincerely.

Snow Gone MARCH

When most of the snow had melted up top, we still couldn't drive to Jamesburg, because the road was out in several places, the worst a half mile or so up the road from Tassajara. There'd been a landslide which included a giant boulder that took the county road crew a few days to clear with the help of dynamite. Finally, they blasted it into some pieces and buried them right there in the road using a backhoe and bulldozer. Till then, we'd have trucks meet on both sides of the slide to transfer goods from one to the other.

I was sorry when they were successful, because I enjoyed being treated to an occasional distant explosion. And aside from the fireworks, it was good to have the road crew staying with us right by where they were working. We fed them and gave them whatever Stone and Pine Rooms they needed. They brought food of their own, too, especially the type we didn't have—meat and beer. They were fun. Always joking.

Richard Gomez, a solid, friendly guy, was head of the crew. I called Henry the clown. He reminded me of Buddy Hackett—quirky. This crew's only job was to work on unpaved Monterey County roads. They'd come in and clear Tassajara Road when there was a slide or tree down. They'd plow snow out of the way. And in the spring, after the last of the heavy seasonal rains, they'd spend a couple of weeks on it—fixing culverts, shoring up walls, widening in places, getting it ready for the wide, low blade of the grader, which left the road as bump free as possible. By the time they were through, it was like gliding down a freeway compared to the condition the winter had left it in.

The first load of supplies that made it through included rice and flour for bread. Thank goodness. Relief at last. Due to the heavy snowpack up top, we'd gone through all the brown rice, white rice, rolled oats, buckwheat, bulgur wheat noodles, other noodles, flour, and were down to eating wheat berries cooked with some brown rice found buried behind boxes in the storeroom. And when that brown rice ran out, there were just wheat berries.

I'd bought the wheat berries on a grain run so that we could make our own flour, but we found it was too time-consuming to make flour more than every now and then. The wheat berries were too tough for normal eating. They should have been ground up into cracked wheat, but we ate them whole. Whole grain won't digest well at all if you don't chew it, at least somewhat. Proof of that was seen by Reb the plumber when he went to fix stopped-up toilets, and when the truck came in to pump our septic tanks in the spring. The pipes and septic tanks were stuffed with a massive amount of undigested wheat berries.

Phone Line

At the start of study period, still dark, Peter asked me to check the phone line and see if we could get reconnected. I told him I'd leave as soon as there was light. The creek had come down enough to cross it without worrying about being snatched by the torrent and shot down toward the Arroyo Seco. When I was out earlier, I'd driven over to Fred's Camp and verified at the connection to Pacific Bell that the problem was on our side. But conditions were such that I couldn't drive to the Horse Bridge to check further.

I got a backpack with a few tools and the portable crank phone and left, as it was getting light enough to see the line. I followed it from the office downstream looking for a break or a ground. To follow the line, the creek had to be crossed four times. Temporary creek crossings with stones and boards had been made by students on their days off wanting to get to the Narrows. I got past the first three without getting my boots too wet. Then, a large sycamore had fallen and served as the last crossing. Rather than balancing nervously as I walked over the fallen log with a cold flowing creek below, I crawled on it. Before the Narrows, the line follows the trail that goes uphill beside a small creek. There was no break or obvious grounding of the line so far.

On the Horse Pasture Trail, I followed the line not far to a wide expanse. Distant mountains visible, the path curving around the mountainside. The line ahead swayed unbroken across a wide expanse to the other side. The problem lay somewhere ahead.

I returned to Tassajara to prepare for a longer haul. Niels came along to carry the heavy pack of gear to the creek crossing before the Horse Bridge. Noah joined us, too. I had a light pack with our lunch and a water bottle. After I'd crawled across the log, Niels taunted me doing a sort of two-step on the log crossing the creek. But I was fine. Nevertheless, the creek was too swift and deep for Noah, there, so Niels ended up carrying him across on the log.

After walking and checking the line for a couple hours, we stopped to rest and drink water. Niels unloaded the heavy backpack and sighed. Noah was barking not far off. I looked up at the sun and figured it was before noon.

I'd brought my sleeping bag rolled up on top of the pack. Niels opened the pack and started questioning the wisdom of bringing so much. "Bolt cutters?"

"Might need 'em—and if I do, there they are."

He grunted and kept looking. One by one he took out the ceramic insulators, wire cutters, electricians' pliers, file, hammer, nails, a few screw drivers, a wonder bar for prying, flashlight and extra batteries, burner for heating water with a small pan, some rice, miso, and green tea, a change of clothes, and Basic H liquid soap to protect skin from poison oak. Attached to the outside were extra line and rope, a canteen of water I'd fill at every opportunity, a pruning saw, a Swedish saw, and a hatchet.

"You don't want this," Niels said, taking out a snakebite kit. I'd heard that too, so I agreed. Apparently the kits with their razor-blade caused more harm than it was worth. It was now considered better to use a tourniquet to block the poison and then loosen the tourniquet now and then to allow the poison to hit the heart little by little.

"A goddamn come-along!" He held it up and looked at me in wonderment.

"I might have to tighten the line."

"You could do that without it. I can make a come-along with the rope that will do anything this will!"

I was going to question this, but Noah's barking and an eerie cry got our attention. "Look!" Niels called out. "Noah got a deer!"

I could see through the trees uphill Noah's teeth clamped on a small deer's front legs. The deer cried out like a baby. Noah lunged for its neck. Pathetic cries continued. I yelled at Noah to stop and ran up, but it was all over. A young doe. Some blood. Noah was panting, unconcerned with my objections. He lay down.

We stood there in silence, which was then broken by me. "What are we going to do with the deer?"

"What do you mean? We leave it here. Do you plan to have it for dinner?"

"Well, someone should."

"And how are you going to get it to them?"

"I'll carry it."

"That's the stupidest thing I've ever heard!"

I kept insisting. He kept calling me stupid. But we trudged on, Niels with the pack on his shoulders, me with the doe over mine.

"David Chadowick, you are a complete crazy man."

"I couldn't leave it," I said.

"You know how many animals are dying all the time everywhere all over the woods? You want to carry them, too?"

"This one is our responsibility," I said.

"Noah's religion is killing. You should follow Noah into the woods every day and carry back all the animals he kills."

After half an hour we reached the creek crossing. The creek was wide at that spot and not flowing fast. It could be crossed—though with some effort. And no matter how easy it is to maneuver, it was still cold, cold as heck. The students who came in that way for the winter-spring practice period did so before the heavy rains. We were doing it well after, but it was still pretty high.

Niels had done the heavy-lifting up till then. I put the deer down and my clothes on a rock next to my Red Wing boots, handed one end of the rope to Niels, then walked the bank upstream for as far as it would let me. I stepped naked into the creek and gasped, then up to my knees and gasped again. The next step sank me above the waist and I screamed involuntarily.

"You sound like you're having an orgasm!" he called out.

I couldn't make a snappy retort, as I was hyperventilating. I struggled and stumbled but didn't fall down. Aiming straight across, but battered by the current, I got to the other bank opposite from where Niels stood. We secured each side, and I went back to the other side holding the rope which made it a lot easier.

"And it's tight, thanks to your masterful trucker's hitch," I praised.

"It was for ships long before trucks. It's a Viking knot."

Niels took off his clothes, lifted the pack over his head, stepped in the water on the up-creek side of the rope, as the creek would push him toward it. He was taller than me, so it hit him hip level. "You call this cold? This is like a hot bath compared to a creek in a Danish winter!"

"Niels, it can only get so cold before it's ice," I said.

"No! In Denmark, the water is so used to the cold that it takes another ten degrees to freeze it!"

He carried on and without screaming or exhibiting any difficulty. I followed him with my clothes over my head. Noah jumped in and was swept downstream. By the time we were both on the other side, Noah came running up to us. I stepped back in.

"Why are you going back?" Niels asked.

"To get the doe."

"That's complete crazy!"

I ignored him and got the deer, which I struggled to get across. Then I put the deer down, dried off, and got dressed as quickly as I could.

"Now you are on your own to carry the ninety-pound pack and the dead deer," Niels said. "And any other dead animals you find. There are probably a lot of dead insects in the bushes you could get!"

I realized I couldn't go any further with the deer. The Willow Creek trail was just above the embankment.

"I'll leave it here and tell the rangers," I said. "Maybe someone will eat it."

"It will be eaten for sure," he said, "but I bet it's not by people."

"OK, guess I'd better get going," I said.

"No! First, we must have a coffee break!"

"No coffee. Just tea."

"I wouldn't have come if I'd known that you didn't bring coffee!"

We got the burner going, heated some creek water, and shared a cup of bancha, even though Niels was still naked in the cold. He then emptied the pack on the ground and started going through it all again.

"What are you doing?" I asked.

"I'm going to lighten your load."

"No. Come on."

"Shut up. You don't know what you're doing. I've used tools all my life. Wire-cutters," he said, picking them up, puting them into the pack. Soon, he'd filled the backpack he would carry with gear, making my own load more bearable.

As Niels crossed the creek, he called to Noah to return with him, and Noah was carried downstream again. Then, Niels and I stood on opposing banks yelling insults at each other as he got dressed. Noah stood by Niels's side shaking off the water. "You're complete crazy!" Niels called out again.

"You're complete Viking!" I yelled back, pronouncing it as he did with a W.

We left the rope there for posterity, which might well include us in the future, but not me on this trip. I'd get rides back as far as they could take me and walk the rest.

I bowed a gassho to the poor little doe corpse, then carried that still fairly heavy pack toward the Arroyo Seco and the Horse Bridge.

The next day, I found where the line was out. It wasn't broken, though. It was sunken in a muddy spot in the earth with a branch on top. Swedish saw to the rescue. I walked the rest of the line and cleared a few bad places, but left everything else to a later spring cleaning.

I reached Fred's Camp in the dark. Got a ride to where the Carmel Valley Road met the Arroyo Seco Greenfield Road and started walking. Came upon a farmhouse with a light on. They were kind and gave me water which I'd run out of. I called Lambert's place in Jamesburg. Silas was there. Then I fell asleep sitting at the kind people's kitchen table until Silas arrived and woke me up.

Steering Wheel

I was returning alone driving the six-ton Dodge flatbed with a truckload of horse manure from Carmel Valley for the garden. A few miles to go on the rutted dirt road, coming down a steep grade toward one of the switchbacks, the steering wheel suddenly came off in my hands. As I held it in front of my face, the sharp turn where the road reverses direction was getting closer and closer. I squeezed on the brakes hard, ready to pump if we started to slide.

As the truck slowed, I glanced toward the drop-off on the right side leading to the quickly approaching drop-off straight ahead. Not slowing down fast enough, I pulled the emergency brake, pushed my foot down harder. The truck rolled up on the berm of the curve and came to a stop just as the front wheels rolled on to the top of it.

Looking below, I made a mental note to thank the road crew for putting that sizable rise there. Then I walked downhill a couple miles into Tassajara, arriving during the afternoon work meeting outside the shop. I passed through the circle of fellow students, went up to E.L., handed him the steering wheel and told him where he could find the truck. No one but E.L. paid any special attention.

Slow Fast

Fasting Can Save Your Life by Herbert Shelton made the rounds in the hands of those of us who tended to get tripped out on something. Shelton had a clinic where people, usually who had a serious illness, would rest while fasting. He monitored the fasts of some terminally-ill patients for up to ninety days.

After reading the book, I became obsessed with the idea of fasting to cure my hemorrhoids and clear up my complexion. To really do it right, I had to go to Shelton's clinic in Escondido. I went to Katagiri and babbled on rather crazed about it. He said, "Please take care of your health." I calmed down a little and decided I'd wait until the practice period was over—which was soon—and then fast in my room. I told Peter that, after consulting with Katagiri, I was taking the first part of my interim break fasting at Tassajara.

On the first day of interim, I went to zazen and service, then to my room in the dorm and lay down. I slept a lot and was hungry the first few days, then hunger faded away. I had hardly stopped to rest for a few years and now it was just one long stopping to rest. On the fourth day, I lay on my sleeping bag on my tatami and felt completely satisfied. On the fifth day I realized I didn't care about anything, including the reasons I had for fasting. *I should be embarrassed,* I thought, but I didn't care enough to be embarrassed. The sixth day was dreamy. On the seventh day Peter came and asked if I wanted to go to the city. I slept most of the way but a pain in my throat kept waking me up.

I lay with the pain in my throat in a room in one of the apartments across from Sokoji. The pain was sharp and getting sharper. Someone suggested I talk to a holistic doctor she knew, so I called him. He told me I was going through detoxification, and it was too much for my tonsils. He suggested to take a 1000 milligrams of vitamin C every few hours. There was no vitamin C in the apartment at the time and I was too out-of-it to go get any. I just lay there in pain. It got dark. I went to sleep and was awakened by the pain. It got so bad it was all I could notice. I lay there focusing on the pain. Then I started to experience it as something like electricity, not painful or pleasant. I could see that fear of it, and trying to avoid it, was what made it painful. Then it became an intense bright light. And then, I became that light.

Someone came in and gave me a glass of water with a vitamin C tablet. I took it. I woke up the next morning feeling weak but not much pain. There was another vitamin C on a dish and a glass of water next to me on the floor. I took it.

A few of us went downtown to a cafe for breakfast. I felt light. I had a glass of orange juice, which is what Shelton advised as a good way to break a fast. Drinking that glass of orange juice was a euphoric experience. I was back to the world.

A Big Scare

On a four-and-nine day in late April some students went downstream with their bag lunches. After some urging, Suzuki agreed to join them. I was getting the afternoon refreshment, a crock of lemonade, out on a table under the grape arbor in the courtyard when they returned, and as they approached I immediately caught a wave of a dreadful excitement. Someone spoke. "Suzuki Roshi just almost drowned at the Narrows!" They were shaken, yet exhibited a stunned relief. As they drank lemonade, several speaking at once, I pieced together what happened. At the Narrows, some were sitting on the smooth granite slopes eating their lunches, others in the water. A voice called out, "Where's Roshi?" Nowhere to be seen. He was quickly found at the bottom of the pool and brought out coughing up water and gasping.

Suzuki said that Peter and some beautiful girls were enjoying themselves so much in the water that he thought he'd join them. So, forgetting that he couldn't swim, he slid down into the Narrows pool and quickly disappeared to the depths. Once down there he realized he needed to get out. He looked up at the dangling legs of the beautiful girls. He tried to reach them, but they were too far away. He held his arms up but no one saw them. So he tried to walk out but he couldn't touch bottom. Then he started taking in water. He got scared but thought he wouldn't die because there were too many students so near. But if he was going to die, he thought he should stop struggling and just be still in his last moment. However, before that last moment came, he was pulled out.

Suzuki said that when he couldn't breathe, he realized how poor his practice was and saw that we would never have good practice unless we became quite serious. From that day, he said he would practice zazen sitting moment after moment as if he were dying in the water. Not struggling. Shikantaza. Just sitting.

Ben Yuhmin

It was not unusual for a young guy with a beard and ponytail to arrive at Tassajara, but that's where the usual ended with Roovane. He came in with some students from the city during winter interim. He wasn't expected. "Roshi told me I could come," he said.

A call to Sokoji confirmed Suzuki had given him the nod, but neglected to pass it on. Still, it wasn't kosher to come unannounced. Roovane was adamant and articulate and said that if he wasn't accepted, he'd sit outside the gate in the cold.

There were deliberations among the officers. It was decided that he had to go back to San Francisco and then could return right away—which he did. He went into a three-day tangaryo the next day. It was so cold in the unheated zendo that he had trouble standing up from his seat for service—like he had to thaw out. After it was over and he was officially entered as a student, he went on and on about how great tangaryo was, and what he learned about himself and the world and cosmos. But he said he owed it all to Meg Gawler who'd also just arrived and sat there with him like a rock. He said that he'd not been sitting long, had practically not even heard of Buddhism until quite recently, and had only sat in the city a short time before finagling himself in.

A garrulous talker with a New York City accent, Robert Front had been making fifty to a hundred dollars an hour in New York as a Madison Avenue consultant. He became dissatisfied. Wishing to know what it's all about, he turned to psychology. He got dissatisfied with that and left a PhD program in clinical psychology at the University of Montana—just walked out, never told them anything. Leaving there, his car broke down in the snow, way out beyond any shop that might service it. He went to a farmhouse and knocked on the door. A naked man answered, introduced himself as Daniel Eggink, and invited Front to join their commune. There were other naked people, there too. And guns. But Front stuck around. He gave himself a new name: Roovane Ben Yuhmin which had roots in his family history.

Eggink had some big ideas for his commune. They had a TV studio in the house from which they could broadcast. He was planning on inviting a thousand people to come build homes on the land. They were going to invite the Beatles and the Grateful Dead. International advertising was planned.

On New Year's Eve 1968, everyone took acid. Eggink led Roovane to sit on a hilltop and groove on the stars. He brought a rifle. After they'd sat for a while, Eggink told Roovane that he was going to kill him. Having left behind, through the magic of chemistry, his normal small self, Roovane said that was OK with him. But Eggink didn't follow through on it. He talked about his spiritual quest, about Alan Watts, and said he had a Zen teacher, revered him so much he'd stolen his teaching stick but then returned it. He concluded with, "You want to meet this man," gave Roovane $300, and put him on a plane to San Francisco.

January 1, 1969, Roovane walked into Sokoji. He had two names of people to meet: Suzuki Roshi and Loring Palmer. He met Loring but not Suzuki, who was ill in bed. So he started sitting. A few days later, Suzuki got up and walked to the corner grocery store. On his return, he seemed to be having trouble opening the massive door to the temple. Roovane had been watching from the steps of an apartment building across the street, ran over, opened the door for him, and introduced himself.

At Tassajara, Roovane couldn't persuade the authorities to let him stay for the practice period that was soon to begin. He thought sitting the three-day tangaryo should be enough to qualify him, but it wasn't a ticket to the practice period, just to being a student. So he said he'd be back as soon as he could.

Roovane was back at Tassajara in mid-April full of enthusiasm and with a shaved head. He threw himself into gardening right away, something he knew nothing about. Paul and Ruthie Discoe appreciated his energy and gave him guidance. There was no limit to what he would take on. The breaks after meals were for him opportunities for extracurricular activities. For instance, Paul suggested he make candles so we could stop buying them. At first, there was resistance to this idea, because people wanted good-looking candles for the altars. But Roovane bought wax, molds, and wicks, and with Paul's advice was on his way to matching store-bought quality. Suzuki heard about it, checked his work out, and told him, "Remember the important thing is the wicks must be in the center."

"Of course," Roovane replied, and appreciated Suzuki's smile in return.

In the city, Roovane had told Suzuki he wanted to be closer to his teacher, and asked if he could move into Sokoji. Suzuki said that would make others jealous but invited him to come at 4 a.m. so that they could clean together.

"We didn't talk, we just worked together. He always told me not to miss the dirt under the rug. We'd dust stuff and water the plants and he'd put his eggshells in with the plants. He'd just leave them on top and water them and the calcium would come off onto the dirt. Smart. We had to make sure the zafus were positioned right on the zabutons and the zabutons in place. We'd vacuum sometimes too."

About Suzuki's lectures, Roovane said, "I couldn't remember what he said, but I'd feel good. It's that way with everyone. We remember a few phrases and everyone has different ideas about what he was saying but everyone feels good. Not only for the lecture but for a few days."

"And people tend to feel like Suzuki was speaking directly to them," I said.

"He was! He was speaking to me!"

"We'd sit in the velvet seats in the pews downstairs at Sokoji for the Sunday lecture and people would come in from the outside who weren't into Zen, and at the end they'd ask questions like when the next earthquake is coming and he'd say, 'I don't know.'"

Roovane would take advice from Bill Shurtleff whom he discovered knew a lot about different diets. It was all new to Roovane. Bill suggested he try macrobiotics, so Roovane tried the most extreme version—eating only whole grains. That wasn't hard to do at Tassajara. But then Bill suggested he try to eat just grapes for a while. Roovane tried it, taking them from the Tassajara vines and ordering more on a town trip—and found it made him feel great.

He delved into other extreme food trips. Some got concerned he was going to become malnourished because he was only accepting food in the small third bowl in the zendo. But he'd graze in the gardens, which were bursting with produce under his newly acquired green thumb. And then he would experiment further. For a while, he even tried eating a teaspoon of garden dirt a day. After all, if it was good for the vegetables.

The officers were concerned. He talked to Suzuki about how little he was eating, said he felt guilty not accepting the same food as others, but that his meditation was better with this diet.

Suzuki, who did not like food trips, and was always encouraging us to practice together, was nevertheless supportive of this renegade. "Dogen said, 'Watch your own bowls,'" he told Roovane. "For Dogen, what you're doing would not be a problem. Don't worry about it. You have to become yourself at some point so what you're doing is not wrong according to Zen practice. It's maybe different, but no one should be disturbed by it. Everyone can eat what they need—but don't get sick."

·

Roovane read Shelton's fasting book and decided it was the ultimate food trip—no food. He fasted for two weeks while following the whole schedule. He found it gave him more energy, said that his zazen was incredible, and that he got even more done than usual in the garden. At oryoki meals in the zendo, he'd open his bowls, bow with the servers, kneel and serve the person next to him. Then he'd turn to that person and put the palm of his hand up, a sign for no more, which in this case actually meant none at all. He only accepted the washing water at the end of the meal. And he drank lots of water during the day.

Roovane got so hyper that Peter finally asked him to start eating again and he complied, beginning with tiny helpings.

He also quickly learned about the local plants—what could be eaten, what would make tea, and what could be smoked. I'd tried smoking yerba santa, which had a pleasant sedating effect before bed, most subtle. I wouldn't even have noticed the effect except that I was so pure from the Tassajara diet. Roovane however, after much trial, came up with a smoking mixture from plants in the woods that was a real high—and there was no marijuana in it. I tried it once and liked it. Eventually, Peter told Roovane to cool it with the smokes, and so he did.

Another time, he tried eating a concoction of herbs and mushrooms, got seriously ill, and passed out. When he came to, he heard the han for zazen sounding. Roovane was determined to go, could barely walk, and met Suzuki on the bridge. Suzuki looked at him sternly and told him, "Never do that again!" Roovane felt like he'd almost died, wondered how Suzuki knew something bad had happened, and took Suzuki's command to heart.

I found Roovane squatting in the garden one day as he worked. He said that was the best way to sit and that native people do it all over the world. I'd noticed how Japanese priests and students would not touch their knees to the ground if they had to work low—they'd squat. I envied them. Roovane said it was also the best way to use the toilet. As a result of that conversation, I started squatting more, including on the toilet but not on the seats—I'd put them up. I watched Roovane squatting in the garden, thought about him squatting on the toilet, and wondered what he might be adding to the compost.

The Walters Return

Audrey Walter promised Suzuki she'd bring a Buddha statue when she returned. On the East Coast, she found an old granite gravestone that she thought was just right. In the library, she studied books with Buddhist iconography to get the dimensions right. The granite was so hard that she kept breaking her chisels even after she bought special carbide tips. When she got to the mudra, she broke a thumb off and had to carve in deeper to redo it.

The Walters drove their van across the country and brought the statue to Suzuki, who was delighted. He placed it on a base stone on the dorm side of the bridge over the small creek.

Later, Bob Walter overheard a student showing some guests around say that the statue was very old, probably thirteenth-century Chinese.

Dress Code

There were always some young, shaved-headed guys who liked to work shirtless and sweating in the sun. There were those who thought this inappropriate attire for *samu,* the Zen monastic word for work. Samu was another at least potential form of zazen. And there was already a shirt requirement for the zendo and other rules—not to enter with footwear, shorts, or jewelry. Once, Bob Halpern told a shirtless guest headed for the zendo, "No shirt, no service." During work, Japanese monks wore *samue,* black work outfits with fitted, yet still baggy, sleeves and pants.

The shirtless issue was brought up in one of our occasional open meetings in the dining room. It was another collision of subcultures, as when student mixed nude bathing had been put to rest by Suzuki early on.

The group meetings gave students the impression their opinions mattered, although decisions were made entirely by the officers, board, and abbot. Paul said that meetings were just to let us feel included. On whether there should be a shirt rule, people had varying opinions. We're not Japanese, we're Americans, was clearly expressed. Yes, and we are not a commune but a monastery, with rules and forms and guests, was said in response. A certain level of decorum is called for. But do we want to continue the uptight, American, puritanical shaming of the body? It's not a matter of shame but of modesty and thoughtfulness. So it went.

Dianne expressed an opinion. "If men can go shirtless, then why not women?" And then the next day she went to work in denim overalls with no shirt underneath so that her ample breasts were visible from the sides. Peter, the director, asked her to please wear something under the overalls. She said no, that next she'd go shirtless like some of the men.

Then came a group of Japanese Zen priests, visiting Tassajara. Peter was showing them around. They observed some students working in the garden, and one of them was Dianne. She was squatting and digging with a trowel. One of her breasts was almost hanging out the side of her overalls. The rule that all must wear shirts was announced the next morning.

Be Yourself

A guy named Ezra arrived to be a student for two weeks. He was from Brooklyn, had sat with Eido at Zen Studies, and then spent some time in Burma.

I wanted to hear about Burma, which I'd gathered from the news was a socialist, isolationist dictatorship. It was supposed to be hard to get into. He said it was but he'd gotten a tourist visa that allowed him to be there a few weeks. He went to a temple in Rangoon, the capital, and met with Mahasi, the teacher, who allowed Ezra to stay there and practice with them.

He said it was all day sitting and walking meditation, but not zazen. It was vipassana meditation, which he called Buddha's meditation. He said it's all laid out in the Satipaṭṭhana Sutta, the roadway to enlightenment. He used the word sutta instead of sutra, and nibbana instead of nirvana, Pali instead of Sanskrit.

My time with Ezra was educational. I'd just sit and listen to him lecture. He said that Suzuki was a Bodhisattva maybe, but not a fully enlightened master because he couldn't get there with zazen. What he did was more like jhana, which is what Buddha did before vipassana. "You just sit here with your minds wandering," he said. "With vipassana you pay attention to your body, your mind, your thoughts, and feelings. Vipassana awakens one to seeing the three marks of existence: impermanence, suffering, and no self." At one point he said to me, "You don't know how lucky you are you met me and hear about the real thing. I had an experience of nibbana in Burma. You don't run into someone who's experienced nibbana in most lifetimes."

The second day that Ezra was at Tassajara, Suzuki gave a lecture in the evening. Suzuki had been speaking for about an hour when suddenly Ezra stood up from his cushion and walked out. After the lecture, I saw Ezra in the courtyard and went up to him.

"Drinking a cup of coffee before I hit the road," he said.

"You're leaving?" I said.

"Yep. I can't stay here. My car's already packed."

"Why?"

"In the lecture, Suzuki Roshi said, 'The purpose of our practice is just to be yourself.' I never heard anything like that from a Buddhist priest. Fundamental to Buddhism is that there is no self. He doesn't understand that."

"Sure he does. Like you say, that's fundamental. 'Be yourself' is using the word self in a different way."

"What different way? He said self. There's no self. You're wasting your time with him. I'm outta here."

"Then why don't you stay and teach him the true way?"

"Nah—he's not ready for it." And he walked out to his car and drove off.

It reminded me how back in '67, those drunk belligerent college students finally left because Norman Stiegelmeyer said, "No, I guess we don't believe in God." Abruptly they ran off, their ringleader calling out, "They don't believe in God! Let's get outta here!"

I wondered if there was some belief I clung to so tightly that a mere mention of something that contradicted it would send me packing.

Mind Trouble

Back in 1968, a chap named Barry was sleeping on the white beach sand of Carmel when the beach patrol woke him and told him to move on. He had just hitchhiked up from Baja and was headed to San Francisco. He walked the empty Carmel streets waiting for sunrise and a place to get something to eat before hitching on. In New York City he'd heard what he called "a funny little Japanese man" give a talk where he mentioned a Zen retreat they were raising money to buy. Barry realized it was somewhere near Carmel and thought, maybe religion, meditation would be the answer to his vague questing. Nothing else seemed to have worked.

Lady Fortune was on his side. On Highway One he got picked up by Katharine Thanas on her way into Tassajara. Barry took to the practice right away. He wanted to stay longer than a week but was told he had to spend time in the city first. He appealed to Richard, whom he'd also heard speak in New York. Richard appreciated Barry's sincerity but told him that needing a place to stay and being afraid he'd go astray in the city weren't adequate reasons to stay. Barry was quiet, serious, and there was a darkness about him. But something he shared with me that he'd written had light in it.

> The days are measured out in the chimes of bells, echoing of gongs, thwocks on a heavy oaken sounding board, booming drum cadences on a huge mounted Japanese temple drum, tock tocks on the hollow carved wooden fish that keep the

> beat for chanting, clapping clappers sequencing events at mealtimes, slaps of the stick during meditation, the slow tintinnabulation of the hand-carried goodnight bell and the faster tinkling of the rise-and-shine one carried by the wakeup person running through the predawn darkness.

Wow. He was a writer. And he wrote about how he had found in zazen a refuge that had eluded him up to that point.

> There is something undeniably transcendent and beautiful in the noble mien of a human being formally expressing, with his or her stable upright posture and respectful silence, an unwavering dedication. It seems to say: Here I sit, with all my sufferings and confusions and monkey mind full of desires, here I sit with my ignorance and the harm I may have done to other beings and to my planet, here we all sit together, submitting to the flow of consciousness in and out with the breath, the whirligig of thoughts coming and going. Letting aching tendons ache as the entire world nestles in your cupped palms, reach for the sky with the crown of your head, sitting until the end. Then what a blissful feeling to stand up, the mind much calmer and clearer, refreshed and even joyous, something ineffable deep inside satisfied—you, we have done zazen!

Barry went to the city and did fine in the supportive environment. He took a room in one of the apartments rented by Zen students. He drove a cab to save money for a return to Tassajara. He delved into psychedelics and pot, but not so much that it interfered with his practice at Sokoji.

At Tassajara, Barry aimed to stay as close to Suzuki as he could get. Barry found him "wise and caring, strict yet not harsh, using his agile mind, expressive ways and friendly sense of humor to communicate the most insightful penetration into who you really are and what life is all about."

Despite the eloquence of his verbiage, I sensed a murky cloud surrounding him. Suzuki told Barry, "I think you have some trouble with your mind." Barry called it a typical Japanese understatement.

Barry helped get the stones for the new kitchen walls. They sought ones that would fit together with a minimum of mortar. They'd have to chip away at a stone to make it fit. "We'd often grunt and thrash at this task, but Suzuki, a mason who loved stones and understood their nature, could quickly size up a specimen and with just a few strategic taps on the proper seam, cleave it to perfection."

The practice period ended and Barry stayed on for the interim and guest season. He didn't want to be anywhere else, but he wasn't happy. He felt like he didn't have any real friends among the other students. He'd make friends with guests who would then leave. He went off more and more on his own. Then, suddenly he decided to go. He went to see Suzuki who encouraged him to stay, but he insisted on leaving. He didn't say why.

Barry hiked out the next morning, early, headed toward Big Sur. It took him longer than he expected. He ventured into what he thought would be a short cut and got tangled up in manzanita and scrub. When he emerged from it, torn and scratched, a pack of wild boar chased him up a tree, where he stayed till it was getting dark. Then, he slept on the ground only to be painfully awakened by the sting of a scorpion. At daylight, he found he was on a ridge above the coast. He descended only to come to a cliff, doubled back, went on, descended again to find a shorter cliff, one he felt he could climb down and drop from. He let his pack go first, then landed next to it, relieved he hadn't broken anything—only to find a rattlesnake coiled up beside him. He grabbed the pack and scooted off.

Barry went back to his native New York where he sat with Eido at Zen Studies and shared an apartment with David Steindl-Rast, the Benedictine brother. After a few months, Eido told him that Suzuki had been ill and suggested he might want to return to California. Suzuki did have a bad case of the flu that spring, and Eido had a warm spot for him, but it's surprising he would send a student away.

Barry got back to Tassajara during the spring interim of 1969 and was assigned the job of being the town-tripper. He'd drive the town-trip truck out twice a week, leaving during morning zazen, shopping all day, returning in the evening. The job involved a good deal of work before and after the trip. He had to gather the laundry, go over the shopping lists, including one for purchases for students, plan the best order and route for the stops, as well as get the vehicle ready. When he got back, he'd have help unloading but still had plenty of distribution to do and squaring away the finances. He was glad to be back in the woods and the zendo, but didn't like being the town-tripper, which he saw as dealing with a lot of dirty laundry from the dining room and guest cabins. Sometimes he was tempted to deliver the dirty laundry and drive off to Mexico with the empty truck. He let Peter know how he felt and when someone working in the office left, he was given that position instead.

When I heard that he was going to be dealing with guests, I suggested, "How about the garden, instead?" He was sincere and wanted to get along with people, but he was gloomy. However, after he'd been in the office a week, everything seemed to be going OK and I forgot about my reservations. He wasn't happy, though.

Always, writing seemed to be a helpful outlet for his pain. Barry wrote this:

> Despite periodic strong "cloisterphobic" desires to flee the isolation, I hung in there, trying to combat my ancient depressions and come to terms with myself. The old feelings of the emptiness and meaninglessness of life and its sufferings were as strong as ever, but I tried to persevere through them and not forever be an escapist.

With Force

MAY

"Who's in charge here?" I was standing at the entrance to the office and a man asked me that question in a dead serious tone. "I can help you," I said.

"One of your students just raped my girlfriend."

"One second," I said, and then turned around and called out strongly, "Peter!" He had a room down below the office where he was concentrating on the next *Wind Bell* and didn't like to be interrupted.

"Don't bother me, David," he called back.

"Peter! Come here right now!"

The next thing I knew, Peter and Silas were talking with the man, the woman he was with, and another man who'd come in with them. She was crying. There was an intense vibe in the way Peter and Silas walked swiftly and talked to each other.

We urged people not to go on walks off campus alone. A student going on a walk with a guest was not unusual. She'd arrived with two men, but they wanted to stay and hang out at the baths and pool. It was Barry's day off.

Barry had overheard them talking in the office, said he was going to take the Horse Pasture trail, and suggested she come with him. When they got back down to Tassajara Creek, they walked to the Narrows, ate their bag lunches, and took a skinny dip in the pool. She was so pretty. Beautiful body. It was still early. He suggested they go further downstream where few ventured. They got to another pool. Barry started making advances which she rejected. She wanted to go back, but he wouldn't let her. She wasn't strong enough to resist. He forced her into several sexual acts.

As she feared for her life, she told Barry that she liked him and suggested they run off together. He fell for it. Soon, they were walking back, and when they came upon some other people, she ran toward them in tears asking for help.

Peter found Barry sitting zazen in the zendo in his robes. They met together with Silas, and Barry at first said he hadn't done anything wrong, but pretty soon, he admitted his guilt. Then he packed up his belongings and went with them to the city.

When she and her friends left Tassajara, they went to the police in Monterey. There, she had to get naked and be photographed, a humiliating experience.

The next day, Suzuki met with her and her two friends at Sokoji. Silas and Peter were there as was Sterling Bunnell, a psychiatrist and psychoanalyst. Also lawyer Dick Wertheimer, who'd been helping Zen Center pro bono for years with legal matters.

Barry met with Suzuki who asked him what happened. Barry started off telling Suzuki the whole story from the beginning. As he rambled on, he looked at Suzuki whose gaze stopped him short. "I raped her," he said. "I used force to impose my will."

"Her friends want to see you," Suzuki said.

"Do they want to beat me up?"

"No, they don't feel that way," Suzuki said. "They're trying to understand what happened and they want you to understand."

Wertheimer told her that if it went to court and Barry fought it, that it would surely be an awful experience and he might not get convicted anyway. The possibility of her suing Zen Center was not mentioned.

She and her friends were stupefied that it had happened at Tassajara where they felt so safe. They were not eager to get revenge but they did want some sort of resolution. She wanted an assurance that Barry would not do this to another woman. It was agreed that she wouldn't press charges if Barry continued his practice at Zen Center and went into therapy. They did not ask again to meet with Barry. He got a room in one of the buildings across the street from Sokoji, dutifully attended zazen and lectures, got a job driving a taxi, and began meeting several times a week with Sterling Bunnell.

Barry's victim had let it go at that, but she also wasn't pleased with how it was being dealt with. She felt that all anyone at Zen Center, including Suzuki, cared about, was protecting Zen Center.

Not long after, I was in the city, staying at Yvonne's. I told her that a guest had been raped by a student. "Was it Barry?" she asked.

I'd assumed she already knew because she seemed to be in on everything of any importance.

"So, you don't know about it?" I asked.

"No."

"Then why'd you say, 'Was it Barry?'"

"It's private," she said.

Flea Bite

There was a group picnic at the Horse Pasture and on the way back some of us took the trail down to Tassajara Creek rather than back to the road. I was walking with a fellow student. She pointed to an out of the way spot where the creek bent away from the trail and said, "That's where it happened."

"That's where what happened?" I asked.

She told me that the year before, she and Barry had gone for a walk down the creek, and on the way back they were walking in the bed itself. She pointed to a small clearing hidden from view and said that he grabbed her there, pulled her down, and forced himself on her. I was shocked and asked why I hadn't heard about this before. She said she hadn't resisted or complained about it. But she'd told Yvonne. I asked how she felt about it, now. "It was nothing to me, like being bitten by a flea," she said defiantly.

I was sure it bothered her more than that, but it was clear she wasn't going to let it dominate her memory.

Then I realized that must be why Barry had left Tassajara immediately and gone to New York the year before. Good lord. Both times Barry had left Tassajara abruptly and both times it was because he'd raped a woman.

I didn't tell her about the other rape. Actually, I hadn't told anyone except for Yvonne and Dianne. Peter and Silas knew I knew and didn't tell me to keep it to myself. Didn't say anything. I thought it was interesting that in a community as small as ours it didn't become a shared outrage or at least hot gossip. It was as if it didn't register.

On a Roll

E.L. Hazelwood was in his late forties, slim, and soft spoken with a twang. He said he was raised on his daddy's pea patch outside a poor, desolate West Texas town. He didn't talk about himself much, but one day he shared something from his past. He said he'd been married to a woman who constantly harangued him to make more money. So one weekend he took her and the few hundred dollars they had on hand to Las Vegas. He left her playing on a slot machine and went off to a roulette table where, within an hour, he lost almost everything. E.L. stood on the gaming floor soaked with dread. His wife found him and asked for more money to play on the slots. He suggested they have a steak dinner first. He figured it would be good to at least have full stomachs if they were going to be sleeping in their car.

After dinner they went to a craps table where he assumed he'd lose the last of their money, confess his failure, and suffer her wrath. He passed his last $20 to a dealer who gave him chips. E.L. put them all on the pass line. The stickman called, "Coming out!" Trembling, E.L. rolled—a seven. Doubled his money. Threw again and got an eleven which doubled his money once more. Still a long way to go. Each roll expecting doom. But no doom, yet. E.L. looked at his $160 in chips as a half-dozen guests stood waiting for his next roll. He could hardly breathe. When the stickman leaned forward and said, "Shooter's hot! Dice are yours," fear fell away and E.L. rolled the dice with an empty hand. Fifteen minutes later, surrounded by a cheering crowd, he gathered his chips which cashed out at over $3,500. He turned to his amazed wife and said, "That's how it's done honey. Let's go home." E.L. knew better than to besmirch that moment of glory by attempting a repeat performance. The memory was sweet, but the money and his marriage didn't last.

Squeaky Gone

Dianne found a baby hummingbird on the ground. She was living in the dorm and put it by the window in a little box, fed it sugar and water, and called it "Squeaky." It only lasted a few days. She came to me crying and I tried to comfort her.

Still crying, she found Suzuki in his garden. He was sympathetic. She asked him, "Where did Squeaky go?" He said, "I don't know."

Flag Rock

Dianne wanted to make the steep climb up to Flag Rock. I'd done it. It's not easy, especially toward the top. But it's not perilous if one goes up from the road and not from the more sheer side facing the creek and lower garden. In our first year some students came back all shook up with frightening descriptions of their close calls climbing, and then trying to get down when they couldn't continue anymore on the ascent from the lower garden.

So I joined Dianne. We made it to the top without any great difficulty and she was indeed appreciative of the new view. Flag Rock is flat, and one can sit on it and enjoy the view which then included Tassajara reduced to a tiny toy settlement in a deep bending valley surrounded by steep, mountainous terrain. There was a short flagpole at the top sporting some Tibetan prayer flags.

We ate our day off bag lunches and took a pleasant nap on the large flat rock. And then rather than return the way we'd come, we went out the back side through brush and met up with the Horse Pasture Trail. That led to a decision—should we go left to the trailhead at Tassajara Road or take the longer route to the right which would bring us down to Tassajara Creek near the Narrows with its cool water rushing over our hot, dry bodies. Right turn. We made it back to Tassajara at dusk, soaked exhausted in a hot plunge, noshed on leftovers in the kitchen as the han for evening zazen was sounding, made it to our rooms to throw on robes, plopped on zafus in the zendo almost on time, and passed the zazen period nodding and getting hit with the kyosaku.

The Pyramid

E.L. had some sort of sporadic mental condition. Sometimes he'd leave the shop and wander around, say strange disconnected things, and then the next day act fairly normal and do a good job. One day E.L. said he had something to show me. He led me up the trail on the other side of the creek from the bathhouse. Then, off trail up further to a cement pyramid about a foot and a half tall where we had a broad view of mountains and valleys beyond. He looked at me, raised his eyebrows, and then turned the pyramid over, revealing it was hollow. It contained a chamber with a crystal, a curious small polished Manzanita burl which vaguely looked like a seated figure, a tiny flying saucer, a drawing of an eye within a pyramid, some dried yucca nuts, a miniscule baby doll on a fat sycamore leaf. He smiled. I smiled back and nodded as if I understood something. What an interesting break in the daily routine.

The Jesters

The time came for me to leave Tassajara and get ready for school. Working in the dining room had never been more fun. For two months I'd enjoyed the antics and chatter of my co-workers, Alan Marlowe and Craig Boyan. Alan older—in his thirties—as tall as Craig was short. Alan had been an actor and model, was grandiose, theatrical, worldly-wise, experienced, well-read, arrogant one moment and self-deprecating the next. Craig was sweet, humble, emotional, devoted to Suzuki and also to the late Meher Baba, whose photo he kept posted in his room. Both Alan and Craig were quick-witted. I was usually the blabbermouth, but with those two I was like a spectator. They kept it up day after day. I would fall down laughing, completely lose it. Both these guys related well with the guests. They almost made me wish I hadn't signed up for the

Japanese course, but at the same time I felt comfortable leaving the diners in their humorous hands.

Permission

When Suzuki arrived back in April, I talked with him about going to Monterey to study Japanese. He was completely against me leaving Tassajara to study Japanese for a couple months of the summer. I said that it was already paid for. That was true, by then, thanks to my mother. I made sure of that because I knew it would strengthen my position. I think if I hadn't spent so much time watching Richard Baker when he related to Suzuki, I might not have had the confidence to disagree with Suzuki myself. He acquiesced.

I met with Suzuki before I left and told him I found a place to stay in Pacific Grove. It had a tiny living room, a tiny bedroom, and a tiny kitchen. I said I planned to turn the living room into a combination study and zendo. I asked if it was OK if anyone else joined me. He said to sit with Jean Ross in neighboring Carmel. Jean was in her fifties and had started sitting with Suzuki regularly soon after he arrived in America. She was the first person he sent to Eiheiji monastery in Japan and she'd done well there. I said that I planned to sit with Jean every Monday night when her group meets, but I will sit every morning and evening at my place. So if someone else wants to join me, is that alright? Same answer came back—support Jean. I tried several other approaches to get his blessing for a little mini zendo open to others. No success. If someone else wants to sit, he said to bring them to Jean's. This time I obeyed.

—CHAPTER FOUR—

THE SECOND HALF OF 1969

Nihongo Marathon MONTEREY, JULY

A stucco cottage just above Cannery Row became my PG home, "PG" for Pacific Grove. There were three old dwellings on the oddly-shaped corner lot. To the left was Marilyn and her daughter, who she said was hyperactive. Straight ahead was Ned and his quiet wife. All three of those adults were in their thirties. I was twenty-four. We had an interesting landlord named Vasquez who was an old character from the area, a restaurateur who said he'd known John Steinbeck back in the day. Ned said he'd talked to Vasquez about his Cannery Row days and that everything Vasquez said lined up with the Steinbeck character Joseph-and-Mary in *Sweet Thursday*. Joseph-and-Mary owned a bar, cashed the cannery workers' checks, and sent hired thugs to rob them afterwards. Ned quoted from the book—"Dishonesty flowed through his veins." He asked Vasquez if he was indeed Joseph-and-Mary from *Sweet Thursday*. Vasquez walked off at that point saying, "I'll be seeing you later, Eddy."

The first night there I went to a party at a home owned by Vic and Shayna. It had an expansive two-story living room. A rock band was playing. Beth and John Veglia were there. They'd come to Tassajara with Vic and Shayna as day guests and I'd visited with them before. Beth was hugely pregnant and eating tons of dairy food. John taught Latin at a private school and had an office in downtown PG with a curious sign on the door: the name "Nestor Marzipan," and below it, "Imaginary Mysteries."

I spent time talking to Willie, a mellow Black guy. I walked with him to another party at a home filled with cannabis smoke that had become a crash pad. The cops came and we walked off before they had time to bother us.

I got to my little place late. I'd only started getting it ready to live in. It was dirty and messy inside, so I slept outside on the scraggly lawn in my sleeping bag. I spent the next day cleaning the place up and slept outside again. In the middle of the night I was awakened when someone tripped over me. I looked up. A guy was looking down at me, brushing himself off. He ran away. I went back to sleep.

The next morning, I got the word from Marilyn and Ned that there'd been a robbery and attempted rape of a woman across the street by a prowler who had been hiding in the bushes. The cops came. I told them about the person who stumbled over me. I went downtown and looked through their mug book. "That's him!" I said.

Next thing I heard, Willie had been arrested for robbery and attempted rape and I instantly realized that I'd confused Willie with the guy who tripped over me. I'd given my car away and had bought a bicycle, so I raced to the police station and told them of my confused mistake. They let Willie go. I told him what happened and how I accidentally falsely accused him of robbery and attempted rape. "Sorry," I said. "That's not a nice thing to do to somebody." He brushed it off. Said he was used to getting hassled by cops.

Japanese class was difficult. Four hours a day, six days a week. Reading, writing, speaking. Three hours with Jun Mink, a Japanese woman who was the head of our program. One hour a day with a Japanese man going over rules and grammar. Day one, I learned the hiragana syllabary. Second day, katakana, an alternative syllabary. After that, ten kanji, Chinese characters, a day. I loved Mrs. Mink. She married an American after the war. I asked her why she didn't teach at the DLI up the hill, the Defense Language Institute, the largest language school in the world. She then taught me the phrase *Heitai ga daikirai*—"Greatly hate the military." She'd been a nurse in Tokyo during the American bombing which included wave after wave of bombers dropping gasoline then napalm on that wood and paper city. Some among the crews in the planes were vomiting from the smell of burning civilian flesh wafting up from below with the smoke.

All day all night *nihongo*, Japanese language. At night I'd dream it—not fluent dreaming. More like absorbed in chewing on it dreams. Mrs. Mink was pleased. She told me not to study on Sunday.

I would be at it till ten at night, do zazen, sleep, arise at four, do zazen, then start studying. I worked at a small desk, and at times on the floor, sitting on a single tatami I bought secondhand. I would eat mainly raw food while studying—like a head of organic lettuce bought at Bud's in Carmel—by itself. Went total pure. I fasted on Mondays. No booze, no pot, no caffeine. I'd found that I had only so much energy, that stimulants just borrowed from the storehouse, and avoiding stimulants and eating wholesome food ended up allowing more clean energy in the long run. That, and not overeating.

Aside from raw fruits and veggies, seeds, and nuts, small amounts of yogurt and homemade sprouts, I baked unyeasted bread I'd eat with *muso*, the sesame butter and miso mix. Other than that, no meals that needed preparation—everything ready to eat over a book. My bowel movements were reduced to just a few, small, dark balls that left no residue for toilet paper.

I had a thick slab of oak on the floor used as an altar. I put incense in a crack in the slab. I came home from school one day and found the place smelling like smoke. The incense had burned down to the wood which smoldered for hours, leaving a charred black pocket in it. It finally went out on its own. Oops.

There were about a dozen of us in the class. I quickly teamed up with an eighteen-year-old. She had a serious heart condition and needed twelve hours sleep a night. Her father was an astrophysicist. She was super-smart—way beyond me. I'd cycle over to her apartment next to the school in the morning and get there an hour before class. She'd have spent an hour on material that I spent four hours on—then she'd explain it to me.

Here's a song I'd sing while on the way to school. The first and second verses were from when I was getting ready to clean up my cottage and had just bought those clothes.

> Got on my new Frisco jeans
> Got on my new Frisco jeans
> The finest duds you ever seen.
> Got on my new Frisco jeans
> Got on my new White Duck shirt
> Got on my new White Duck shirt
> Pretty soon be full of grime and grease and dirt
> Got on my new White Duck shirt
> Ridin' on my new blue Peugeot bike
> Ridin' on my new blue Peugeot bike
> Wet Monterey Bay air blowin by my side
> Ridin' on my new blue Peugeot bike

Moon Rocket

My neighbor Ned had a PhD in one of the sciences. He had a job with a professor in the Midwest who spent a decade with his students counting something only visible with a microscope and then publishing his findings in scientific journals. Ned built a counting contraption that utilized computer and photo technology which showed the professor's method of counting was so far off that it invalidated his ten years of research. Ned got fired. He was depressed and bored and smoked pot all day. He'd offer me some, but I declined. Marilyn's grubby, alcohol-reeking ex-hubby would come over to bug her, she'd kick him out, and he'd go smoke pot with Ned and fall asleep.

Dot Luce had been coming from Carmel to Tassajara to join us for zazen and work since the first year. On Monday eves she'd come pick me up and drive to Jean Ross's apartment in Carmel for zazen. On Sundays we'd go to San Francisco to hear Suzuki's talk.

In July, just after the historic moon landing, Suzuki gave a lecture in which he pooh-poohed the whole thing and said, "I'm not interested in anyone who's interested in going to the moon." I thought about that statement as Dot and I drove back. Ned, Marilyn, and I had watched the moon landing on a cheap, small, black and white set. It was a thrilling, memorable experience. But of course, Suzuki had a point, it was just more empty phenomena.

Ned had a scale model of the moon landing rocket with removable parts that he put together. It was about two-and-a-half-feet tall. I asked if I could borrow it and he generously complied. The next Sunday, Dot and I went back to San Francisco for a period of zazen followed by Suzuki's lecture at Sokoji. After the lecture, I asked Suzuki if I could see him. I brought the rocket model into his office and showed it to him, pulling the first stage off, then the second, then the moon landing vehicle, explaining what I knew about the flight, landing, and return. He was genuinely interested, playful in response, curious—not a shred of negativity. I put the rocket back together, said goodbye, and then Dot and I were on our way back.

Theater Break

Every once in a while something would happen to add a dash of variety to my scholastic toil. One day I joined a theater full of students of Russian language from the DLI to see the Russian version of *Dr. Zhivago*. I heard there were five buildings for Russian alone up there. I kept hearing that Russian and Vietnamese, both languages of critical importance to our government, were two of the most difficult. I also heard that graduates from this costly government school would consistently be assigned to countries with languages they had not studied. When *Dr. Zhivago* started, I was perplexed why there was laughing and booing from the audience. Then I realized. It was because the movie was dubbed in English.

There was another foreign film I saw there that got a bunch of soldiers from Fort Ord and DLI all excited, the Swedish film *I Am*

Curious (Yellow), mentioned earlier. I'd never seen genitals in a film before. Aside from depicting sex in famous Swedish locations, it had quite a hodgepodge of material including urination in a sink, an interview with Martin Luther King, Jr., and breaking the fourth wall with the camera crew entering into the action.

Magazine Salesman

A knock at the door. A young man wanted to give me a bunch of magazine subscriptions for practically nothing. I asked him what would I do with twenty magazines, told him I didn't have time to do anything but study Japanese. But then we got talking. I gave him some orange juice and proceeded to carefully study the deal he was offering. Read the small print out loud.

I recalled how my best friend Ward and I in high school had been invited by a fellow student to join in making fantastic money as door-to-door cookware salesmen. We got the prep talk in the office from his boss which included a good deal on how to sucker customers into spending more than they could afford, to buy more than they needed. High quality stainless steel, copper bottom frying pans, pots small and large. Then we went with our friend to watch him do a sale. It was all based on frightening young housewives and wanna-be-housewives into thinking that if they didn't buy the whole set plus implements, they'd either lose their husbands through clogged arteries, or not get a husband to begin with. The pitch preyed on their insecurity and innocence. Ward and I were not interested.

I laid into the salesman, telling him I knew he'd be making most of his money off young housewives who felt ignorant and were being promised that just having these magazines around would make them and their families, or families-to-be, smart. I told him I bet he was targeting Fort Ord army base and low-cost housing areas. And the seeming pennies the magazines cost would eventually add up to a sizeable chunk every month, taking a costly bite out of meager budgets. Customers would become locked in a contract that took time and effort to get out of. I ranted at my trapped con-man about the immorality of what he was doing.

One of the magazines he was offering was *Look*. I happened to have spent time at Tassajara with the West Coast editor of *Look*, George Leonard, who'd come in with Mike Murphy from Esalen. I got hold of him in his office. He said he wished he could control such things, but it was beyond his reach. He suggested to tell the salesman to practice Aikido to find the balance of body, mind, and spirit, and that compassionate moral conduct would follow. I did so and the guy broke down crying and said this was the only job he could find. I mentioned the concept of right livelihood, number five on the Buddhist eightfold path. On his way out, he thanked me and said he'd look right away for another job.

Accusing Finger

The police were back. This time they wanted to know if I'd let them use my place to watch out for Marilyn's ex. She'd gotten a restraining order against him, but he still kept coming. So I sat studying on the floor and let the police sit in my only two chairs at the little desk by the window. They were no trouble. I enjoyed the new experience of studying in the midst of a stakeout. They did that for two days. On the third, her grubby ex was back again, staggering around in front of her house, cursing. He smoked some pot with Ned, then broke into her house. She came home, found him passed out on the couch, and called the police from my phone.

Ned, Marilyn, and I entered her place cautiously with two policemen. We stood looking down on the snoring intruder. A policeman nudged him till he awoke. He looked up at us, slowly surveying each person and rubbing his eyes. Then he jerked back when he realized there were police there, raised his right arm, shakingly pointed it at Ned, and gutturally uttered, "Marijuana!" The police were undeterred. They cuffed and removed him.

Back to nihongo.

Trudy Dixon

Trudy Dixon and her artist husband Mike had two young children. They attended sesshins and practiced at Tassajara when time allowed. They started sitting at Sokoji back in 1962 while in their early twenties. Before she came, she'd been a student of philosophy. She had been involved with editing the *Wind Bells* and had become the head editor when Richard Baker stepped down from that role in 1968.

That same year, ailing with cancer, she completed the editing of a book of Suzuki's lectures. Trudy worked closely with Suzuki and Richard Baker to bring the book to fruition. The working title had been *Beginner's Mind*. Richard sailed to Japan with the manuscript. There he found a publisher, Weatherhill, and established a relationship with its founder, Meredith Weatherby, who made Richard a guest in his Tokyo home. Weatherby insisted that the word "Zen" be in the title, so it would be called *Zen Mind, Beginner's Mind*, and was scheduled to be published in January 1970.

While finishing her work on that book, Trudy was dealing with cancer and went through a remarkable transformation that was evident to all. Kobun Chino said Trudy had a light surrounding her. She joined us for the 1968 end of summer guest season sesshin, and had a whole tatami next to the altar. She'd do zazen lying down. She also had the following exchange with Suzuki in the shosan ceremony on the last day.

> "Docho Roshi: Let me see who I am. [She paused.] To die each moment, and to be reborn, is the great freedom of the dharma. I'm like a small fish, I swim in and out of the big death."
>
> **Suzuki:** [Softly] "Yeah, that's right. I am grateful that you are making your best effort in accepting this dharma. Of course, it is not easy, but dharma cannot be so easy. Dharma is that which everyone of us have been striving for, and will strive for, to

> know what it is, to accept as theirs. So, it is not only you, but all the patriarchs and sages have been striving for it, and you are one of them. And you should have pity on people who do not strive for it. To realize the necessity of striving for it is the point on which we are making our best effort. There's no other point to strive for. Since you have realized the necessity of striving for it, you are already one of the patriarchs and you gained that state. Don't think Buddha and patriarchs were quite free from birth and death. They are still striving for it in the name of various sentient beings. It is the most valuable thing that you realized the necessity of striving for it. The suffering you have is everybody's suffering, but perhaps most will not realize it. And it was and will be true with the past Buddhas and future Buddhas."

Trudy returned to Tassajara in early July 1969. She was thin and frail, but her spirit was strong. Angie Runyan who had been helping the Dixons with their children back in Mill Valley, was now assisting Trudy, helping her walk to the zendo where she'd join in zazen. Again Suzuki had designated a whole tatami for her, close to the raised altar platform. Now she was too weak to sit at all and lay up there next to him. Marian Derby said Trudy was "too weak to sit up. She lay curled on her side upon the tatami-covered meditation platform—expressing the true reality of Buddha's full-lotus posture."

Mike Dixon said "It was very satisfying for her to do the book. It brought her closer to Suzuki. At Tassajara when she was quite sick, she had trouble moving around. We were in Suzuki's cabin. She was lying down. She seemed very happy to be there with him. He seemed happy to have her there."

Trudy died in San Francisco the day after she left Tassajara, July 9th, at the age of thirty.

My biggest disappointment that summer was not going to Trudy Dixon's memorial at Sokoji. It was on a Friday, and I felt I could not afford to miss class. I could barely keep up. But waves of Suzuki's emotional and powerful elegy for Trudy are still echoing through our collective consciousness.

Gracious Heart

Charlie and Carolyn Page were regular guests at Tassajara. They'd come several times in the summer, often with the Wenners. One day that summer, the Pages invited me to dinner in their home with other friends of theirs. After dinner, Charlie brought out his rare prize port and gave each of us a tiny glass. No longer on the pure path, I slugged it down. Uh oh—they all looked at me in shock and then returned to savoring theirs. They were most forgiving.

This was a group that regularly got together and, after dinner, would sit around, talk, or play a parlor game. They were all intellectuals, much better educated and well-read than I. Charlie suggested they each say who they would like to be. One by one they answered—astronaut, filmmaker, organic farmer, a teenager again, deep sea diver, superwoman. When it came to me, I said, "I'd like to be someone who doesn't want to be anyone else."

Later, Charlie kindly spoke to me about not one-upping everyone like that. He said that no matter what came up, I seemed to say something more interesting or wiser than who I was with. I told him I knew just what he meant. I said I'd try to pay attention to that habit and rein it in. I added that I'd read *Reader's Digest* every week when I was in elementary school and I recalled a piece called "The Gift of a Gracious Heart." "It's about just that sort of thing," I said. "Norman Vincent Peale talked about it. Thinking of others' feelings first. Not having to have the last word. Let the other person have the upper hand. Japanese are pros at that. Suzuki Roshi is too."

"You did it again," he said laughing.

The Deep Gash

There was a guitar on the wall at the Lamberts in Jamesburg and Bill Lambert discovered that if he plied me with some booze, I'd sit and play songs for him, and with more booze, I'd start improvising raunchy stuff that would get him whooping. Then he discovered that if I had some pot, it was even better.

Pot had made inroads into the cowboy scene and eventually Bill would keep a cup full of joints on the kitchen table—not for him, for his guests. He didn't, as he said, give a rat's ass about the law, but Marion cared, at least at first. I was there for the christening of that table with smoke from the evil weed.

By this time, my intensive course in Japanese had come to an end. Carmel friend and fellow Zennie, Dot Luce, our mutual friend Yolanda, and I had made a day trip into Tassajara on the last day of the guest season. On the way out, we stopped by the Lamberts and sat with Bill and an old inebriated farmer friend of his from Greenfield. I noted how multi-generational we were. I was in my twenties, Dot in her thirties, Yolanda in her forties, and the Lamberts and Bill's friend in their fifties. *True Grit,* a film about a tough, hard-drinking cowboy, had just come out and we told Bill he should have played the lead, was true-grittier than John Wayne.

Dot was talking to Marion, who was tending a stew on the stove. I was talking with Bill, and Yolanda was talking with the inebriated farmer. At one point, Yolanda spoke up in her Austrian accent, "Bill, do you mind if I turn your friend on to hashish?"

Bill, who was also somewhat inebriated, replied, "Go right ahead."

Marion turned her head and called out. "Bill!" with obvious disapproval.

"Shut up Marion!" And then to Yolanda, "You go right ahead and smoke your hashish!"

Marion was not convinced. "Bill!" she protested.

"Alright!" Bill stood up. Grabbed what looked to me like a Bowie knife from a window ledge. "I'm drawin' a line!" He dragged the knife blade across the table leaving a deep gash. "Everybody who wants to smoke hashish on this side of the line," he barked out. "And everyone who doesn't want to smoke hashish on that side of the line."

Marion gave up.

Three Sisters

Just after leaving Carmel Valley Village on the way east to Cachagua, Jamesburg, Arroyo Seco, or Greenfield, there was a nice Spanish stucco place down a bit off the road to the right. On a good day, Joan Baez, whose place it was, might be sitting outside talking with friends or playing music. You could drive in and say hi. She was friendly, political, always ready to sing.

Baez came to Tassajara as a guest now and then. The Becks liked having her as a guest—and her boyfriends and girlfriends. I first heard her sing in Dallas in 1964. At Tassajara, she'd come in and be silent and austere one time, and the next time be drinking wine, singing, and playing a guitar in her cabin with friends. No one complained that she kept them up.

Once she was at the pool playing requests for a small group of students and guests. When someone asked for Dylan's "Love Is Just a Four-Letter Word," she made a face and shook her head. One time she sang "Amazing Grace" at the steps by Gossip Oak on her way out. What a voice! Another time, she left with a student who'd only been there a few days and had planned to stay longer but—she was mighty attractive. Were people outraged? What I heard was, "Lucky guy."

Bill Shurtleff had lived in Baez's Palo Alto commune. He admired her greatly. His brother Jeffrey sang and recorded with her, sang with her at Woodstock. She was refusing to pay income tax as a protest to the Vietnam War. The men in the commune were draft resisters, wouldn't register for the draft, burned their cards.

Baez had two sisters—Pauline and Mimi. Pauline lived in Jamesburg with her husband, Peyton. For a while he had a cool joint in the village, the Encounter Coffee Shop. The name was appropriate for the area, as encounter groups had been made famous at Esalen Institute. Ed Farrington, a neighbor of Peyton's in Jamesburg, was leading encounter groups in the area. The Encounter, as we called it, and The Stirrup Cup across the road, were the last commercial places on the way to Tassajara. But Peyton couldn't make the Encounter pay for itself, so it closed.

Peyton and Pauline's abode in Jamesburg was a good place to drop by on the way in or out of Tassajara. Real backwoodsy feel. Dark wood walls, a loft. Comfy couch and overstuffed chair, hammock. We'd play some music, drink a little, smoke a little. He had a few makeshift huts and hang-out spots on the side of the hill, had dug a shallow cave good for some cozy time alone. The Tassajara nefarious element was comfortable there.

Pauline co-authored the song "Pack Up Your Sorrows" with Richard Fariña, who recorded it with his wife Mimi, the third sister. It was on *Celebrations for a Grey Day*, released in 1965, to me a most magical album. And I loved that song. I thought it was a traditional folk gospel till I learned it was half Pauline's. It offers a metaphor for not dwelling on, yet dealing with, suffering.

On April 30, 1966, there was a book release party for Richard Fariña's novel, *Been Down So Long It Looks Like Up to Me*. It was hosted by the Thunderbird bookstore located in the village. Later that day at his wife Mimi's twenty-first birthday party, Richard went off for a quick fun ride with a friend who drove his motorcycle way too fast headed toward Cachagua. That road has turns that you can't even make driving the posted speed limit. There's an S curve at one spot that sometimes catches me by surprise and I've got to brake pretty hard. That's where they went off the road and through a barbed wire fence at what the cops estimated to be ninety. The driver lived.

Two Balconies

I decided to continue at the Monterey Institute of Foreign Studies for the fall quarter, but that wouldn't start for a couple of weeks. I was staying in a room across from Sokoji. My older sister, Susan, had moved to San Francisco the year before. Our mother came from Fort Worth to visit us. I took them on a tour which included the apartment where I was staying, my almost bare room, and the neat and clean kitchen—hippies no more. Then over to Sokoji, which was originally a synagogue built in 1895. Katagiri greeted them warmly. The auditorium had tall, beautiful stained-glass windows. Mother found the altar platform in the zendo on the second floor to be fascinating—the small Buddha statue, a scroll, the mokugyo, bells, offerings. She was always drawn to Japanese art and handiwork.

Mother had brought my father's old but still quite good 16mm camera. It was in the glove box not visible but there was an unlocked door in my sister's car. Bye-bye 16mm camera. The rule of locking all doors and leaving nothing of value visible, was not just for high crime areas in San Francisco.

We got together with Niels Holm and Bob Halpern for dinner at the Mandarin in Ghirardelli Square. Afterwards, we rode a cable car to nowhere and back. The next day, Mother, Susan, Bob and I saw the musical *Hair* on stage, sitting in the balcony at the Geary Theater. When the show was over, Bob removed his shirt to be more in tune with the spirit of the show and proudly walked out with us.

Mother and Susan were staying in a posh rooftop apartment owned by the family of a well-to-do Zen buddy. We were waiting there to meet Bob and Niels and then go to Fisherman's Wharf for lunch, another meal that Mother would treat. Bob and Niels arrived, and we all went out to the back porch. It was way up with a great view of San Francisco and the Bay. I said I didn't like to get too close to the railing, that I'd get the feeling I was being sucked down over the side. Bob immediately went to the outside of the railing. Niels joined him saying he felt more comfortable there.

Mother, Susan, and I asked them to please come back on this side.

"What? Are you afraid I'll fall?" said Niels, letting go, falling back then grabbing the railing at the last instant. Our scaredy-cat faction screamed. Then Bob did the same—falling back and grabbing the railing at the last fraction of a second. We were horrified and begged them to stop, but they repeated their feigned fall together. Then again. And again. I ran out into the hall. After a few moments, all four of them came out. I was so relieved to see Bob and Niels still on the same floor as me. I didn't want to talk to them. I'd lost my sense of play. It was too real. I didn't even want to think about it.

The next day, Niels said he couldn't sleep all night long reliving that foolishness and shuddering.

City Center

The board of Sokoji had given Suzuki an ultimatum—us or them. The older, conservative Japanese Americans felt like their temple had been overrun, taken over. It had gotten to be too much. Claude and Silas found an excellent building fifteen blocks down Laguna Street from Sokoji. It had been a home for young Jewish women designed by Julia Morgan of Hearst Castle fame. It was three stories tall with a large basement and stairs leading to a flat area on the roof.

There were single and double rooms, enough for seventy-five students, an apartment for the Suzukis, a dance hall perfect for a zendo and much more—room for everything that would be needed. Suzuki saw it and was delighted. With help from some friends, the Zen Center bought it.

Jack Weller moved in on September 5th. A Mrs. Michaelson and a two-man staff were still living there. Jack found the staff and especially Mrs. Michaelson to be warm and friendly. He said she'd been the house mother for all the girls and now was house mother for him. They showed Jack around and familiarized him with everything they could think of that would be useful to know about the building—like where the fuse boxes were.

Jack wanted her to stay, but pretty soon they all moved out. Kobun had given Jack some incense from Eiheiji and suggested he bless the building with it. On his first night, Jack lit a stick of the incense and sat zazen for forty minutes. Then he walked around the whole building sanctifying each room with the smoke of the Eiheiji incense.

During that time Suzuki came to see it again and Jack escorted him around the building. Jack said Suzuki was "clearly very happy about the building, continually smiling and chatting in a way I hadn't experienced before." Jack showed him a room on the third floor. Suzuki looked out the window at the apartment building across the street and said, "We should buy that building too," and laughed.

I'd met Jack in the spring of '67 when we worked together loading debris from the demolished Beck dining room floor onto a pickup truck. He was twenty-eight and told me how the year before he went into a hospital for a routine test and was told he had to have immediate open-heart surgery. He said it didn't bother him till they described the procedure afterwards—sawing down the middle of his chest and cranking the rib cage open before getting to work with surgical instruments and so forth.

The neighborhood was scary, on the edge of the Fillmore, a lot of crime. Right after Jack moved in, someone was shot and killed on the corner of Lily Alley and Laguna, the back corner of the building. There were blood stains on the sidewalk for weeks. The Chinese woman who owned and ran the small grocery catty-corner from the building had twice shot and killed attempting robbers. Her husband had died in a robbery there a few years before.

Bob Halpern and Niels Holm were next to move into the new City Center building, while it was being prepared for the day of the big move from Sokoji and Bush Street. Bob, like a handful of his Zen brothers, was doing high-rise iron work. It frightened me just to hear him tell about the job. But apparently, the iron work paid well. He'd get a check every two weeks. One day he cashed it on the way home. He got out of the bus and there were the hookers and shady guys. Bob had that cash in his jeans pocket. The guys could smell it and started walking toward him, calling out. He ran. They pursued. As he approached the Page Street building, he realized he'd left his key in another pair of pants. They were gaining on him. He leapt up the steps and banged on the door. By chance, Claude was standing on the other side. He opened it. Bob thrust a wad of bills into his hand, saying, "Hold this for a moment please," pulled the door quickly shut, locking himself out, turned around as the two pursuers reached the bottom of the steps, opened his arms wide and called out, "Brothers!"

The Actor

Paul Shippee had been involved with a group that did political street theater in New York City from a flatbed truck. Then he switched coasts, moving to San Francisco in 1959. He had a degree in civil engineering, and originally came to be an engineer for reconstruction work on the Bay Bridge. He wanted to be with the Mime Troupe with Saul Landau, but Ronni Davis, the founding director, was living with Paul's ex-wife and didn't want him around. So he started doing political street theater with a group that included Country Joe McDonald and was directed by Landau's wife, Nina. He was living in a house in the Haight with Jig Schneider and some other friends of his from college in Connecticut. Jig's younger brother, Peter, who Paul also knew from back East, came out and joined them. Paul and Peter were talking one night around 10 p.m. when Paul said, "Let's hop on a freight train and go to Seattle." Peter said, "Why not?" So they got over to the East Bay where the trains were, and they were off. They messed around in Seattle for a few days and then rode an empty box car back.

Later, Paul was living in the Haight in another house with two women he knew from the Actor's Workshop. It was near Christmas. He was sick with hepatitis but didn't want to stay home when they asked if he wanted to go with them to hear a lecture by a Zen master in Japantown. For a while, he'd lived in Japantown in an apartment where he could look down on the street and see people walking into that Zen temple and had been curious about what they were doing.

Paul and his friends arrived early, climbed the stairs, and entered a room with chairs and cushions, a number of which were already occupied with people sitting quietly and still. He plopped down in the front row on a cushion. Before him was a platform with an altar and a Buddha statue, flowers, offerings of fruit, and curious ornamentation. There was a small man sitting next to a big bowl bell with his back to Paul. The man had a shaved head and was dressed in a brown robe. Paul sat gazing at the motionless man. So amazing, the stillness of him. And then the man lifted his arm and rang the bell. A deep mellow sound. The man got up, arranged his robe, stood in front and gave a lecture while laughing a lot. It was a most entertaining lecture.

On his way back to his apartment, Paul reflected on what he just experienced. He had never seen anybody laugh so hard in his life. He was amazed with the contrast between the stillness and that laughter and the expressiveness of Suzuki's talk. It wasn't about the words—it was about his being.

A couple days later, Paul went back to Sokoji and received zazen instruction from Katagiri. Katagiri told him to be still, follow his breath with focus on his *hara*—patting his belly—and to come back for the group meditation. That was it. The meditation was going to be for forty minutes. He'd never been still that long, but he remembered as an actor he had experimented with being still once.

He was in his apartment practicing gestures and lines for a play when out of nowhere he wondered what it would be like to be still for five minutes. So he went to the window and stood there unmoving. That was good—for five minutes. What would forty minutes be like? He came back to do zazen at 5:30 p.m., where he sat the entire forty minutes and found it excruciatingly uncomfortable. And his ears burned. The longer he sat the more they burned. So meditation was painful with ears on fire. Still, he was attracted to meditation and resolved to learn how to do it.

Paul had been on a search for the vitality and keen perception that he had as a child. He wanted to expand. He dropped out of the acting scene and anything to do with the Haight-Ashbury. He was sick and disillusioned with everything he'd ever done, including college and science, art, and drugs, which were the cause of his hepatitis—needles. None of it made sense to him anymore. Meditation made sense.

Paul's brother sent him a ticket and he flew back to Connecticut for Christmas. His parents took care of him and he recovered from the hepatitis. He had changed since they'd last seen him five years previously. He had long hair and an earring. His father thought there was something wrong with him mentally and urged him to speak to a friend of his, the head psychiatrist at a mental hospital. Paul did so. The psychiatrist was impressed with Paul and hired him to be a psychiatric aide. At home, Paul practiced meditation every day for twenty minutes. He found that if he took a hit off a joint, it calmed him down enough to do it.

After a year, Paul moved to New York City and got a job as a social worker in Bedford-Stuyvesant, a poor, violence-ridden neighborhood. He started doing formal zazen at Zen Studies with Eido. In Greenwich Village, he heard a scholarly talk on Buddhism by a Tibetan professor named Geshe Sopa. After the lecture he spoke with the professor. He'd never met a Tibetan before. He asked if there were any Tibetan Buddhists in the area and Geshe Sopa sent him to the Lamaist Buddhist Monastery of America in Washington, New Jersey, the first Buddhist monastery in the West, established in 1958. Paul spent the day there with Tibetan monks in robes, hanging out and eating with them. They didn't speak much. Good feeling, though.

At the door on his way out, Paul met a Westerner named Jeffrey Hopkins who studied there with his friend Bob Thurman. Paul told Hopkins he had a crucial question: he wanted to know why he was meditating. Hopkins said, "There may not be a real big answer to that. How do you feel after you sit or while you're sitting? Do you like it?"

"Actually, I do like it for a variety of reasons."

"Let that motivate you to sit the next day and just go from one sitting to the next. Don't try to figure out some big philosophical answer to why you're sitting."

Soon after that, Paul was in his apartment in the East Village on a weekend reading the *Village Voice* when all of a sudden, he saw a photo of Peter Schneider. The article said Schneider was the general manager of a brand new Zen monastery named Tassajara Zen Mountain Center. Paul said, "Well, if he can do it, I can do it."

Paul had read *The Three Pillars of Zen* by Philip Kapleau. He liked what he read in that book. The Rochester Zen Center was a lot closer than Tassajara. But he wasn't sure if it was for him. So he phoned, and Kapleau answered. They talked for half an hour and Paul thought, *He's not my cup of tea. He's not gonna be my teacher.* He wrote a letter to the San Francisco Zen Center and applied for the next training period. Yvonne wrote back that he was accepted. "I'm gonna do it," he said when he read her letter.

He wanted to deepen his meditation, so every day after work he would come home and sit in his apartment in front of the fireplace, put a stick of incense in a bowl of ashes, and sit for thirty minutes which was how long it took for that incense to burn down, an ancient practice.

Paul quit his job, spent the summer in Maine, and then headed west in his truck with his girlfriend. He had left a motorcycle in San Francisco with a friend and sold it to pay for the fall 1969 practice period. He showed up at Tassajara a day early. Sure enough, Peter was the director, just as it had said in the *Village Voice*. And once again, Paul thought, *If he can do it, I can do it.*

But then right away there was a hurdle to leap. He didn't believe he could get up at four in the morning. *I cannot do this,* he thought. *I cannot do this.* He fretted about it all afternoon, then he got a bright idea. He told himself, *OK, Paul, if you don't get up, nobody will get up. Nobody's going to get up unless you get up.* It worked. He fooled himself into getting up. He had to, or nobody else would.

A month later, Paul was in the back of a dump truck shoveling manure onto the garden. He looked at his work partner shoveling with him and said, "This gets better every day, doesn't it?"

The Valley

I walked out to enjoy sunrise with the sheep. The morning fog from Carmel was coming in, blanketing the hills. I'd moved to upper Carmel Valley for the fall semester at the language school. There was just one other student and me with Mrs. Mink. It wasn't an intensive course, but at that ratio it was intense.

Vasquez had wanted his place in Pacific Grove back. Bill Lambert made a call and got a friend of his to rent me a cabin on his land. Beautiful view, lovely countryside, but a bicycle wouldn't do it anymore. Dot generously loaned me her station wagon.

I was not getting out much. Jean Ross's Monday night zazen group was still meeting even though she was shuso at Tassajara. She was driven to her apartment in Carmel for the sitting and brief talk she'd give and then back after it was over.

I was lonely. Looking at the sheep made me remember I was affection starved. Not for sheep, thank goodness, because there were all these jokes about sheep and farmers being involved that way. Once when a group came to Tassajara on horseback, Jerry Fuller made the comment that he wondered if the horses were stump broke. I asked, "What's that?" He said that some horses were taught how to back up to a stump in order to soothe the loneliness of their cowpoke out on the range. I had desires other than sheep and doubted they were stump breakable anyway.

My cabin was just off a drive that went uphill from Carmel Valley Road, across from Russell Wolter's farm. He was just starting to get known for his organically-grown lettuce and other vegetables. He'd done it that way for decades. He found it humorous that people talked about growing crops without poison as if it were something special.

Russell's brother Lou ran the small grocery store on the road—Wolter's Hacienda Market. When I got tired of studying Japanese, or staring at the wall, I might go down there and hang out a while, eat or drink something. No cracker barrel, but there was a bit of crude philosophy. Lou told stories about the Korean War. Guys would talk about trucks and women's body parts.

Only Now

Paul Shippee was planning ahead. He wanted to stay for the spring practice period but he didn't have the money. Peter told him he could be on scholarship. Many students paid for their practice periods by staying for the guest season. Shippee had heard the razor's edge got dull in guest season, so he wasn't interested. He was not there to mess around. Being the mechanic and taking care of the shop would pay his way and gave him a degree of independence that he enjoyed.

During work periods, he could usually be found in the shop. For him, though, what went on in the zendo was the beating heart of Tassajara. He'd gone there with one purpose in mind—to get deeper into meditation. Thirty minutes a day at home hadn't been enough. He wanted to be in the pressure cooker and the practice period schedule was just that.

The morning work period was rather short due to a period of zazen before noon service and lunch. Shippee got to that zazen early, if he could, so that the sitting for him would be more like fifty-five minutes. When the bell rang to end the period, he slowly unwound from zazen and stood in the aisle to chant the Heart Sutra at noon service with fifty or so others. Then he returned to sitting on his zafu, facing out, for lunch. He reached back, picked up his oryoki, and placed it on the meal board before him. The meal chant began and he unwrapped and set out his bowls.

One day as he sat on his cushion with opened bowls, waiting for the servers to bring the baskets of bread, tureens of soup, and wooden serving bowls of salad, his eye was caught by a spot of sunlight from a beam that came through a window on to the shiny plum-colored linoleum of the aisle. He gazed at the spot of sunlight and all of a sudden his hair stood on end and a shiver went through him as he had a powerful realization. He felt his whole being light up and thought, *There is no past and future, it's just always now.* He told himself, *You better wake up to that because that's what reality is. It's always now.*

He went up to Peter after lunch and said he wanted to see Suzuki.

Suzuki's little cabin was cold. There was warmth though radiating from smoldering charcoal in his hibachi—and from Suzuki. Shippee told him what he'd experienced in the zendo and asked, "What about that experience? Is that an enlightenment experience?"

Suzuki nodded yes.

Shippee said, "Well, what about you? Do you have that all the time? How does it work for you?"

Suzuki said, "Well, it's like sometimes I hear a bird sing."

Barking Sea Lions

Walking on the beach in Carmel, I met an interesting woman dressed in layers of unmatching apparel. I treated her to dinner from a delicatessen which had a small area where we could sit. Then I gave her a ride to her home, a tiny place with a kitchen, bathroom, and bedroom-living room. There were knick-knacks everywhere—figurines, souvenirs, framed photos, little decorations. I didn't know where the evening was headed, and didn't care, when a knock on the door solved that problem. The door opened before she'd even responded and—my gosh—Sterling Bunnell stepped in. I sized up the situation quickly and told Sterling I'd love to stay and talk with him but I had a date with some friends. He said he was staying in the area. We agreed to meet the next day for lunch on the Old Fisherman's Wharf.

Sterling showed up disheveled as ever. I didn't think about that aspect of him at Tassajara, but out here in the civilized world he stood out—shirt half-tucked in, loose pants falling down. Uncombed hair. Not that I cared. What he lacked in sartorial splendor, he made up for with keen observations. We never had trouble talking, as he was interested in and, it seemed, knowledgeable, about everything.

With the hoarse barking of sea lions as accompaniment, the conversation soon migrated to the subject of Barry and his rape of a Tassajara guest. I told Sterling that since then I'd learned Barry had raped a student, as well. He said he wasn't surprised. I asked how Barry's therapy sessions went.

Sterling said he saw Barry for a number of visits but that Barry was in denial, hiding from Sterling in their meetings. After a few months, Sterling gave up. He saw Barry had great hostility toward his mother which he took out on other women.

"Do you think he's still dangerous?" I asked, "like, could he do it again?"

"Sure," Sterling said. "Potentially. He's sitting at Sokoji and living across the street. Maybe the community can help him in ways I couldn't."

Baby Sister

Bob Halpern came to visit. He was still living in the city doing scary iron work way up on high-rises. He and I went to Wolter's Hacienda Market to get some beer, at my suggestion. Billy and Don were at the counter talking to Lou. They were big, tough guys. Don was tall. Billy was heavy, swarthy. Both were muscular and sun-scorched from working outdoors—backhoe work, selling firewood, boar hunting. Billy and Don were the most threatening guys in the valley. Always looking for trouble, getting into fights, especially in bars.

Once, Stan White had the flatbed truck full of 55-gallon drums of gasoline and kerosene he was bringing into Tassajara. He pulled into Lambert's gravel parking area. Billy was out there, drunk. He taunted Stan, whooping it up with his six-gun out, shooting bullets dangerously close to the flammables, while Don stood by laughing. Stan ignored them and walked to the back door unconcerned.

So I said hi to Lou, then Don, and Billy. Billy snickered at me. I picked out a six-pack of Dos Equis.

Billy spoke up. "God damn hypocrite."

"Huh?" I said.

"God damn hypocrite. We're bad and we know it, but you people pretend to be good and then go out and buy beer."

"Good lord, Billy, nothing bad about drinking a little beer," I said to him. "Lou, Billy, Don—this is my friend, Bob."

"Pleased to meet you," said Bob, nodding to Lou and then sticking out his hand and stepping up to the bad boys, looking them in the eye with a fearless grin.

They each extended a hand unenthusiastically. Billy looked for another angle to get to me. "How's them girls over there at Tassajara?"

"Oh fine," I said. "Working hard. Getting up early to meditate." Trying to change the tenor I added, "Come over some day and take a bath. Stay for dinner. Be my guest."

"You don't eat meat. No beer, either."

"You can bring your own beer," I said. "People bring beer, wine, hard liquor."

"Those girls, there," said Don, "can we come in and fuck some of them girls, there?"

I was just getting ready to say something else diplomatic and passive when Bob stepped up into Don's head-higher face and said, "Sure, you can come to my house and fuck my sister—if she's interested, that is—if I can go to your house and fuck your sister—if she's interested, that is."

Don's eyes grew large. His fists clenched. Lips trembled. Neck vein bulged. His wide shoulders were shaking. He looked like a volcano ready to go off. I leaped in between them, put my hands up on Don's shoulders.

"Please forgive my friend," I begged sincerely. "He's insane—and suicidal."

Don turned to me, his whole body now shaking. We were no longer joking. He'd taken what I said seriously. Bob was in his eyes now like an invalid in a wheelchair. "OK, OK," he backed off, and with a voice slightly trembling uttered, "But my baby sister is the sweetest little girl in the world—"

"I understand," I interjected, throwing some money on the counter for Lou, who'd been watching silently. And I pulled Bob out of there.

Back home, Bob chastised me for interfering with his exchange. He said he was going to take care of it himself and didn't appreciate my intrusion.

"Really?" I said. "I thought I just saved your life."

A Date

There was an attractive woman who lived up the hill in a small cabin, an older woman. She was twenty-nine, did Tarot and massage. We'd say hi. One day she knocked. We talked. She was acting friendly. We walked up the hill to her place. She suggested we go to a dance club in Carmel. OK. She got dolled up. I drove us there. As soon as we pulled into the driveway and parked, she got out of the car and went ahead of me to the door. A man met her there. They embraced, went inside. She didn't even wave goodbye. I just got in the station wagon and drove back to what I called home.

Twenty Dollars

Niels dropped by on his way into Monterey from Tassajara. Getting all worked up talking made us want to indulge in the usual conversational aids, so we walked down to Lou's market and bought coffee and rolling tobacco. Niels had a sharp intellect and, despite the cursing sailor character, was well-read. Philosophizing and making psychological, social, and spiritual practice-oriented observations were his calling.

"What does Suzuki Roshi teach?" he asked me with his strong voice that told me whatever I said would be pounced on.

"The nature of mind," I said.

"No! He said, 'Actually there's no such thing as the mind.' I remember his words exactly!"

"OK," I said, "Tell me."

"Precepts! That is what Suzuki Roshi teaches! Just listen to him—everything he says gets down to how to conduct oneself, how to be, how we live together in such a way as to be enlightened! And where does his right attitude, right practice, right insight come from? From zazen! Not from memorizing rules and trying to follow them. Without zazen we will inevitably fail. The precepts are not written!"

"The ones that are written have some use," I said. "They warn us of areas of behavior where we've got to pay attention and be careful."

"No! Not careful. Mindful! Careful sounds like some nervous person who doesn't know how to be mindful."

"Come on—taking care, being mindful—they're the same thing, Niels."

Then, turning playful and grinning, he said, "You say that because you don't understand the profound way of the Buddhas!"

We laughed, drank more coffee, and rolled another couple cigarettes.

While in the midst of this deep exchange, there was a knock on the door. Wow. It was Richard Baker. That was a complete surprise. "What are you doing here?" I said. "Back from Japan already?" He said he was on his way to Esalen Institute in Big Sur to lead a workshop with Suzuki and Bill Kwong.

We grilled Richard about what it was like in Japan. He said he'd been sitting at Daitokuji, a Rinzai temple, studying with Kobori Roshi. He was living near Myoshinji and said the abbot there, Mumon Yamada, was an impressive roshi with the same sort of feeling that Suzuki had. He talked about how Japan was filled with fascinating intricacies like a thread shop that sold only purple thread—over five hundred choices. There were thousand-year-old ceremonies and the world's fastest, smoothest train rides, artistry expressed in so many different ways from Noh plays to surrealistic TV ads. There were T-shirts with shocking profanity and senseless messages in English. He said that he and Ginny had seen a T-shirt that read "Peppy Casual" and had tried in vain to find one to buy.

Niels asked him who paid for his flight to America, whether our hard work during the Tassajara guest season was paying for that. He said that it was covered by Ed Johnson, head of Fidelity

Investments. Richard was going to visit him in Boston, be Fidelity's guest, and hang out in their offices. Johnson had been a major donor since he'd met Suzuki and Richard. Niels accused Richard of being a capitalist pig and not a priest. Richard said that Buddhists should be socially vertical and that, by being vertical, he was doing his part in planting Buddhism in America. Also, he wanted to voice his opposition to the Vietnam War in a power center. Anyway, he said, he was broke, so not much of a capitalist pig. He said he hardly had enough money to buy gas. Niels pulled his wallet out and handed Richard a twenty-dollar bill. Richard declined. Niels insisted. Richard continued to decline until Niels in a loud voice said, "What? You cannot accept a gift? Is that some sort of hang-up? This is dana! What sort of priest are you? You're denying me good karma!" Richard reluctantly accepted.

Female Company

One morning, Dianne and her pal Margaret Crowley dropped by. They had borrowed a car to do some errands and see Dr. Wenner on their day off. He was friendly and always happy to see Zennies—especially Dianne.

He didn't charge us. He wouldn't even take insurance or government money. It was during practice period, so students had to have a good reason to go out, and going to the doctor was a reason that couldn't be questioned too closely. But I could tell by their vibe that Dianne and Margaret mainly wanted to play. They were planning on a picnic at the beach in Carmel after seeing Dr. Wenner.

They returned in the evening all giddy and talkative. Having been alone studying—and not studying—so much of the time, I was delighted to have them as honored guests. I served them green tea in Marley mugs and we jabbered away mindlessly. They were particularly excited about their new word. They'd agreed they didn't like the word penis or the more vernacular and crude words which weren't respectful enough. "So now," said Dianne, "we're calling it wajima."

They looked at me awaiting my reaction.

"Wajima. OK!" I said. "Less clinical. A toast!"

We lifted our cups of tea.

"A wajima is a wajima is a wajima," I said, "but by any name would be just as… Uh, I'll stop there."

After some more deep, penetrating conversation, Margaret said they'd better get back because they still had to get up at four-thirty. I told her to go on, that I'd drive Dianne in later. Dianne concurred. Margaret didn't like that idea, and bade Dianne to come on with her. I told her not to worry and go. But she wouldn't give up. I insisted she leave, eventually yelled at her, finally pushed her outside and locked the door.

Hours later, Dianne and I were cruising on the dark Tassajara road. Contrary to what people tend to think, it was safest to drive the road at night. The stones and bumps in the road were clearly defined with shadows. The headlights of approaching cars around turns could be seen well in advance—if there were any approaching cars at that hour. And there was no worry about the engine overheating.

I coasted in quietly and parked outside the gate. Just then, we heard the han for morning zazen. Dianne ran off to get her robe on. I went to the baths—how good the hot spring water felt. Steam room in the utter dark. The creek was low but dammed up with rocks outside the steam room, so I could dip into a shallow pool. The ringing of bells from the zendo penetrated the darkness. Then I slept in the car for a while, got back to the cabin at eight, and fell asleep as soon as I hit the mattress on the floor.

I'd hardly slept at all when I was awakened. Someone was calling, "David! David!" The voice was urgent and demanding. It was unpleasant to come to consciousness. I groaned, opened my eyes and, as they focused, realized I was looking at a woman covered in blood. She kept calling my name. When she saw she'd gotten through to me she said, "We had an accident—motorcycle—Doug's hurt—on the road below!"

It was Pat, a Zennie from the city. Thoughts raced by quickly. How'd she know where I lived? She was totally covered in blood.

Doug's hurt. Good lord. Look at her. He must be about to die. I still had my clothes on. Helped her down to lie on my bed not worrying about the blood.

I ran down to the road where I found Doug, who was OK, just sitting on his motorcycle. A little mussed up. "Where's Pat?" he said.

He drove me back up the hundred yards or so to my place, where Pat was not only covered in blood, but in gravel, much of it embedded in her skin. I made a bed in the back of the station wagon. Doug helped me get her in.

He was on his way to L.A. from San Francisco and she had hitched a ride saying she wanted to visit me. He'd been to my place before and knew the way. They'd had a spill while making the turn from the asphalt Carmel Valley Road onto the dirt and gravel road I lived on. There was gravel from our road spread out on the asphalt.

I told Doug to rest in my place while I drove to Monterey Peninsula Community Hospital, but he went on. Arriving at the emergency entrance to the hospital, orderlies carefully transferred Pat from the station wagon to a gurney and rolled her in. A doctor looked at her and started screaming at me. "Goddamn motorcycles! Goddamn motorcycles! We're going to be picking gravel out of her for hours because of a goddamn motorcycle!"

Pat was in the hospital for the night and then I drove her back to my place. I put a mattress in a small back room for her. She slept till the next day. Then she was up, and I discovered why she'd come. She'd decided that she was destined to take care of me. She would cook, clean. We could sit zazen and chant the Heart Sutra together. She would tend to my needs so that I could concentrate on studying. For a couple days, I let her recuperate while telling her that Dianne was my girlfriend and that she could not stay long. Then I drove her against her wishes to the city. I took her to Yvonne's next door to Sokoji; Yvonne was like our den mother, always willing to take in any stray or wounded people or animals.

Pat cried. I told her we'd be friends forever. Driving back I thought about karma—intentional action and the results of it.

Drop Out

Dot needed the car back. I moved from Carmel Valley into Monterey. I got a room that was walking distance from the school, but I had a bad relationship with the landlady. I was so tired of being there.

I loved Mrs. Mink, but I'd run out of juice, couldn't concentrate on studying. I had an upset stomach. It was gurgling a lot and there was white wispy stuff in my stool. I tried diet change, fasting, medicine. Nothing worked. I had to get out. I called my sister. We decided to go together in her car to Texas and invited Bob Halpern to join us.

I told Mrs. Mink I was leaving early to drive to Texas for the holidays and then I'd be returning to Tassajara. She said I could come back anytime and finish up to get credit for the course, and that I was the best student she'd ever had. I told her I'd never had a better teacher and that I'd keep studying, but I needed a break. And credit meant nothing to me. I'd not even finished a year of college.

I'd made six trips into Tassajara while studying Japanese. The first was in the summer about a third of the way through the six-week intensive course. I ran into Suzuki on the bridge over the small creek and completely failed in an attempt to communicate in his native tongue. So embarrassing. The second was a midnight drive in with friends to sneak into the baths. We played around for a couple hours and departed as the wake-up bell was being rung on its rounds. I left an empty gallon bottle of bad wine at the top of the steps to the zendo as a calling card.

The third trip was when Dot, Yolanda, and I went in for the day. The fourth was the time I drove Dianne back in. The fifth was a clandestine visit to Dianne, whom I missed. It was a night she was *jikido*, the zendo cleaner, and slept in the zendo. That was an excellent location because no one else was within earshot. And the jikido has to be up an hour early to light and distribute the Coleman lanterns, so I had time to go into the hot plunge and cold creek and share coffee with her up by the gate before heading out.

The sixth trip into Tassajara was to attend Jean Ross's impressive shuso ceremony. I visited with Suzuki later that day. This time my Japanese was better. He was pleased. He said he hadn't imagined it was possible for me to learn so much Japanese that quickly. Now, he wanted me to stay at the school for two years and then go to Japan to study Zen and Japanese culture.

Brother David had said that St. Benedict's *Rule* for the monks started off with the admonition to obey, and that obey meant to listen. I did listen to Suzuki, but didn't obey. I told him I'd keep studying but that I had to go back to Tassajara, had reached the limit of how much I could do out there.

I'd heard about the guest Zen master who was coming from Japan to lead the spring practice period. I wanted to be there with him. Suzuki nodded. "OK," he said, obviously a little disappointed.

Dangerous Answers

Bob Walter paid a visit and told me what a great practice period it had been. Like me, he'd been impressed with Jean Ross's shuso ceremony. He said she handled every question with ease. He added—that's how she was as shuso: steady, at home in the role.

He told me some of the Q and A from the shosan ceremony. The exchange with Ken Berman stuck in my mind. Ken was in his late teens, the youngest male student we'd had. He was sincere and idealistic. In the shosan ceremony, he posed a challenging situation. "We were all quite conscious of the Vietnam War," Bob said, "and Ken was a pacifist. Speaking hypothetically, he asked something like: 'I'm married and have a wife and kids. An intruder comes into our home and wants to kill us. What do I do? Do I kill him? Do I let him kill my family?' Suzuki Roshi responded, 'Kill your self.'"

Hearing that was like a lightning bolt to Bob, who saw, then, that by dropping the illusory self, whatever comes, one wouldn't have to ask someone else what to do.

"Yeah, but that's sure subject to misinterpretation," I said. "In a shosan, people will understand, but I think if that story is repeated elsewhere there should be a disclaimer: this does not mean kill your body."

Bob told me another exchange between Dan Welch and Suzuki that would also not play well outside the context of *mondo*, of question and answer with a master. Dan asked Suzuki, "You said all beings are bodhisattvas. So, was Adolf Hitler a bodhisattva?"

Suzuki answered, "Yes, Adolf Hitler was a great bodhisattva."

"Oh no," I said. "That's coming from the same place when Buddha said all beings are buddha. That of course means Vlad the Impaler was a buddha, an unrealized buddha. That's not at the level of all beings suffer from greed, hate, and delusion. That can't be repeated just anywhere, or someday there will be a poster with Suzuki Roshi's face and below it: 'Adolph Hitler was a great bodhisattva.'–Shunryu Suzuki."

Concert Bummer DECEMBER

I waited at my place for my sister and Bob to arrive. The last time the three of us had been together was just ten days earlier, at an all-day free concert. People said it was going to be a lovefest like Woodstock. The Rolling Stones had quickly arranged for it. Couldn't miss that.

The venue had just changed a day or two before, from the Sears Point Raceway in Sonoma County, to a field at Altamont Pass beyond the East Bay. How on earth would they have time to get everything ready? We headed out. It was new territory to us, so unlike the Bay Area—rolling hills of dry grassland, fairly barren.

We arrived before the music started and miraculously got a parking spot right next to the entrance. A few hundred thousand people were expected, and indeed there were more people than I'd ever seen at one time—way more. We went to the back of the crowd which gave a clear view, as it was on a gentle incline. The stage was a good couple of football fields away.

I think Bob would have liked to go down front but we stayed nice and uncrowded where we were with a big cloth to sit on and plenty of food and water. Santana came on. We could hear them OK way back there but not hi-fi for sure. I slept through the Flying Burrito Brothers. The Jefferson Airplane was next, and something awful was happening onstage that stopped their music—sounds of fighting. Grace Slick and Marty Balin could be heard trying to cool things down, but things didn't seem to be cooling down. A couple next to us with binoculars said there were some Hells Angels being way too rough with people going past some barrier before the stage, especially with one guy who'd gotten onstage. Band members were yelling at them to calm down. They said that an Angel knocked Marty Balin down and he wasn't getting up. After Balin got up and the frenzy had died down some, the Airplane started playing again but kept getting interrupted by fighting while they pleaded with those up front to be peaceful.

There were not nearly enough porta-potties so Bob and I walked further away from the crowd and peed in the field alongside numerous other concert goers, not all of them male. I pitied my sister off standing in a long line.

Crosby, Stills, Nash, and Young were next and they seemed overwhelmed by what was happening. They'd start a song, stop it, start again. They tried to cool things down with no success as well and clearly stopped before their set was over.

Someone who'd come from the front said there were a bunch of Hells Angels beating people up with pool cues—and added they were from the Oakland chapter—the bad ones. It got dark and cold. We learned that the Grateful Dead, who were next, were getting reports of the chaos and had their helicopter turn around. After a while, The Rolling Stones came on and had to interrupt every song in their first set to attempt crowd control. Their second set lasted for only three songs and went pretty smoothly. Then, they just walked off and it was over.

Looking at all the cars heading toward San Francisco, I decided to drive the other way. We did a big round-about around the Bay Area returning to San Francisco over the Golden Gate Bridge a couple of hours later instead of going the jam-packed route through the Bay Bridge. We were numb from the day-long sitting and listening to all that broken up distant music and unpleasantness.

A Vanishing

My sister and Bob arrived. I was packed and ready to go. We drove some possessions of mine to the Veglia's place for safekeeping, and then we were on our way.

We reviewed our Altamont experience as we headed out. We'd learned since then that during the Stones' set, a guy pulled a gun and was stabbed to death by a Hells Angel. What were The Rolling Stones thinking, rushing into a giant event like that with so little planning? Turns out, Bill Graham and others in the Bay Area concert scene had urged them not to do it.

We stopped to munch on burritos and pick up goodies and drinks for the road. An hour after leaving, we'd only gone a couple of miles. Back in the car, my stomach was gurgling as it had been for weeks. In the distance, I could see the Monterey city limit sign. I felt a great sense of relief and, as we passed the sign, my chronic stomach grumbling instantly vanished.

Pure Wind

Bob Halpern, Susan, and I looked up tall, red-bearded Bob and short, sweet Sandy Watkins at their cozy home in Studio City, part of greater Los Angeles. I asked Bob Watkins what he was doing now and he said he was working on sets for films. He spoke nostalgically about Tassajara and Suzuki, who he said was the greatest teacher he'd ever had or hoped to meet.

"One of Suzuki's one liners that I really applied a lot in my life," he said, "was 'Just do it.' Just do it was like this little island in my stream.

"You remember that Ruthie used to pick yucca flowers and how we would eat them in our salads? She brought some to Suzuki Roshi. The base of one of the yucca leaves was kind of frayed. Suzuki Roshi said it would make a great sumi brush, so I grabbed a handful of them and he made up some sumi ink. He started giggling and got out some good white paper and did two pieces of calligraphy. Then he laughed and gave those to me and said, 'Now don't tell anybody.' In other words, what he used for a brush. One of them is hanging in the other room. It says 'Everything is absolutely perfect.' He signed it and put 'Tassajara Zenshinji 1967' on it. I got them mounted. The other one is put away. It has two characters that say 'Pure Wind.'

"Do you remember how he used the word 'pure' a lot? If you get up from zazen and leave the zendo in that frame of mind, that's what he called pure action—without thinking—you just do it. If you just do it, it's shikantaza. It's the same attitude that you had in the zendo, and he used to refer to that as pure practice."

Bob told about the time Suzuki had crushed a finger working on the wall below the dining room deck. Bob drove him to Dr. Wenner's office and Bill fixed him up. "Afterwards, we had to pick up a few things for the kitchen and shop and we were driving over in Seaside, and he said he was hungry. All I could see was fast food places. Before I could get out of there and find a good place to eat, he said, 'Pull over here,' and so I did. It was a hamburger joint. We sat down at a booth and looked at the menu. He said, 'Oh, you don't eat meat, do you?' and I said, 'No Roshi, I haven't eaten any animal food in two years.' Everything on the menu had animal food. The best I could do was order a grilled cheese sandwich. He ordered a hamburger with double meat. When the food arrived, I took a bite of my grilled cheese and he took a tiny bite of his hamburger and asked, 'How do you like your grilled cheese sandwich?' and I said, 'It's fine,' and he said, 'I don't like mine,' and then he switched them and took a bite of the grilled cheese and said, 'Ah, good. I like this.' And so I ate the hamburger with double meat, and we drove on back to Tassajara. After that, I couldn't be so rigid about what I ate."

"Serving up the roast beef," Sandy said, putting a platter on the table.

"Looking back on it all," Bob said, "my viewpoint now is that everything is perfect—as Suzuki Roshi said."

An Interview

Still in L.A., our traveling trio dropped by Joshu Sasaki's Cimarron Zen Center. His group had grown larger, with residential facilities.

Gayle was there. I knew her from Tassajara. She'd left because she didn't have enough contact with Suzuki, said she was lucky to see him for dokusan once a year. She saw Sasaki twice a day. But she said she loved Suzuki and missed the daily practice with us. Said she had combined Suzuki's teaching of shikantaza, just sitting, with working on koans with Sasaki. I asked, wasn't she supposed to be working with the koan all the time? She said she practiced just sitting for the first part of a zazen period, and worked on her koan the second part.

I told her we wanted to interview Sasaki for the *Wind Bell*. I just made that up on the spot. She said she'd convey the message. It worked. Before long we sat at a table across from Sasaki, two translators at his side—James Yamamoto, and George Stanicci, who mainly just listened. My Japanese was nowhere near good enough to understand more than some words and phrases as they whizzed by, but I greeted Sasaki in Japanese, and he responded in kind.

Sasaki started off with something to say about the upcoming interview. He didn't want to get superficial questions like a reporter would ask. "Don't ask me why I came here, and when did I come. Don't waste my time. Ask about the dharma."

Bob looked at Sasaki and asked, "Why did you come here and when did you come?"

Without hesitation or complaint, Sasaki answered those questions and more. He arrived in 1962. His sponsor, Dr. Harmon, had written Myoshinji in Kyoto requesting a Zen teacher and they'd sent Sasaki. Sasaki had thought about it for six months before agreeing. He had tried to study English but said he couldn't muster the courage to use it—comparing his reluctance to put effort into learning English to Americans' hesitancy to learn Zen. But he thought, *Well, I'll do what I can and maybe become friends with a few of them.* There were difficulties at first, but he said that especially due to the early assistance of Dr. Harmon, problems were solved, his center grew. He'd had to change locations several times due to neighbors' complaints about traffic, chanting and bell sounds, and his acceptance of hippies. "Zen welcomes everyone," he said. So in 1968 they settled in at Cimarron Street.

As opposite as his style was to Suzuki, some of what he said was quite similar—like his tolerance of hippies. He said he never had a plan. "People come and practice. If there's a problem, we'll deal with it. This isn't a business. I don't want to build temples and expand." He didn't want other Japanese priests to come—better to develop local people. At first, he only taught zazen. Things picked up after he added koans and sanzen. He said there were two types of students—the ones interested in hearing lectures and knowing history, and those interested in Zen training and practice. "The latter I will give koans and they can confront me in sanzen. True Zen of necessity includes sanzen and koan practice." Without sanzen, he stressed, it's just curiosity Zen, adding that if we were merely journalists, he'd not say all this but asked are we academics and journalists or students? "You might be dead in one hour, so I wish a correct answer from you."

Bob said, "We came because there is a Buddha here."

"I'm not a Buddha," and he quoted Basso, "Not mind, not buddha," then added, "I don't like people who are looking for Buddha here. You're hooked on buddha and must be free from even such ideas. Entangled in that word, buddha, you will be no more free than a believing Zen student. You must be free to accept or throw away buddha. The attitude should be that you will neither affirm nor deny buddha or god, free from any such notions."

He went on to say that it's difficult here because people in the U.S. need a symbol such as a god-savior or a Buddha, and it appeared that we came seeking buddha like we were Christians seeking god. As long as you depend on someone from Japan, your Zen will remain weak. Maybe all that could be expected was that people here would just be interested in doctrine and theory.

I wanted to protest that we weren't theists—but thought better of it. The translators suggested we might bring it to an end, then, but we kept asking and Sasaki kept answering.

Bob asked if Sasaki planned to continue the Japanese form of separation of priests and lay. Sasaki answered, there's no difference between priest and lay, men and women. He named it Zen Center on purpose rather than Zen Temple with its hierarchy, and said cats and dogs could come practice there. "I welcome all—particularly hippies." He said he wasn't transplanting the Japanese system of hierarchy, but was introducing practices and disciplines that were appropriate for America.

I asked, "Practices such as what?" He said to come join them in a sesshin and we'd find out.

Sasaki said what he was doing was teaching zazen and "thinking twenty-four hours how to make people enlightened Zen students, whether by pulling their noses, hitting them, or pushing them. I am just combing my brain trying to find ways and means to produce such students."

I asked if he saw any other problems with Americans. He said the Western mind was well developed at dealing with data, and had produced wonders in the fields of science, philosophy, and psychology. Yet there's a split there between subject and object. Zen has no object or goal. "However, Zen does include everything from sutra study to journalism."

I asked about translating the sutras and such that we chanted. He said that since they had no meaning at all, it's not necessary to translate sutras for chanting. The key was to manifest oneself. Better to do them in a loud voice, he said, and imitate the sounds of animals, than chanting without the belief that you're manifesting yourself. Whatever you do, believe that you're manifesting yourself. It's better not to think that one must understand what one reads. While not fully understanding, adhere faithfully to what one is doing, chanting or chores, and realize one is manifesting oneself in these activities.

He said that we must also go into the secular world to earn a living. Then the much more full type of Zen practice begins. He said that one of the problems of Zen doctrine is that one is apt to become isolated from the world of social responsibility. Since the self doesn't exist, one can harmonize with whatever situation and environment one finds oneself in.

I asked if he was getting tired. He said he could answer these types of questions half asleep, suggesting some high-class twelve-year-old scotch would help. Towards the end of our time with him, Sasaki said, "I am very appreciative of Tassajara and the San Francisco effort towards helping the American people and impressed." He added that he'd met Richard Baker and was impressed with him as well.

I left that day with Susan and Bob feeling quite pleased, a distinctly different experience than the prior visit when he'd kicked my friend Warren and me out. I had expected and was almost looking forward to receiving a bashing like before, but the meeting was friendly and comfortable, no-nonsense. I found it profound and inspiring.

Another Reading

Four of us visited with psychic Fred Kimball, the fourth being Gayle. She was eager to meet him.

He did a reading on me first. "What?" he started off. "Did you become a Hindu?"

"Why do you say that?" I asked.

"You've got all these spirits around you."

"Oh. I guess that's because you told me not only to ask for help from my psyche and subconscious, but all higher beings."

"Well, they're there. I don't know what they can do to help, but it can't hurt."

After less than half an hour, it was Bob's turn. He was asleep. "He doesn't want to be read," Fred said.

I looked at Gayle. She nodded. He looked at Gayle and was quiet for a while. He said she had some conflict, but he couldn't see what it was yet. After a minute, he said, "You can't have two religions. You've got to choose one." That got her attention.

After he'd read Bob and Susan, an hour-and-a-half had passed.

It was fascinating being with Fred. None of us were ready to leave. I asked him, "Can you keep going?" "As long as the money's coming," he answered. I thought that was funny coming from him who charged so little.

"Tell me about Kelly," I said. That's what people called my father, whose name was Kelroy, which he didn't like. Fred didn't get an immediate hit. Put his hand on his forehead for a moment, looked up, and said, "Has this person died?" I said yes. "They don't like to be bothered, and I'm no good at that," he said. "There are people who are good at that."

I told him to go on and try. He said, "Well, OK. Kelly, appreciate the courtesy of your picking up the phone." And he waited a minute and then said, "You got to make sure you get the right person. I see a big radio. Does that mean anything?" I told him yes, that my father had a short-wave radio, and it was big. "OK. That's him. He says he took care of his wife and kids. Worked too much. Had more fun when he was younger. Says he was too interested in religion."

That's my father alright. He would sit and read the New Thought Christian books and pamphlets and the early motivational and early self-help books. *TNT: The Power Within You* is one I recall. I thought about how my life had led me to be with people who had that same sort of drive, what Suzuki called the way-seeking mind.

"He asks if he can go now," Fred said. That sort of hurt my feelings and made me laugh at the same time. It also reminded me of what medium Arthur Ford told my mother. She said he conveyed things from my father that he could not have known. She said my father had left that life behind and would rather not respond to more questions. Fred said that he'd spent time with Ford, that he was a strong medium though he'd tell women stuff like that they were the reincarnation of the Queen of Sheba.

"Ahdel?" I said, asking about my mother.

After a moment he said, "She had a big setback about twelve years ago. It took her a couple of years to recover. She suppressed a lot of her feminine side because she felt the weight of a lot of responsibility on her shoulders." That's clearly what happened when my father died.

So we asked him about people we knew. Fred of course knew nothing of any of them or about Zen Center.

"How about Reb?" Bob said.

Fred paused a moment and said, "Boy is that guy ambitious. He ought to get a motorcycle and ride up mountains all day."

"He's turned that ambition toward Zen," I said. "How about Richard?"

"Now here's a guy," he said, "who can get knocked down three times and still get up. Most people don't get up after the second time."

"Well he certainly hasn't been knocked down, yet," I said.

"He was when he was younger. And he will be again," Fred said.

"Paul," Bob said. He meant Paul Discoe.

Fred was quiet for a bit. "Is he enlightened?"

"We wouldn't know," I said.

"He's sure of himself. I can't see why he didn't go further. He should have a PhD, but something stopped him."

"Maybe because he's dyslexic," I said. "I hear Ruthie even signs his checks. How about Ruthie?"

"She's got a lot of energy spillin' out all over. She's one person that definitely ought to be doing your meditation."

That was interesting because she was the one person who didn't do zazen, at least not regularly. She was there as a spouse. She did tons of work in the garden though.

I asked, "How about Shunryu?"

"Is that your teacher?" he said after a moment.

"Yes."

"He should take better care of his health. These gurus get enlightened and then they don't care if they live or die."

"He wants to live, I'm sure," I said. "He's got a lot of students and responsibility."

"Yeah," Fred said, "He's happy with that, but he's OK with whatever happens."

—CHAPTER FIVE—

1970

Dana Paramita

Don Penner was just getting ready to fill a cavity in one of my molars. For no charge, he was seeing anyone at Tassajara who needed their teeth cleaned, or for more extensive work. There were a few people who needed such extensive work, and he'd have them come in for a whole day or two and put them up. He'd cleaned my teeth and found a cavity. As he was preparing to fill it, he asked a question. "Do you want any painkiller?"

I didn't like seeing a long needle coming up to my gums, but the alternative I saw as having a drill go way down into a tooth that had sensitive nerves in it. "Don't I have to get a shot of Novocain?" I asked.

"Not really. Usually don't get to a nerve."

"How do you know if you do?"

"You'll know it for sure. It's just like hitting your funny bone but only a hundred times stronger."

"Well then, what?"

"Then I can stop and give you a shot of procaine if you want."

"What's procaine?"

"It's the pain killer in Novocain. Novocain's a brand name."

"Well I don't know..."

"My wife and children don't use any painkiller."

That did it. "OK. No painkiller." I braced myself. But he was right. It didn't hurt. Later, I had another cavity filled by him and he didn't ask, just drilled and filled.

Penner had an office in Salinas which is as close to Tassajara as Monterey but with a lower cost of living. He and his Japanese wife were Buddhists and exemplars of *dana paramita*—the practice of giving with no idea of return. They hosted visiting Buddhist monks and laypeople from time to time.

Penner did ask something of Zen Center at least once. A Japanese artist named Eitaro Tada had been staying with them a while and they wished to share him with the Zen Center. He'd been with them long enough. Word was that he smoked a lot and left burned spots on their tatami. So he went to the City Center and then came to Tassajara for a week during the cold, dark winter interim in January.

Tada Sensei, as we called him, was a sumi artist who did piece after piece of what we thought of as China's first Zen ancestor, Bodhidharma. He painted Bodhidharmas all day long. Every once in a while he did an Avalokiteshvara, the mythical bodhisattva of compassion—*Kannon* in Japanese—or the older Kanzeon we chanted in the Heart Sutra. Then he'd do another Bodhidharma. Tada said, "Every morning I wake up with Bodhidharma." All the students got at least one of his *sumie*, sumi ink paintings, and everyone liked them. Some were large, some small. Almost all were black sumi ink on sumi paper with some on harder white paperboard.

Tada didn't speak much English. Dan Welch wasn't at Tassajara to translate, but I was back from the trip to Texas. So I found myself in the difficult position of being the only person there who knew any Japanese. I helped attend to him. It didn't take much.

It was cold as heck. He was in the end Stone Room with a wood burning stove, so I'd make sure he had wood and that the fire kept going. I bummed occasional cigarettes off him, too. He made his own tea. He said he started painting as a teenager and eventually had his own school, but that after his wife died he left the school to others and started painting just Bodhidharma and Avalokiteshvara.

The frightening part of my role was that I had to translate people's questions and his answers, and that was way beyond my beginner's level. Still, somehow, it went fairly smoothly. I'd tell them to ask short, simple questions, and he kept his answers the same. I had a couple of dictionaries. Also, I'd fudge it if I were lost. After he'd been at Tassajara a week, Tada went back to the City Center where he stayed till March. He left behind a City Center and Tassajara overflowing with Bodhidharmas.

Stanley White

Stan White was born in 1913. He grew up in Boston and went to private schools, where his studies included Latin and Greek. After he returned from World War II, his uncle arranged for him to be president of a small bank. He said he'd rather go to art school and study portrait painting. His father said he could do that, but he'd be forfeiting his inheritance. They shook on it. Stan told me that his sister sent him enough to get by on.

He started sitting at Sokoji in 1964. Back then, he was a bearded Bohemian character known as Sebastian to people in North Beach. He had stories about the Beats and street people. Some of them were salacious, including what he had to say about Janice Joplin. He was frank and could make unflattering comments about others, as well as praise. Silas had urged Stan from the first to come to Tassajara to work in the office and do the books. Stan finally made it there in the summer of 1968.

Stan said that sometimes Tassajara was difficult for him—the sitting and the students. He'd hear "the kids" talking a lot about the Vietnam War. He'd been in two wars and he'd hear people say how they wouldn't fight. That was foreign to him. He felt that a lot of students disliked him because he'd been in war. He said he was the only veteran there since Bob Watkins left, but there were a few others. E.L. had been in the army. There was another older student named Tommy Dorsey who'd been in the navy, though he was kicked out for smooching with another sailor. Also, Lou Hartman was as old as

Stan, and he'd been in the Merchant Marine, and his wife Blanche had worked in the defense industry making flight simulators and bomb-sights, those crosshairs made with spider silk, a job she lost when the war was over and there were men to take her place.

Stan the Bohemian surely didn't approve of Allen Ginsberg being a conscientious objector during WWII.

I didn't think most people judged or disliked him. He could get grouchy and complain, but mainly he was respected and accepted. He did his work well and followed the schedule. He was confident and a good storyteller.

One day, Stan had a group of young students enthralled with stories of working around carnivals. He said he started off selling souvenirs, balloons and pens, and that you could tell who'd bought his pens because they had ink stains on their shirts. The attitude there was to regard customers as suckers and see what you could con them out of. But later, Tim Aston told me how he thought that this time we were the suckers, that Stan's carnival stories happened to be awfully close to the ones in a book he'd read.

Sotan Tatsugami

Sotan Tatsugami arrived at Tassajara from Japan several days before the 1970 winter-spring practice period's official opening date of January 15. He was in his mid-sixties, hefty but strong, and exuded self-confidence. He had a formidable presence but wasn't aloof. He related in a direct and somewhat friendly fashion with us. He had some experience with students from the West at Eiheiji, including the first three that Suzuki had sent there—Jean Ross, Grahame Petchey, and Phillip Wilson. Tatsugami was also a teacher of the quasi-legendary monk, Brian Victoria, known for his involvement with leftist student groups in Japan. Jean Ross said that Tatsugami was the best friend that *gaijin*, foreigners, had at Eiheiji. "He brought us in so to speak, accepted us."

Tatsugami had barely unpacked before he instituted the first ceremony rehearsal. Later, we came back attired for the entering ceremony, entrance into the new practice period, the first practice period that would be a full, traditional ninety days. Up to then they'd all been close to sixty days. In the opening ceremony, all students walked single file around the zendo in gassho, heads bowed, in front of Tatsugami, Katagiri, Mel the shuso, and each other. Before, we'd just done the entering ceremony without any rehearsal, but now he was fine-tuning the ceremony, reminding me of a choreographer making sure every move is correct. He said we should all be wearing *tabi*, white socks with a separate space for the big toes so that they could be worn with sandals, sandals that were taken off before entering the zendo. Tabi would be ordered for future ceremonies.

There was a lot more Japanese entered into the vocabulary because Tatsugami didn't speak English. So four-and-nine days with their relaxed schedule were called *shikunichi*—the term Kobun used. Many of us continued using the English but the newer students were using shikunichi and it began to take hold.

Tatsugami brought more order, form, and ceremony to Tassajara, modeling the place as much as he could, little by little, after the great Japanese training temple Eiheiji, though indeed a greatly simplified version. "The officers" was no longer a vague term for those in authority. They were now the *rokuchiji*, the six who know things, thus, the six governors. Each position now had a classical, monastic Japanese name.

Tatsugami had the shop make wooden plaques about eight inches long to place where each officer sat in the zendo. In his cabin, he calligraphed with brush and sumi ink the title for each one. The rokuchiji sat on the left side of the zendo as seen from in back facing the altar with their plaques at their seats. *Tsusu* was director, *kansu* the assistant director, *fusu* the treasurer, *ino* for the head of the zendo, *tenzo* the kitchen head, and *shissui* the work leader. That's in pecking order. If the tsusu is gone, the kansu is the acting director, and so on. And there they sat—Peter Schneider, Paul Discoe, Stan White, Bob Halpern, Angie Runyan, and Bill Shurtleff. Tatsugami had a plaque made for himself which read *Docho*, and one for Katagiri that said *Godo*.

I asked Katagiri what godo meant and he said the godo at Eiheiji oversaw the practice of all monks, with other practice leaders below him. He did not approve of Tatsugami having the docho plaque made for himself. That should have been saved for Suzuki, he said, the abbot. And Tatsugami's plaque should have read *seido,* guest teacher. It seemed Tatsugami thought that Suzuki had founded this Zen monastery just waiting for someone qualified to arrive. I could tell right away that Katagiri was not overjoyed that Tatsugami had moved in.

Creek in Winter

Their laughter was a frequent ingredient of the Tassajara scene. Dianne and Margaret were usually doing what was expected of them, but sometimes they'd stray from the tracks. Even during zazen their jubilant voices would occasionally filter in from afar, climbing on a hill or naked in the creek. And then one day they were asked to skip the next practice period. Dan took Dianne for a walk to tell her, and she cried.

I was not pleased when I learned Dianne wouldn't be there. It was the same curious decision that had come down on Bob and me the year before—sending both of us instead of one of us. Except I'd learn it wasn't faulty logic—it was Suzuki's soft heart. He didn't want to separate Bob and me, or Dianne and Margaret, because we were so close.

As the spring practice period was about to begin, I got a letter from Dianne. She and Margaret had hung out together for a while in the city, and then Margaret had gone to Maryland to be with relatives. Dianne was lonely. Then about three days into the practice period, she showed up at Tassajara. People were surprised. I was worried she'd just decided to come in on her own, but nope, Peter knew she was coming. Silas had called.

I didn't have a chance to talk to her till after evening zazen. We talked and talked. Absence had made our hearts so fond that we were still awake when the wake-up bell rang. Poor thing. She had to do a day of tangaryo as we all did before a practice period. She had a difficult groggy day and fasted so she'd not be so sleepy. "I'm sorry," I said to her that night when it was over. But she didn't respond. She just trudged to her room.

I wondered what magic she'd conjured up to be able to come back. The next day she told me that she'd gone to see Suzuki in his study at the City Center. He inquired how she was doing. She said she was unhappy and missed Margaret and hated the city and wanted to go to Tassajara, that the problem had been her and Margaret together. "She's on the East Coast. Why can't I go back?"

Suzuki asked, "Why do you want to go to Tassajara?"

"Because," she said, "I've never seen the creek in the winter."

The Doanryo

The ino was in charge of the zendo, ceremonies, and rules and had underlings called *doans*. Bob Halpern was the ino. Bob's old friend Reb was a doan. So were Meg, Jane, Bob Shuman, Niels, and I. This is the group that was to set the tone for the zendo, services, conduct in general. We were the engineers of the holy stuff and schedule, there to make it all run smoothly.

Tatsugami had been the ino at Eiheiji for thirteen years. This was the area he put the most energy into. After the rokuchiji, we, the doanryo, had more contact with him than any others. Right away we were getting trained by him in how to chant, ring bells, pound the mokugyo, strike the han and the *umpan*, the flat bronze "cloud plate" that had a cloud shape. It was struck before meals. "From the *hara*!" he said in Japanese and patted his stomach, "Not the head!"

"Don't sing!" he admonished me in chanting practice. Then he'd demonstrate, I'd try, and he'd shake his head.

We were to go onto the hillsides to practice chanting, bellowing out the ancient Japanese lines. I thought of Demosthenes who plied his oratory over the roar of the waves with pebbles in his mouth. "Spirit of a flea," he scoffed in Japanese when I first struck the wide bronze bowl bell with the deep sound used in service.

Katagiri and Dan would translate for many of these meetings. Dan was Tatsugami's jisha. Having practiced Zen in Japan, Dan had a good sense of how to do all these things. But Dan did everything well. To me, he was the Eagle Scout Zen student, always applying himself a hundred percent but never judgmental with others. Driven. Exemplary.

All the doans did their best, but Reb was the most enthusiastic and exacting student of Tatsugami's. He got a tape of Tatsugami chanting and spent extra time in the hills honing his voice to as close to Tatsugami's as he could.

The doan tasks had plaques that rotated. The *kokyo* would lead the chanting, the person with the doan plaque hit the bells, the *tenken* hit the mokugyo and densho bell outside, and checked attendance. The officers had always paid attention to who showed up and people would be talked to if there was a pattern of being late or missing in non-action. In such a small community most of us would know who was there or not. But now it was codified. On the bright side, only one person now was to think about this.

Attendance was taken for each zazen by the tenken with clipboard in hand. If someone wasn't there, the tenken would go to their room to see if they were ill, bring meals on a tray if they were, and urge them to get to the zendo if they weren't. The abbot and officers were traditionally presented with a tenken report at chosan, morning tea.

Having someone in black robes standing with a list checking to see who was there and not was a bit much for some—especially if it was someone in black robes standing at their door looking down on them in their sleeping bag. That happened to Reb one time. He stayed up reading late and didn't hear the wake up bell the next morning. The tenken came. Reb told me he did not like that experience at all and said it would never happen again.

There was a lot going down that was new, so a certain amount of confusion would be expected, but not the amount that ensued with Bob and me. I can recall times in the zendo with Bob looking at a chart in his hand, he and I whispering loudly to each other walking around confused during zazen, not clear on who should do what when. Tatsugami and Katagiri sitting zazen facing out toward the room would not intervene or even appear to notice. Neither would Mel, the head monk. Students facing the wall in zazen endured the chaos.

One afternoon session, Tatsugami instructed the doans in the correct use of the kyosaku. We thought we already knew, but as with everything else, what we knew wasn't good enough. He showed us one by one the way to receive it, whacking us hard once on each shoulder. Those who would carry the kyosaku during zazen knew it was their turn when they found a plaque with the title *junko* at their seat.

Bob demonstrated one way to receive the kyosaku. Lou Musto was carrying that long stick. He rested it on Bob's right shoulder. Rather than put his hands in gassho and lean to the left as is customary, Bob turned his head and growled, "I wasn't sleeping." People who are nodding in zazen often think that because they're in an in-between stage. But it doesn't matter—one is not to second guess the junko. Lou did not back off. He pressed the stick down on Bob's shoulder again. Bob reached over his shoulder and grabbed the stick. Neither would let go. Lou was strong but Bob's iron worker muscles came into play as he thrust the stick forward bringing Lou crashing down onto the tatami between Bob and Niels. Tatsugami sitting on the altar looking right down on them didn't budge. Lou walked on with the stick.

Behavior Unbecoming

E.L. had gotten so crazy that he had to go to a hospital where they gave him Thorazine, a super-heavy tranquilizer. To continue staying at Tassajara, he'd have to keep taking it. He told me it felt to him like having cement poured in his head. We could tell when he cheated because he'd be acting weird instead of sedate. One day, there was a ruckus on the path in front of the cabins. I went over to see what was happening. E.L. was being held down by two senior male students and force-fed his Thorazine by a third. That was not an agreeable solution for anyone and it wasn't repeated.

Thorazine was the same drug they were using to bring people down from bad LSD trips. Bill Wenner was the go-to doctor for psychedelics in Monterey County and one day he got a call from a woman whose husband had accidentally taken LSD and wanted to know if she should bring him to the emergency room. Bill told her to take her husband to a nice spot in the countryside and sit quietly with him under a tree. He said the man would process it best naturally. He thought Thorazine probably wasn't a good thing for E.L. either. In fact, no one liked for E.L being forced to take Thorazine, so he wasn't monitored anymore. But then he became less and less functional. It got to where he'd put on his robes for work meeting and wander around in his work clothes for zazen, stand on the hill above the zendo staring down at us.

I was at the City Center passing Claude on the steps, and said, "Claude, what are we going to do about E.L.?" "Funny," he answered, "that's just what Suzuki Roshi was saying about you." Hmm. I thought Suzuki already had an answer to that. Alan told me Suzuki said to him, "Don't worry about David. He'll just take longer."

In staff tea one morning not long after he'd arrived for the fall 1970 practice period, Tatsugami asked, "Who is that person who's standing around in robes looking strange?" He was told that's E.L. Tatsugami asked what he was doing at Tassajara. "Oh, just being E.L.," came the answer. They tried to explain to him that E.L. was part of our family and so forth. Tatsugami said this wasn't a village and that man did not belong in a monastery. So E.L. was driven to the city the following day.

The Han

I told Katagiri I wanted to study the kanji of the Heart Sutra and other chants we recited. He suggested I start with something short and work my way up to longer pieces. He said the kanji on the face of our han was a poem traditionally written on the han at Eiheiji.

The *han*, the wooden board that called us to zazen, hung under the arbor by the entrance to the zendo. The mallet it was struck with dangled from a loop of rope attached to the bottom of the han. The person striking the han would gassho, take the mallet out of the loop, hold the loop with one hand to pull the han slightly toward them, keep it tight and strike the center with the mallet. In time, the mallet would dig a splintered crater into the face of the han. Eventually, the han would break in two. We heard that monks in Japan had a party when the han in their temple broke but we didn't follow that practice at Tassajara. The original han that Paul made had broken and was replaced before it was a year old. Kobun had worked with Paul on the design of the next han and mallet. It was thinner and hollowed out some on the striking side to improve the sound. The mallet for it was hefty but with a thin handle. The handle wasn't to be gripped tightly on impact any more than if the mallet head had been at the end of a string.

The pattern of strikes to call us to zazen took fifteen minutes. There were three introductory strikes well-spaced, then seven less than a minute apart from each other, ending with a roll down and a punctuating hit. The next round was five strikes, a roll down and two hits—light then strong. The third round was for the *doshi*, whoever was leading service. They'd arrive and offer incense at the altar with the final strikes: strong, light, strong.

I stood before the han not holding the mallet but a pen, copying the characters from the poem on its face. I wasn't sure how to write all of them because Kobun's brush work was so artistic.

Han is just a word for wood, but not the one that's used in modern spoken and written Japanese. It's what the Japanese made of the Chinese sound long ago. It was common knowledge that *han* meant "wood," but the meaning of the kanji on the han was not known. When asked what that poem meant, Suzuki had said, "Don't goof off."

I went to Katagiri's cabin. He looked at what I had written, grimaced, and wrote the characters clearly on a blank sheet of rice paper while enunciating how they were to be pronounced. I told him I'd find out what I could about the meaning of those kanji and, if he would be so kind, I'd come talk to him about it later when I knew more. He nodded and gasshoed.

I had a stack of reference books bought in San Francisco. The one I used first was the large Nelson's kanji dictionary. The regular Kenkyusha Japanese/English and vice versa dictionary was sometimes useful, but usually not. This was old stuff I was looking at. I had Chinese- and Japanese-to-English Buddhist dictionaries that were helpful, but not at all complete. Serious students of those classical Buddhist texts were beyond using books with English.

After going over the meaning of the kanji on the han in those books, I went to Katagiri. And after talking with him, I had a fairly good idea what the poem on the han said.

There were four lines with four characters each. The kanji in the first line were easy ones "life death thing big." What comes across is more like, "Life and death is the great matter." The next line had two compound words meaning something like "Transient, fleeting." Then four kanji that meant "each of us should pay close attention." The last line was tough. It started with "respectfully don't be ... " All I could find for that last word was "dissolute." But I didn't like "Respectfully don't be dissolute." I considered, instead, "Don't be lax." "Don't be negligent." Katagiri suggested, "Don't waste this life."

After that, every time I heard the han hit, I heard those words in Japanese and English. Thump! "Life and death are the great matter." Thump! "Transient, fleeting." Thump! "Each of us should pay close attention to this." Thump! "Don't waste this life!"

Katagiri was resolute. He took those words seriously and he wanted us to do so, too. Surely, his assignment during the Pacific War had made him think seriously about life and death. He never saw combat, but he had abdominal surgery without painkiller. He was a seventeen-year-old kamikaze pilot who was out of a job when the war ended.

I also studied other short poems that we chanted, and some that we didn't. Katagiri gave me a book that included these short Soto Zen chants called *gathas*. This book wasn't like our books. It

was about eight inches tall, four inches wide, and opened like an accordion. The whole thing was one continuous page that was read from right to left.

There was the robe chant we did in the morning, the Bodhisattva's vow, and my favorite, the bath gatha. It was calligraphed in romanized Japanese and English at an altar at the entrance to the baths. It read, "Now as I bathe this body, I vow with all sentient beings to wash from body and mind all dust and confusion and feel healthy and clean within and without." What I liked about it was how fluidly it chanted in Japanese. Kobun said to chant it to oneself, but I liked to hear it, so I'd do it softly so that no one would notice. People went in and out quickly so the entrance to the baths wasn't a crowded place. When I stepped on the bridge I'd remember it and think, *Oh boy, now the bath gatha. "Moku yoku shintai togan shujo, shinjin muku naige koketsu."*

One gatha I said every evening was my last thing before going to sleep. "Now as I sleep, I vow with all sentient beings, to awaken to all things without throwing off the world." I thought it was neat that I vowed to awaken as I fell to slumber.

Apology Ceremony

Two students went on a long hike on a four-and-nine day, misjudging how far they could go and get back in daylight. Then they straggled in the next morning. This was brought up in the morning tea, now called *chosan*, an Eiheiji word meaning "morning visit." Who should talk with them about this? Katagiri? He shook his head, no. Bob, the ino in charge of discipline? Mel, the head monk? Peter, the director? Tatsugami said the ino should just tell them they'll have to do an apology ceremony. So without any official scolding, the two students had to do the apology ceremony which was a lot like the entering ceremony but just for the two of them walking around in gassho, heads bowed before us all. No words were spoken.

The tenken taking attendance, the apology ceremony, all the new emphasis on hierarchy and rules rubbed some students wrong. A couple of them decided to leave as a result of this new regimen. Things actually went more smoothly under the new order and, in spite of some grumbling, it didn't feel more authoritarian. Tatsugami didn't get angry or guilt trip people. He strengthened and increased the forms, set up a way to police them, but didn't punish or even pay attention to resistance.

Right Answer

Tatsugami had a few students at a time for tea, no one excluded. He'd write down their names and ages and ask how long they'd been practicing. One day, one of Suzuki's early students, Paul Alexander, was at a tea. Tatsugami wrote his age—fifty-three. Asked how long he'd practiced. Paul said ten years. That was a rarity. Tatsugami said Paul's practice must be very good, to which the truly humble Paul replied, "No, it's going backwards."

Cheryl Hughes was quiet at her first practice period. She'd gotten turned on to Zen by reading Alan Watts's *The Way of Zen*, and had decided to go to Tassajara because psychic Ann Armstrong suggested it. At a tea with students, Tatsugami asked each person to tell what had brought them to practice. One by one Cheryl heard their impressive reasons. The person before Cheryl mentioned his burning desire to attain enlightenment. Cheryl was last and thought—*Alan Watts and a psychic—he's going to kick me out.*

"Oh I don't know," Cheryl finally said.

"That's the right answer," Tatsugami responded.

The Locks

The practice at Tassajara was to eat what was served when it was served. Sometimes that did not seem to be enough, especially for those of the male persuasion. We might get physically weak and go to a stash in our room or to the kitchen to beg for mercy, which might work depending on the kitchen worker who was begged. Or, a famished student might sneak into the storeroom for a gob of peanut butter, an apple, or some leftover bread slices. One day, I was so crazed I drank a whole can of evaporated milk. Another day, I was even more crazed and drank two cans of evaporated milk. That was too much. It made me crash. Paul couldn't get over that. He'd look at me and shake his head going, "Two cans of evaporated milk."

Students at times staggered into the kitchen and announced that they were going to faint if they couldn't put something into their stomach. Some said they had hypoglycemia. Yvonne called it being a boy. If Tommy Dorsey was working in the kitchen, he'd help out, but sometimes he couldn't.

Once, a young student went into the kitchen and said he really had to eat something right away and was scolded with, "No! It's bad for your practice!" "You're not saying no because it's bad for his practice," Tommy said. "You're saying no because you like to say no."

The problem, however, was not only people coming in from outside the kitchen. People inside the kitchen had stomachs, too. There was a policy of no munching while preparing meals. That policy held at times, and broke down badly at other times. If one took a nibble other than the customary sample for taste, another might do the same, and if the head cook did so, the dam could burst and everyone would be washed away. I've seen it become a compulsive habit like tobacco addiction where people couldn't stop even when they didn't want to eat anymore.

It was once brought up in an officers' meeting that food was being taken at night from the kitchen and kitchen storeroom. Tatsugami said to put locks on the doors. The officers argued with him. Some said, "We can't lock the doors." "That's not our way." But Tatsugami couldn't understand why not, and said, "Put locks on the doors instead of your minds."

Stan was the treasurer and buyer. He got hold of Joe, with whom Silas had shared warehouse space. Joe imported locks, so he sent down a couple. The kitchen and storeroom then sported spiffy imported locks which were fastened by the last person to leave the kitchen in the evening. Usually, the baker would be the one to remove them upon arrival in the early dark morning.

Peter did not enjoy announcing the new policy at the morning work meeting. Almost no one liked this solution and some were angry. Ed Brown, now in the garden, would get angry about people stealing food, but he thought putting locks on the doors was worse. I remember him standing outside the kitchen after evening zazen, glaring at the locks, standing there a while, and then going off to bed.

Stubborn Me

I enjoyed time spent with Tatsugami at teas in his room, and *dokusan,* the private interview. He was awfully relaxed. Not only would he smoke when I was in dokusan with him, but he'd blow the smoke in my face, not in a nasty way, just unconcernedly. He smoked either cigarettes in a holder, or tobacco in a long clay pipe that took just a pinch in its small bowl. He said he hadn't smoked when he was at Eiheiji.

Kobun Chino returned from Japan to be the priest at the Los Altos Haiku Zendo. He came to Tassajara to see Tatsugami, whom he'd practiced under at Eiheiji. There was a meeting of doans with Tatsugami in the abbot's cabin. Kobun joined us. When our meeting was over and we were leaving the cabin, Tatsugami said something to Kobun.

Outside, Kobun told me that Tatsugami told him to tell me not to rise from seiza the way I did, which was awkward. I told Kobun the reason was that I had a sprained ankle. I didn't know how to say that in Japanese and asked Kobun to go back to the cabin with me so Tatsugami would understand why I got up the way I did. Kobun said that wouldn't be necessary. I insisted. Kobun resisted. Then I got more insistent, so we went back and explained that, and Tatsugami just grunted which I took to mean, "Why are you bothering me with this?"

Afterwards, Kobun fumed and said to me strongly, "You have no mind for teaching!" Instantly, I realized I'd gotten way out of hand. That hit me so heavy that I went off and cried. Before Kobun left, I begged forgiveness and he gasshoed.

Open Eyes

Unlike the other priests I sat with, Tatsugami didn't sleep in zazen. Zazen is done with eyes half open. During zazen he would frequently admonish us with, "*Me o akete!*" (Open your eyes). He'd also give other brief impromptu zazen teachings, often invoking Dogen. And he made observations about our practice in general, such as when he said that we farted like horses.

Some people preferred being with Tatsugami to Suzuki, because of Tatsugami's higher energy level. It was hard to get to see Suzuki for dokusan. Not Tatsugami.

Stan White enjoyed Tatsugami and Tatsugami liked Stan because he was straightforward, older, and he smoked. Sometimes, Stan would roll a couple of cigarettes from his Top Tobacco, and they'd smoke and not say anything. Tatsugami told Stan, "I take a student and I squeeze and I squeeze and I squeeze and then I catch what's left."

Shortly after Tatsugami arrived at Tassajara, Jean, whom I thought of as somewhat straitlaced, drove in from her apartment in Carmel, went to the abbot's cabin, presented him with a bottle of whiskey, and the two of them visited and drank and laughed for a couple of hours.

A year before, Phillip Wilson told me about his experience with Tatsugami at Eiheiji. He said Tatsugami had ridden him pretty hard. Phillip, who was strong as heck, had challenged Tatsugami to a wrestling match. Tatsugami, the sumo champ of Eiheiji, said OK, let's go into the rock garden. That might not sound like a good place to wrestle, but there were few rocks and lots of fine, raked sand. Phillip said that Tatsugami beat him up so badly that it scared him and turned his hair prematurely gray. Suzuki, he said, had just hit him with puppy blows.

Endless Teisho

Surely the most difficult part about being at Tassajara with Tatsugami were the long lectures. We weren't to call them lectures, though, they were *teisho,* dharma talks. He'd orate in a dramatic fashion, his voice rising and falling in pitch and volume.

L-R – Reb Anderson, David Chadwick, Bob Halpern, Mel Weitsman. Photo by Bob Shuman

His teisho would go on and on, sometimes lasting two hours. It was torture for Katagiri to do the translating, as Tatsugami would speak for ten or twenty minutes before pausing for translation. Students' legs would be aching and patience tested as the subject matter frequently wasn't all that inspiring, especially after it got to us via Katagiri's unenthusiastic and highly abbreviated translation.

After evening zazen, Bob and I were doing zazen in my room, and suddenly in the silence Bob came up with a good facsimile of Tatsugami's deep rolling voice expounding the dharma with ascending pitch: "*Dogen Zenji Sama wa …* " I filled in with the descending: "*Honto no Zen no teriyaki to iu sashimi Toyota tsunami …* " Then we started laughing and someone on the other side of the single-board thick wall banged on it.

Ladder Up

Dianne and Meg were sitting up late in Dianne's dorm room, the one nearest the creek on the courtyard side. There was a blanket over the window so that the firewatch couldn't see a kerosene lamp still lighting the room.

They were determined to circumvent Tatsugami's lock on the kitchen door, and were waiting for the firewatch to finish the rounds. Their plan was to take a ladder to the creek side and enter the kitchen through a window.

Just as they were about to leave, Dianne looked out to make sure all was clear and saw light from a flashlight bobbing up and down on the backside of the kitchen. Upon close inspection, it became clear that someone else with a ladder was beating them to it. They went down and peeked into the window in the locked door and saw Craig Boyan climbing in the creek-side window. They watched as he heated leftovers, carried them down the ladder on a tray, then back up onto the deck and into the zendo. He had to return to the kitchen twice more to complete his task.

Craig was *jikido*, the zendo cleaner who sleeps there the night before the day to clean. Dianne and Meg tiptoed to the door of the zendo and peeked in. Craig's oryoki was set on the meal board in front of his zafu. He slowly walked down the aisle with each serving bowl held high and placed the three one after another on the floor in front of his seat. He stepped up on his zabuton, bowed toward the zafu, then away, sat, put his hands in gassho, and began reciting the meal chant. He didn't use the kaishaku to punctuate the ritual, likely because of their penetrating sound of wood on wood. He opened his bowls following protocol at the right time in the chanting and served himself. Slowly he ate, slower than he could get away with at scheduled mealtimes. He finished eating then cleaned his empty bowls with his cloth-tipped *setsu*, cleaning the setsu then in his mouth covered by his left palm.

Craig had prepared a kettle with hot water and a bucket to collect the wash water and left them on the serving table at the back of the zendo near the door. Before he could get up to fetch the kettle, though, Dianne walked down the zendo aisle with the kettle held high with two hands, bowed before Craig, who froze for a few seconds, and then bowed in return, holding up his large bowl to receive the water. He indicated when he'd had enough by raising his right palm a bit. Then he cleaned the bowls again with setsu and hot water, pouring the water from large to middle bowl. He cleaned the spoon and chopsticks in the middle bowl, dried them with the small drying cloth, and placed them in their sleeve. Then he poured the cleaning water into his third bowl, cleaned it with the setsu, dried the end of the setsu and placed it in the sleeve.

At that point, Meg walked down the aisle with the bucket as she and Dianne began to chant, "The water with which we wash these bowls," and Craig joined in, "tastes like ambrosia. We offer it to the various spirits to satisfy them. *Om makurasai. Svaha.*"

Craig emptied the wash water from his small bowl into the bucket with his right hand while covering the action with his left, saving a little for a customary final sip. Meg bowed with him, walked out, quickly watered a plant, and placed the bucket next to the kettle back on the serving table for Craig to deal with.

Craig chanted, "May we exist in muddy water with purity like the lotus. Thus we bow to Buddha." He dried his bowls, placed them together in the center of the wrapping cloth, tied it correctly, placed his oryoki in its place by the wall, fluffed his zafu, and stood up.

Dianne and Meg hid and waited for Craig to clean and return the serving bowls to the kitchen, climb out the window and down the ladder, return it and go back to the zendo to sleep. They then got the ladder and entered the kitchen to make their snack. In the process of doing so, Dianne dropped a gallon jar of honey. It broke and she got honey all over her robes and the floor. She was cleaning up long into the cold winter night.

A few days later, Dianne told me what had happened that night. She said she and Meg did not mention the clandestine meal with a twist to Craig, and he didn't allude to it, either. "Maybe he thought it was a dream," she said. The most difficult part of the whole affair, she added, was having to contain themselves to keep from laughing. I admired them for being able to do that.

One morning, the locks weren't on the doors. An anonymous act of sabotage. Peter brought it up at a group meeting and with trembling voice said he'd learned a lot from this experience. I had a hunch Ed had done it. I asked him. He just looked at me and asked if I missed them. The locks were not replaced.

Kitchen Schedule

Tatsugami said that because the kitchen schedule was so rigorous, students working in the kitchen should get every fourth day off instead of every fifth. Scheduling worked out fine for each person getting a day off every fifth day because there were five people, thus each day one person would have a day off. But they couldn't figure out how to make a schedule with five people getting a day off every fourth day. Since Bill Shurtleff seemed to be a whiz at everything, he agreed to take it on. He got close, but it still wasn't right. Then someone remembered that Jerry Halpern had done graduate work in statistics at Stanford. Jerry worked it out in a jiff—thus achieving minor celebrity status.

The Nudge

We learned Suzuki was coming. He'd be staying for one night. The students were as excited as kids who'd been at camp for the first time and learned their parents were coming to visit.

Tatsugami announced to the officers that in honor of Suzuki's visit, he would give a special lecture. Dead silence. No way was that going to happen. The officers suggested that the students missed their primary teacher and would want to hear his lecture. Tatsugami tried to throw his weight in the matter, but he met a solid wall of resistance and gave up.

Suzuki arrived in the afternoon, offered incense in the zendo, and paid a visit to Tatsugami. They went to the baths together. When the bell for evening service began, both prepared to lead it. One would have thought they'd have worked that out beforehand. But on the third round of the densho bell, when the doshi, the priest to lead service, walks to the zendo, both did so. Suzuki entered the zendo followed by his jisha holding the incense, and then Tatsugami and his jisha also entered.

Suzuki went down the right aisle, the one customarily used. Tatsugami went down the left aisle, speeding up some. They converged at the single step in the middle, brawny Tatsugami and diminutive Suzuki. Lightly nudging Tatsugami over, Suzuki moved to the center and stepped up to stand before the altar. Tatsugami went up, stood to the left, and Suzuki led the service.

Suzuki gave the talk that night in which he praised and thanked Tatsugami for his great effort and training. Suzuki also led service the next morning, and then departed after some meetings. There was never a word spoken in those meetings that hinted at any power struggle, what was Tatsugami's role, and what was Suzuki's.

Sharp Shovel

Bill Laws was somewhat older and had sobering stories of studying Rinzai Zen in Japan. He'd seen novice monks thrown off the deck while in full lotus. He suffered malnutrition from the diet. He said the abbot and his two main disciples had stomach cancer. He talked to the youngest one about the diet and his health, but the monk told him he wouldn't change anything, that he'd found what he was looking for. Not wishing to waste away, Bill moved to a nearby apartment, made his own meals or ate out, and came to the temple for zazen and sanzen, meeting with the teacher.

Once Bill and I were among students planting pine trees. We'd dig a hole with pick and shovel, fill it with rich earth, then put in a sapling with a stake pounded in with the flat blade of the shovel. The small sledges, the right tool for that job, were taken by others. The saplings were about two feet tall, the stakes about three feet with a pointed end.

I was squatting down holding a stake when Bill came down hard on it with the shovel which slid off the stake, the side of the shovel blade smashing onto the top of my head. I fell over, was out for some seconds. When I came to, I was dizzy and a little nauseous. I made a gesture that communicated, just leave me alone. I sat on the ground for a minute, blood dripping down my face. Then I reached up, saying, "I'm OK now."

Bill helped me stand and walked me back to my room sporting my blood-soaked head and once-white T-shirt. I enjoyed people's shock and concern as I trudged on. I was washed off and put straight to bed. Dr. Wenner was called. He said someone should stay with me and not let me go to sleep for a few hours so others could watch for signs of a serious concussion—like vomiting.

Katagiri came to visit. I apologized to him for being so out of it and babbling. Jerry Fuller was sitting with us and said that was nothing unusual. I got to stay in bed for the rest of that day and, doctor's orders, the next. Got some good reading done.

The pine trees didn't do so well. It was decided not to water them so that the strong would survive. They all died.

Friend and Fugitive

At morning tea in the abbot's cabin, Tatsugami was sitting behind his hibachi where he dumped his tobacco ashes. Formality was relaxed. The officers and Katagiri were chatting while Tatsugami read a letter that had come in on the town trip truck the night before. All of a sudden he broke out laughing. Dan asked him what he was laughing at and Tatsugami said, "My best friend who is taking care of my temple while I'm here in America was eating New Year's mochi and choked to death!" Mochi is somewhat sticky and made from gluten rice flour. That's a famous way for old Japanese to die. Tatsugami finally stopped laughing.

It was brought up that there was a guy living in the woods up creek. He'd come in every few days and beg for food from the kitchen. The FBI and sheriff were looking for him because he was a draft dodger who was involved with some anti-war underground group. Tatsugami said we should cooperate with the sheriff's department, that Tassajara couldn't be involved with harboring criminals. No one agreed, but also, no one argued. We just didn't do anything. Eventually, the guy walked out to Big Sur.

Work Leader

It wasn't surprising that Bill Shurtleff was made work leader even though there were a number of us more senior than he. When Bill first arrived to live at Tassajara a year and a half earlier, Dan saw he was good at stonework and grabbed him as a sort of assistant. Bill was thorough and exacting in taking care of Tassajara's physical plant, although his micromanaging style with frequent feedback did cause some tension. I didn't have a problem with him, because I could be exacting too, and usually he was just being more exacting.

I was around a few altercations that were unusually fierce for Tassajara between Bill and students who were not appreciative of his management style. For instance, back when we still had a brief work period during sesshin, Bill and Paul Shippee were struggling together to get a large stone out of a hole. Bill was making what he thought were helpful suggestions when Paul suddenly reeled back and screamed, "Shut up!"

Bill was shocked. "You can't talk like that here, especially during sesshin."

Paul then let loose a string of nasty epithets that were quite inappropriate, yet inspiring in their rapid and well-articulated delivery. Paul was a sweetheart, but did not like to be told what to do.

Another time, at a work meeting when I was in charge, all the students were gathered around in a circle, I was asking people to do this and that and when I got to Paul, he responded with indignant anger. I walked up to him and kissed him right on the lips and a smile slowly came across his face.

I once saw tall, muscular Alan Marlowe explode in Bill's face, loom over him, and threaten to pulverize him with the shovel he was holding if he didn't leave him alone. Dianne came up and rubbed Alan's shoulder going, "Down boy, down boy." Alan could get riled up—especially at an officer and Bill, being work leader, was an officer.

I wheeled a barrow load of dirt one time, with Alan at my side going on about some spat with the officers who'd denied him something, saying he was destined to be the avatar of the age and that he'd out-live them all and be spreading their god-damn ashes one by one up on the Hogback.

Party Time

Tatsugami emphasized that Zen practice should be fun, that there was an element of sport to it. Suzuki didn't like parties though he let us have some now and then. He'd attend for a while and usually leave early. Tatsugami, however, loved parties. Not that there were a lot, only two in that ninety-day practice period. He had alcohol brought in, though there was resistance from the officers. Katagiri didn't object, as sake served to all on special occasions was not unusual in Japanese temples and monasteries. He said it gives teachers a chance to see their students in a different light. Peter made sure the amount ordered was modest.

Tatsugami started off the first party with a toast, "I hate zazen! I hate practice! I love alcohol and dancing! Drink up and enjoy yourselves!"

Tatsugami enjoyed day off picnics. I'd sit near him, trying to understand his Japanese and use my little bit. Once he offered me some coffee, and I said, "No thanks. I've had enough caffeine, and more would make me nervous." He replied, "Oh—you think it's the caffeine that makes you nervous?"

Brain Damage

It seemed to me that Bob, the ino, had gone to extremes to try to get kicked out. He swaggered around making a point of his status in a not very serious way. He ordered beer on the town trip, insisting it was his prerogative as ino. But why? He wasn't a drinker like me, and wouldn't order beer when he and I were in town.

Also, normally Bob wouldn't miss any part of the schedule, but as ino he slept in a few times and missed this and that seemingly just to flout the rules. He did so while being the guardian of the rules. In a communal setting like that, rather slight discrepancies are noticeable—and Bob's were not slight.

Bob went to see Tatsugami and told him that he was failing as ino and should be expelled from the monastery. He pointed out that other doans would be better ino, that he was not following the schedule completely, had beer in his room, and was sleeping with another student. Tatsugami told Bob that he was the ino and that he would fulfill his obligation this term. He added that he'd once had a friend like Bob, and eventually it was concluded that the only hope for his friend was neurosurgery. That was perfect—really got to Bob.

Zen Song

Katagiri was so earnest. He had a strong sense of responsibility, an exemplar yet humble. He was strict with himself in a non-judgmental way so that students felt comfortable around him and encouraged. In practice situations, he maintained good form. If we were on a picnic, he'd loosen up, be more outwardly friendly, joke with people.

He tended to be relaxed alone with me, perhaps because he'd known me longer in various situations. I might be with him walking and when some other students came up, he'd immediately adjust his posture, get more formal. One day off, I saw Katagiri coming across the bridge by the dorm with four students. I thought they looked awfully somber for a four-and-nine day and before I could stop myself, I leaped out in front of them and belted out a little ditty as if I were on stage:

> I hate Zen—even though it is my friend
> Just can't win—it follows me until the end
> Now some say it's wrong, some say it's right
> Some say it's uptight, some out-a-sight
> But I hate Zen—even though it is my friend, that's right
> Even though it is my friend.

With that last line, I danced off behind the side of a cabin and ran to the back. Later, I denied doing that and said they must have hallucinated it.

Seven Days

The time came for the seven-day sesshin at the end of the practice period. It was no surprise that Tatsugami had some changes in mind.

I looked at the schedule and the term "bare bones" came to mind. As usual, it included arising earlier for a 4 a.m. first period of zazen. Bed at ten. An abbreviated morning service. A lecture in the afternoon. Dokusan interviews throughout. Rather than simpler food, which we were used to, Tatsugami said that we needed plenty of the best food to fuel our enormous effort those seven days, so there was more cheese and special tempura meals. He eliminated the hour-and-a-half afternoon work period and the bath time—for men. Women, he said, had more odors, so they got to go to the baths two times that week. It was a strong sesshin and set a precedent.

I found I liked it better without the breaks for work and bathing, that previously I'd looked forward to. They broke the concentration, pulled me out of a zone that came from being still—still with my dharma mates. Excess falling away. Down to our bare bones.

After Mel Weitsman's shuso ceremony. See Notes for names

Last Supper

In mid-April, we had the practice period closing ceremony. A few days later, Tatsugami left for the city. The night before he returned to Japan, the City Center dining room was full of students and guests at a dinner in his honor. Suzuki had invited him to come back to Tassajara to lead the fall practice period, and he'd accepted.

There was already a waiting list of students who wished to attend. Some had no desire to return if Tatsugami were to lead it, but many were eager. Bob, Reb, Suzuki, Katagiri, and I, among others, sat at the table with the guest of honor. There was no alcohol. Lots of laughter.

Tatsugami seemed to have held none of Bob's antics against him, was playful and friendly equally with all of us. The talk turned to what people's positions would be in the fall practice period. People were making serious and silly suggestions for others and themselves. It all took time because of translation. I suggested Reb as ino, and myself as dishwasher, which got a laugh, though I did wish that lowly position still existed.

Bob said he'd like to try being the work leader. Tatsugami looked at him and said something. Pause. Then, Katagiri translated, "He says you won't be coming to the next practice period." That got a laugh, too, one that tapered off quickly.

Shire School

During the interim between practice period and the guest season, Alan Marlowe and I went out on the annual phone line maintenance. Unlike finding and fixing a break, this spring cleaning took days. We were going along the line, clearing branches that imposed on it, reattaching the line to insulators. Sometimes, usually due to a fallen branch, the line would be running along on the ground for a ways, and still be working as long as it wasn't raining. We'd get it back up where it belonged.

Climbing trees, I learned to recognize the vinegar-like smell of ants, and if I did, it meant a tree was infested, and since I'd learned they can attack as a group, I'd quickly scoot down and leave that one alone. Same with bees or wasps. Had to be alert at ground level, too. Once I'd smelled rattlesnake, sort of musky, I remembered that. They aren't aggressive, but you don't want to surprise them. We had to climb sometimes to follow the line and knew not to put a hand where we couldn't see.

Then, there were the heights. I've never loved heights. I got vertigo way up in a tall tree one day and realized I was losing the distinction between gripping and letting go. I slid down that tree in a split second. I'd always wondered why boys who climb tall water tower ladders sometimes fall to their deaths. Then, I knew. The line could be touching branches and leaves here and there without any noticeable interference, so some lofty places we'd just leave as they were.

I did the poison oak places. Some people seem to be born with a bad allergy to it—not me. Steve Brown had to be driven to a hospital one winter morning looking like he'd been stung by a swarm of bees, because the day before he'd handled leafless poison oak vines and roots while digging a ditch. I wasn't very susceptible, but respected poison oak, and would warn folks that they could lose their immunity through contact as it's an allergy. The deer eat it and I heard that the Indians used to eat homeopathic bits in the early spring to build up a tolerance. We'd had students who did that without any bad results. I think it's best not to mess with it, even though I had to. I'd cover myself with liquid soap and go into a patch—sometimes taller than me—to get to the line, and do the work, and then go straight into the creek to wash my body and clothes in cold water. The soap cut the oil, and the cold water didn't open up the pores.

Alan was tall and strong and usually most talkative, but not on this trip. There wasn't enough energy left for that. We worked our butts off from soon after sunrise to soon before sunset. We'd clean up in a creek, lay a tarp down, no tent, cook up some miso soup and brown rice, do zazen, climb into our sleeping bags and fall immediately to sleep, awaken at the first sign of light, sit, eat the left-over rice and miso and get to work. We were full of energy charging through a couple of miles of line in a day. It was rugged, exhausting, and blissful. Then, late on the afternoon of the third day, we arrived at the Horse Bridge where the line crossed the Arroyo Seco River.

We could hear children's voices and followed a path to see where they were coming from. Set back from the trail was a camp with wooden buildings, picnic tables, and children. Getting in closer, there was a friendly face—Tony Johansen, an old Suzuki student. He greeted us warmly with hugs. He told me they had rented the facility for the Shire School's spring outing. The Shire School, located in the Haight-Ashbury, was the ultimate hippie dream school, a free school, founded by Tony and his wife, Toni.

As soon as we put our packs down, we were passed a joint. It was late afternoon. We'd earned it. At Tassajara, for students there was no dope, no booze, no meat or fish. With the Shire School teachers and parents, we lay back and enjoyed the music and then feasted on hamburger, cheese, beer, wine, pot, and a nap around the fire. There was some participation by students in the contraband as well.

The Shire School concept was so outlandish. A school that's free? It seemed so noble. There had been a positive article about it in the *San Francisco Chronicle*. It followed the example of the Free Store in the Haight and free food from the Diggers and Hare Krishna. So they thought, why not have a free school? I asked, how did they cover expenses? From donations, of course. I asked if the donations were enough. No.

The next morning, Alan and I got up late. No time for zazen. Ate bacon and eggs and pancakes, coffee instead of green tea. Bid farewell to our friends and then back to the line.

But something had changed. We weren't light and zippy anymore. We'd lost our buoyancy, felt heavy, lethargic, faded like our batteries were low. We trudged. Every small incline an effort, every tree an ordeal. The joy of hard work in the great outdoors had been extinguished. It was a most convincing lesson in the importance of eating lightly and minimizing indulgences.

During a mid-morning break, Alan reached into his pack and pulled out a small brown glass bottle. He gave us each a dose of homeopathic rescue remedy which he seemed to believe would heal, repair, renew just about any malady. He said it was so effective in reducing pain in the legs in zazen during sesshin that it made him feel like cheating. I hadn't taken it for leg pain before, but was eager to cheat the hangover from our visit with the Shire School. It did seem to help, and we made it to the end of the line late the next day.

Close Calls

People were accusing a student behind his back of slacking off when he kept staying in bed. Then, he got a fever. When his temperature went to 106, Stan drove him post-haste to Monterey Peninsula Hospital ninety minutes away. Upon their return, Stan said Dr. Wenner gave strict instructions for the student to rest for three days before returning to the schedule.

Wenner said we needed to have somebody at Tassajara with medical training and some authority. We shouldn't wait that long to act. He urged us to rest more, especially when a flu set in, saying that continuing to work prolongs it. And he told us to keep resting till it had been gone for three days. I couldn't do that. I'd be up the first day I felt good.

We shared a lot of contagious illness, I guess, because we all lived and ate together. Some people got more than their share. I'd get less. Wenner said he was using the word "flu" in the colloquial sense to mean flu-like symptoms. He said the cause might often be any number of common viruses that are similar to the flu virus.

Another time, Dianne hadn't been feeling good for over a week. She had an ache in her abdomen that got worse and worse. She was working with me in the dining room and finally I had to tell her to stay in bed. Suzuki was giving talks and she got too sick to go into the zendo, so she sat on a chair outside. At the next talk, she was in too much pain to even do that and returned to her room. She'd been partially fasting and now had been on water only for days. Suzuki was concerned. I was concerned. Some people urged her to go see Dr. Wenner, and others told her to stay away from Western medicine, take some herbs, keep fasting, and she would heal. However, there was enough trust of Bill Wenner to tip the scales. He was called and he insisted she be brought to the hospital immediately.

She went straight into surgery, with Wenner as the surgeon. He discovered an abscess on her right fallopian tube and intestine. It was the size of a cantaloupe, and it broke during the operation. She was in the hospital for five days and then recuperated at Wenner's for a week—all free of charge.

I visited with her at the Wenner's on a day off. Dianne said Suzuki had come to the hospital and that she'd been out of it from the combination of the prior fasting and morphine.

"When he came into the room, I was there but not there. I was on a cliff and there were large birds flying around me and I was feeling them fly and then I saw Suzuki Roshi at the door and he walked in and said hello and I came back from the cliff to see him. He sort of played with me for ten minutes. Offered me a dime to see my scar. The dime's on the bedside table here. Okusan said they should go, and he said to come back soon to Tassajara."

Bill Wenner told me that Dianne would have died if we'd waited any longer to bring her in. He said we were a young community that was very inspiring, but we had a lot to learn besides Zen.

The Staircase

The last round of the han sounding, Shunryu Suzuki in his soft brown robes was on his way to the zendo to give the evening talk. Behind him in black robes followed Mel Weitsman holding a stick of incense, forehead high, between index fingers and thumbs. Alan Marlowe, over six feet tall, followed with a time-worn incense pot.

Suzuki was less than five feet tall. The two members of his retinue each added another eight inches, so the three of them looked like a human staircase moving along.

The Staircase—by Mel Weitsman

Outdoor Coleman lamps were lit in the twilight, mosquitoes and bats swirled in the air. Suzuki entered the zendo where most students were already settled in their seats. A few guests lingering over the red tablecloths in the dining room were told by a server eager to get to the lecture that the last person to leave should blow out the kerosene lamp. Stan stood outside the side screen door to the zendo so he could still answer the phone or take care of late arriving guests—and smoke his hand-rolled cigarettes one after another.

Suzuki took the incense from Mel and placed it straight down in the center of the ashes sitting in a small earthen pot before the

Buddha statue. He opened his *zagu,* bowing cloth, onto the tatami, and bowed down on it three times while a deep, wide, bronze bowl bell tolled. He stepped over to his seat, pulled his robes up some, sat on his brown zafu, brushed the soles of his feet clean with his hands, crossed his legs, arranged his robes in his lap, rocked back and forth sideways a few times, coughed, cleared his throat, and settled in for the lecture. Students whose seats were further back, moved up front, placing their zabutons and zafus on the shiny time-darkened magenta linoleum aisles. Suzuki placed his hands together.

We began a brief chant at the ring of a small bronze bowl.

Mujo jinjin mimyo no ho wa
Hyakusenman go ni mo ai gatashi
Waga ima kenmon shi juji suru koto o etari
Negawaku wa nyorai no shinjitsu gi o geshitatematsuran

There were times we'd use the English as well:

An unsurpassed penetrating and perfect dharma
Is rarely met with even in a hundred thousand million kalpas
Having it to see and listen to, to remember and accept
I vow to taste the truth of the Tathagata's words

The Blackboard

Then there was silence, except for the evening orchestra of crickets and the rustle of the last of the dining room crew, guest cooks, and dish washers entering, bowing, and sitting as close in as they could get.

Suzuki had recently completed a series of lectures on the *Sandokai,* an ancient poem we chanted on the unity of one and many, to me as Zen as it could get. As usual, he coughed when he gave a lecture, sometimes a lot.

This night was the first of six lectures he would give on the *eko*, brief chants recited by a lone person after each group chant in service. The purpose was offering the merit accrued from chanting that sutra to a whole slew of beings—living, departed, and symbolic. The recitations were in classical Buddhist Japanese. The eko were far from the chop wood carry water Zen most of us were there to practice. I was studying these chants with Suzuki at the time, so I was surely more motivated than most to pay attention and not just soak up the vibes. As usual, he took the subject far from any literal understanding.

The first eko, after the Heart Sutra, was for Shakyamuni Buddha, who Suzuki said could be the historical Buddha, or the dharma body, or our own original nature. Also mentioned were Bodhidharma, the first Chinese ancestor; Dogen who founded Soto Zen in Japan; and Manjushri, a mythical bodhisattva representing wisdom.

"We are supposed to resume the true nature of Manjushri," he said. "That is why we have Manjushri in our zendo."

We didn't literally have Manjushri, or a statue of Manjushri, in our zendo, as is traditional. The room also served as a Buddha Hall for services and a dharma hall for lectures, so it wasn't just a zendo for zazen. A small seated Buddha statue sat on the altar. That seemed fine. Buddha and Manjushri were good friends.

Possibly picking up on our lack of enthusiasm for the subject, Suzuki said that someday we would have many good teachers at Tassajara and an American Buddhism, but not if it's just something we do for the sake of convenience. "It should be connected with some spiritual relationship. Without this kind of effort, you cannot establish American Buddhism in its true sense. So if you think about this, you have to understand Japanese Buddhism, Chinese Buddhism, and Indian Buddhism too as a Buddhist. So it is not so easy. We should be concentrated on this point from now on."

These lectures on the eko—reciting and studying them—seemed to be one way we were reaching out to better understand the culture and practice of our ancestors, especially of Soto Zen in Japan. I felt as if Suzuki was giving in somewhat to a new direction

Tassajara practice had taken. None of these lectures on the eko, or the prior series that summer on the Sandokai, would have happened if Tatsugami hadn't introduced these chants and other new elements into the services.

I remembered nostalgically what we'd done before Tatsugami and at Sokoji. Then, we chanted only the *Prajna Paramita Hridaya Sutra,* the Heart Sutra, the national anthem of emptiness, in Sino-Japanese three times at morning service. I missed the simplicity and elegance of the way it had been when I first practiced at Sokoji. And the dynamism. The daily experience of chanting the Heart Sutra three times in a row in the morning had been powerful. The introductory title of the sutra only came the first time it was recited—"*Maka Hannya Haramita Shingyo*" intoned with its extended final syllable extended dramatically.

Then, we all started chanting together, "*Kan ji zai bo satsu gyo jin han-nya ha ra mi ta ji sho ken go on kai ku do is-sai ku yaku sha ri shi shiki fu i ku ku fu i shiki shiki soku ze ku* … " The tempo, accentuated by the mokugyo, gradually increased as we chanted, and there was no pause as we pounced into the next round. We were solidly together and energized in a way I had never experienced—charging ahead as one toward the finale. It was like a train taking off into the wisdom that has gone beyond. And I love trains.

Before Tatsugami, we'd only had one eko, the brief Universal Eko recited by the officiating priest. It was translated by Suzuki on the old chant card thus:

> What I pray is that this merit pervade universally and we Buddhists and all sentient beings achieve Buddhism.

I greatly enjoyed studying the new chants. I copied the Japanese for the Sandokai and the ekos from the Soto Zen chant book that Katagiri had loaned me.

Meeting with Suzuki in his cabin, he took out a thick, western-type bound book and showed me the Sandokai in Chinese. It had the same kanji without all the verb endings, particles, and grammatical connectors that the Japanese has. We chanted it the Japanese way. But it was good to study it in the Chinese, because of the simplicity and the English type word order of subject, verb, object. Japanese has subject, object, verb.

When Suzuki told me he was going to lecture on the Sandokai, he asked me to sit next to him and draw the characters on a blackboard. What?! No way. He tried to convince me to do that, but I absolutely refused to sit up there with him. I'd have felt so out of place and it wasn't necessary. I said I'd prepare the blackboard with the kanji for the lines he was going to speak on. He could use his nyoi or a longer stick to identify one. He agreed.

I was still running the dining room, so I'd get the blackboard ready during the afternoon break. My handwriting was terrible and my chalkmanship with the kanji was worse. I was embarrassed at how awful it looked. I'd bring it to him for his approval—not how elegant it was, but did I get the strokes right.

People commonly said that they felt uniquely accepted by Suzuki. That he didn't grimace when he'd look at what I prepared, seemed to me to be acceptance beyond the call of duty. I'd take the blackboard right away to the zendo and put it in the back corner of the altar platform, ready for public viewing that evening. Then I'd get to the dining room where Dianne, who worked there with me that summer, would gently berate me for being late.

Jack Weller was teaching at the CIIS, the California Institute of Integral Studies, which grew out of the old American Academy of Asian Studies. He brought a class to Tassajara during the time that Suzuki was speaking on the Sandokai. Suzuki let them film the talk he gave that evening. I learned from Jack afterwards that their film would have no sound. At first, I thought that was too bad, but then realized we'd recorded that talk so there would be a way to join the sound to the film.

The Sandokai was written by a Chinese monk called Sekito Kisen in Japanese. Suzuki said that Sekito's union of one and many, of opposites, of the relative and absolute, was also about bringing together northern and southern Zen. And by lecturing on this poem that Tatsugami had introduced into our morning service, I sensed that Suzuki was also placing his and Tatsugami's seemingly contradictory ways of Zen-mastering under an umbrella of harmony.

Priest and Lay

Mel mentioned to Suzuki that there hadn't been a lay ordination since 1962, and he felt that something was needed, that it would pull things together in some way. There had been a number of priest ordinations. What about lay ordinations? A couple of days later Suzuki said to Mel, "We're going to have a lay ordination."

To be shuso and now jisha at Tassajara, Mel had taken a leave of absence from the Berkeley Zendo which he'd been in charge of since 1967. In the fall of '69, in a ceremony at the Berkeley Zendo, Mel had been ordained by Suzuki as a priest. He was considered a senior not only Zen-wise but in age, too, as he was forty-three that year. He'd been a Bohemian artist who hung out in North Beach. He'd played the recorder with his pal, musician Terry Riley, on the famed experimental piece *In C*.

When Suzuki ordained Mel, he said even though he was ordaining him before Bill Kwong, he should consider Bill to be senior to him. In early January 1970, Suzuki ordained Bill and Silas at the new City Center. In May, Peter Schneider and Dan Welch were ordained, and in August, Paul Discoe and Reb Anderson would be next. So now there would be a lay ordination. Suzuki was coming up with Zen names for each of the thirty-six ordainees, those of us who'd been around for at least three years. The ordination was planned for August.

Jisha and Anja

Suzuki told Mel that in Japan the jisha is close to the abbot. He's the eyes and ears of the abbot for the monastery. The jisha tells him what's going on. He takes names for people to see the abbot. He's an intermediary and secretary as well.

Suzuki said, "When I walk around Tassajara, I don't see anything and I don't hear anything." Mel kept Suzuki abreast of what he felt was appropriate but, "I never told him about people sleeping around or anything like that." Suzuki was fine with not hearing about that stuff too.

It wasn't a big problem anyway. The life there was rewarding and demanding enough without a surplus of entangling extracurricular activities. For balance, some of us had excess energy, and a modicum of entanglements. That usually didn't cause much of a stir, as Suzuki's low-key approach didn't let people's tendencies toward Puritanism take hold. All considered, I'd say it was a wholesome mix.

Alan was Suzuki's *anja*, cabin cleaner, and second assistant for miscellaneous duties such as making tea for Suzuki, his guests, and for meetings. The anja cleaned the abbot's cabin while the abbot was out. Thus, they missed a lot of zazen, which was considered a sacrifice as well as an honor. That was the anja's practice. The anja was around the abbot a good deal, and Alan spent more time with him than others because of his many talents and assertiveness. Alan had a creative, theatrical style, and was exacting in tending to Suzuki's cabin, adding flowers and little stones here and there.

He was an enthusiastic hedonist who loved men and women and anything they could do or take together. But that was all on hold while he was at Tassajara. There, he channeled his overflowing enthusiasm into his practice and amassed an enormous private library of spiritual and occult books, almost all of which were well outside of the approach we were involved with. This was, he said, thanks to the generous support of his wife Diane di Prima.

One day, both Mel and Alan joined Suzuki at the baths. Suzuki obliquely brought up Alan's love life and quipped, "It's alright to have as many girlfriends as you want, as long as you remember all their names."

Chogyam Trungpa JUNE 13

A Tibetan Buddhist teacher, a rinpoche named Chogyam Trungpa, came to Tassajara. He was accompanied by his young Scottish wife, Diana, Sam and Hazel Bercholz, and a few of his students. They arrived late and were put up in the Pine and Stone Rooms. I'd met Sam before several times at his little Buddhist bookstore in Berkeley called Shambhala. He'd heard Suzuki speak at Sokoji and liked him alright, but wasn't compelled to stay. Sam didn't like the social vibe at Sokoji, especially that of one person in particular whose name he diplomatically didn't disclose. When he met Chogyam Trungpa, that was it. They had *en,* or more politely, *goen,* as the Japanese would say—good chemistry.

Dianne and I served them a special late dinner that the kitchen whipped up from leftovers. At the end of the meal, Suzuki and Mel, Suzuki's jisha, joined them in the dining room. I was busy going back and forth with trays of dishes and beverages. Dianne did the actual serving.

Suzuki and Trungpa smiled and spoke a few words. The room was pretty dark, lit only by a few kerosene lamps. Dianne experienced light beginning to fill the room. She saw Suzuki and Trungpa looking at each other with sparkles in their eyes. I didn't catch all that, but I did pick up that they were having a most comfortable time. And Dianne was smiling broadly. After dinner, Trungpa went into the kitchen and thanked Rick Levine who had made their special meal.

Before he returned to his room, Suzuki asked Trungpa to give a talk in the zendo the next evening and Trungpa accepted. He and his entourage went to zazen that evening. Trungpa sat in a chair in the zendo. Roovane was carrying the stick and told Trungpa to turn around and face the wall like everyone else. Trungpa obliged.

After zazen, Alan Marlowe, who was more eclectic in his spiritual experience and interests than anyone else, went to the Pine Room and asked Trungpa questions about Tibetan Buddhism. Alan had a bad hangover the next morning from that visit and told me that Trungpa would alternate between pouring him another drink and poking and hitting him with his cane in response to his questions.

Stan was in charge of guests. The night of Trungpa's talk, Suzuki asked Stan to come to his room. When Stan did so, Suzuki handed him a box of powdered incense to give to Trungpa and Diana. Diana answered the door and invited Stan in. Trungpa was in back, so Stan presented the incense to Diana, bowing his head respectfully. Diana did the same and they bumped heads which caused Stan to drop the box spilling the powdered incense on the floor. Trungpa came up and saw the two of them on the floor getting the incense back in the box. Stan looked up and said, "This powdered incense is a gift from Suzuki Roshi."

Trungpa said, "Would you like to have a drink?" They drank and smoked till it was time for Trungpa to give his talk. Trungpa was lame from an automobile accident in Scotland where he first taught. He walked into the zendo using a cane and wearing corrective shoes. He gave his talk while sitting in a chair. It was well-received by the students. Stan found it "crystal clear."

Roovane thought Trungpa's talk was "most lucid" and wanted to meet him. He knocked on the door and Trungpa answered and invited him in. First, Roovane apologized for asking Trungpa to turn around in the zendo, saying he didn't realize who he was. Trungpa said he was happy to sit facing the wall. Trungpa offered him a drink. Roovane said a glass of water would be good.

Trungpa's entourage came in from the baths. Roovane went to the kitchen and made a late night meal for the whole crowd in the Pine Room. He knew Tibetan Buddhists ate meat. There was chicken in the freezer, so Roovane requisitioned some of it. He went to the garden in the dark and picked vegetables for a salad, plus some gruel bread made from leftovers mixed with the batter. Trungpa called it "cosmic bread." Stan stayed till the han was hit for 5 a.m. zazen. Later, he reported to Suzuki about delivering the powdered incense. Suzuki said, "He's a Buddhist."

Before leaving, Trungpa gave some interviews to students. Roovane asked Trungpa about desire. Trungpa said that it's like the soles on our shoes, the only way to wear them out is to walk on them. Trungpa told Roovane he was going to start a center in Colorado and asked Roovane to come join him, but Roovane liked Suzuki's way and felt comfortable staying put. A few other students who met with Trungpa, or who had just heard him, were interested in following him at some point. He made a mark like no other visiting teacher.

All in all, there were mixed impressions. Not everyone was enamored with his drinking and smoking and especially with him throwing his empty Johnny Walker Red Label bottles in the creek from their back porch. One of Trungpa's students said it was a teaching—that it was a response to how uptight we were in our "tidy little Zen world." Fortunately, Alan Marlowe was there. He fastidiously gathered every piece of broken glass from the creek that he could find.

Front Desk

There was a desk and chair in the City Center front hall that weren't used for anything in particular during the day. After 5:30 p.m. zazen, a student would sit there to answer the door during service and dinner and stay until 9 p.m. During work hours, if there was someone at the door, a person in the office would answer it.

Bob hadn't yet gotten a job since returning from the spring practice period at Tassajara. He hung out at the desk some and chatted with people who were coming and going and, if the bell rang or there was a knock at the door, he'd answer it. Suzuki suggested they find something for him to do so that he wasn't just hanging out. There wasn't anything available that seemed right. So he was given the job of doing what he'd been doing—sitting at that desk, answering the door, and meeting delivery people, guests, anyone who didn't have a key.

I was in from Tassajara and spent my spare time chatting with Bob, who was on duty as the official greeter. I enjoyed watching him relate to those who came, marveling at his ability to make someone feel welcome, and cringing at the way he'd toy with people's assumptions and identity.

The doorbell rang. I answered it as he'd appointed me his temporary assistant. A tall fellow with a backpack and beard was there. He started to say something, but I interrupted him with, "Wait—you must speak first with the official greeter," and nodded toward Bob sitting in a chair behind the dark wood table.

"How can I help you?" Bob said matter-of-factly.

The young man stood erect with his heavy backpack still on. He spoke with serious precision and resolve. "I left MIT shortly before finishing work on a PhD in astrophysics. I have hitchhiked from Big Sur where I've been camping for three months in the wilderness, living off the land, contemplating the course my life should take. Now, I have arrived at this temple to end my wandering and devote myself to the study and practice of Zen Buddhism and to attain enlightenment."

Bob looked at him blankly. He tilted his head. "Oh yeah?" he uttered. An empty pause. Then Bob's mouth slowly opened, top lip going one way, bottom one other, his head jerked back, tongue protruded, slobber dripped out. He started moaning and shaking, gurgling, grunting, head wobbling. His eyes rolled. His arms began making spastic motions. He fell to one side, the chair overturned. He lay on the floor vibrating violently, wild eyes open, writhing, flopping about.

I took the arm of the poor, perplexed guy, saying, "Come with me," and walked him down the hall. Loring was just coming up the stairs from the basement. I asked him with a tone of subtle urgency to please take our visitor to the courtyard and speak with him. Loring was a generous, kind, and sympathetic listener with no dramatic flair. I went back to find Bob sitting at his desk looking at the morning paper as if nothing had happened. I took the section with the funnies and bridge column and sat in a chair next to him. Never saw that guy again.

Bob was away from the desk. I answered the door. A plain-clothes policeman introduced himself. I invited him in. He asked if he could speak to someone in charge. I said I could talk with him. He said he was investigating a death that had happened a block away. A man was found dead in his car and the officer wondered if I'd look at a couple of photos and see if I recognized him. He warned me that the photos were disturbing. He showed them to me. They were of a man sitting in the driver's seat of a car with a rifle barrel in his mouth, blood coming out of it. From the front view, I could see the car was packed with camping and other gear. I told the officer I did know who he was but not his name. He'd been coming to the City Center for a few days asking if he could stay until he got his head together. He'd been told that he had to stay somewhere else and come for zazen and so forth from the outside and establish a relationship first. He kept coming back asking for help. I'd talked to him the day before. He wasn't mentally stable, confused. I wished I could do something for him, but like the people in the office, I didn't know what to do or where to send him. I felt terrible. He'd given up.

When Bob returned, I told him what happened. He said the guy had been there one last time and that someone had yelled at him to go away and not come back.

The Sewing Nun

Eshun Yoshida was a Soto Zen nun who came to Zen Center as a guest of Dainin Katagiri. She was abbot of a temple in Japan. Katagiri told us to call her Yoshida Roshi. She was moved by the sincerity of the practice of the students at the City Center and Tassajara. She was surprised, though, to find out almost no one was lay ordained.

She didn't understand something that Suzuki and Katagiri had learned in their years in America. In Japan, the Buddhist sects had an established role and people were dependable, predictable. One could go to a temple and be ordained almost on the spot. For Americans, Buddhism and Zen were new and no matter how committed people said they were, at first, they felt free to change their minds at any time. Many passed through Zen Center like it was a school. Indeed, that was one of its functions. Suzuki had been disappointed that some who received lay ordination from him in 1962 had moved on. It had been eight years since then.

Yoshida and Dainin Katagiri had both practiced with the revered Eko Hashimoto. His lineage had a tradition of sewing their own robes of ordination, the large rectangular *kesa* and the *rakusu*, which is a sort of miniature kesa worn like a bib with straps around the neck. The origins of the rakusu go back to China. Kesa and rakusu were constructed by sewing together many small pieces, making a patchwork of rectangles. Yoshida said that Hashimoto's method of making the kesa is the closest to the robes sewn by Buddha and his disciples from discarded scraps of cloth.

Yoshida asked Suzuki why no one was wearing a rakusu. He told her there was a lay ordination planned for late August. She offered to teach students at the Zen Center how to sew these garments. The rakusu for the ordination had not yet been ordered. Suzuki agreed. We'd make our own. There was little time to choose material and teach people how to sew their rakusu. Suzuki suggested they use sewing machines, but Yoshida said they had to be done by hand. "OK. Let's do it," Suzuki said.

Tomoe and Dainin Katagiri had both done this sort of sewing in Japan, but they needed a refresher. Tomoe assisted Yoshida in guiding students to be ordained, and then others who would help them. Kesa and rakusu would be sewn for those to be ordained and those who'd already been ordained as priests. In the city, the Buddha Hall and dining room soon became busy centers of sewing activity.

Tomoe came to Tassajara to teach us how to sew these vestments. I still had to run the dining room, but sewing my rakusu gobbled up my free time till the task was done. The rakusu were first outlined on a length of dark blue cotton. An old measurement system was used.

Rather than centimeters or inches, we were measuring in *bu*. Then, the pieces were cut. It was a highly intricate process involving various distinct parts and folds. Tomoe had dozens of pages of notes. The parts were sewn together with exacting stitches that were close together. With each stitch, we were to recite, "*Namu Amida Butsu*," homage to Amida Buddha. I knew that came from Yoshida because I'd sewn briefly with Yoshida in the city. I wasn't acquainted with Amida Buddha and thought of that mythical character as being central to Pure Land Buddhism, not Zen—more a faith thing. But I had nothing against him, so I dutifully chanted Namu Amida Butsu *sotto voce* with every stitch. I'd get into it and forget about the sewing and Tomoe would take a look and say the line of stitches wasn't straight enough or a piece had been sewn in crooked and had to be redone. It was not my favorite thing to do but it was my duty—and sweet Tomoe took pity on me and helped considerably.

At Zen Center, we called a kesa "*okesa*" with the honorific O in front, and thought of them as only being for priests. Yoshida said that Dogen wanted lay people, all who practiced zazen, to wear them too. But she emphasized not just any kesa, but what she called the *nyoho-e*, which I thought of as meaning the suchness dharma robe. During her time at Zen Center she made a special nyoho-e for Suzuki which he would wear at our lay ordination.

We who were lay ordained by Suzuki in the City Center Buddha Hall, and donned our new rakusu, were—in a sense—each blessed by Yoshida through the exacting folds, precise cuts, mindful stitches, and the echoes of countless Namu Amida Buddhas.

Good Summer

Suzuki brought a statue of Prince Shotoku who imported Buddhism to Japan in 522, bringing many Buddhist texts from Korea. The statue stood in his cabin on the altar. On four-and-nine days it was brought to a student cabin. Suzuki would visit and they'd drink tea.

Mitsu invited us to attend her tea ceremony performed in a lovely kimono. Millie Johnstone came from New York that summer, and did tea ceremony, too, wearing a long, flowing, pleated beige skirt. There was a Japanized cabin with shoji doors and tatami on the floor where they stayed and conducted tea ceremony for students and sometimes guests. I wondered what would happen if both of them were there at the same time, but it didn't happen. Suzuki attended Millie's tea ceremony at Tassajara once, but then kept being too busy to be her tea guest again. I did it once with Mitsu.

Nancy Sheldon's brother visited her. He was a student at Philip Kapleau's Rochester Zen Center. Kapleau had received permission to teach from Hakuun Yasutani, and Kapleau's students worked on koans with him. They had a reputation for having a fierce approach to practice. I learned Nancy's brother had recently been playing bass for the Fugs, an outrageous and most wonderful band of barely musicians. I told him I'd seen the Fugs in the panhandle of Golden Gate Park and loved them, especially their song "Kill for Peace," and their expression of the *via negativa,* which went "Monday nothing. Tuesday nothing," through the week and elaborated from there, not departing from the constant nothings. Poet Ed Sanders was their founding leader. Nancy's brother was not impressed with them and their wicked ways. He was a serious Zen student.

Jim Murphy roomed with Tommy Dorsey that summer. Tommy told Jim that Okusan, as Mitsu was called, had noticed a teacup on the windowsill as being Suzuki's cup. She was miffed till Tommy showed her that Jim had mended the broken cup. The next day, she came by to tell Jim with enthusiasm that her husband said that mending the cup was very good practice.

Using Coulter Pine from the mountain, milled at the Cummings Brothers Mill in Carmel Valley, Paul Discoe and crew were building cabins on the flat of the hillside above the Stone and Pine Rooms. In the blazing sun, Paul built a fire under a 55-gallon drum to treat the flat roofs with hot tar.

It was a good summer. The upper and lower gardens were flourishing. Amidst the flowers and bees, one could find in those beds sweet potatoes, tomatoes, eggplant, beans, peppers, gobo, daikon, lettuce, cucumbers, summer and winter squash, pumpkins and turnips.

Spiderman Strikes

One evening, Suzuki finished his lecture and asked if there were any questions. Mel raised his hand and said, "The other day when I was hitting the mokugyo, there was this small spider that crawled across the top. And there was nothing I could do. I went a little bit off to the side, but he went right into it. It was too powerful for him to escape. And the next—"

In the midst of people's laughter, Suzuki cut him off and said, "You didn't kill it," halfway between a statement and a question.

"Something did."

"By mistake."

"Yeah, but I couldn't stop."

"But you hit some other place."

"Yes, but he still went right into it."

"Yeah. You know, it can't be helped. Buddha killed him. He may be very happy. Yeah, you know, to live in this world is not so easy."

Suzuki riffed on watching children playing by bridges and things they could fall from, all the cars on the freeway going so fast, and how easy it was to be frightened and worried about death. But, he said, we can't survive with just feelings like that. We have to go deeper. And we can't survive without killing. You have to do that sometimes. And then, after having taken Mel off the hook, he said, "And if it is absolutely necessary, you know, you should stop hitting the mokugyo, even though all of us get confused."

Cabin Move

Paul Discoe built a tripod out of thick pipe fitted with block and tackle and chains. He attached a winch with a long cable to the power wagon. It could do some heavy pulling. Before they buried it in the road, the road crew let Paul cut off the top of an old abandoned car up by the bathtub switchback. The severed top was turned upside down to make a sled that could ride over rough creek or mountainside terrain with heavy cargo—such as stones.

Using those tools and their bare hands, Suzuki, Mel, and Alan repaired and made new stone walls in the small creek near Suzuki's cabin. They would work for hours on a rock to get it in place and Suzuki would say, no, that's not quite right, so he'd take it up again with the tripod and no matter how much they worked on something they might still have to do it over again. Mel said Suzuki never left anything that he felt wasn't right. He noticed how Suzuki would move a rock with his whole body, and could move such large ones even though, as Mel said, "he was such a thin little guy." There was nothing Mel and Alan did that Suzuki didn't do as well.

There wasn't any excess of conversation. When they talked, it was about what they were doing. They were always focused on it. It was hot and Mel would take a wet washcloth and put it over Suzuki's head. And then, sometimes, Suzuki would take a nap in the afternoon in the cool of the dormitory.

Paul and crew were preparing to move Suzuki's cabin by the creek to make way for a new, larger abbot's cabin. The small one-room plus half-bath redwood cabin was sitting on cement blocks at the corners. The water pipe had been disconnected. There was no electric line to disconnect. Beams were placed under it and four jacks raised it. The steps were removed. A makeshift wagon was rolled under it. The winch on the power wagon was ready to pull it fifty feet to its new location. The power wagon started up. The crew stood around waiting. With a jerk, it inched forward. Slowly it made its way. Suddenly, the door opened and Mel and Suzuki peeked out. Naptime over.

Smokey the Artist

Tim Aston said that Stan White had "the gift of gab." Sometimes I'd go bum a cigarette from Stan and, if he wasn't busy, I'd catch some of that gab.

"Back in '68," he started off one time, "Paul Discoe asked me if I could drive a truck and I said, 'Hell, I've driven trucks and jeeps through Korea.' I did the town trips which eventually led to me being in the office and doing the books and Silas liked that cause I'd kept his books carefully. And then Tatsugami Roshi came, and I became *fusu*, the treasurer. I had a title and was in charge of the guests which I really loved because I'm kind of people-oriented. The students, I had a hard time with, because everybody seemed to be bucking for something and I wanted to get rid of my suffering. I had a lot of problems and I wanted to get rid of them, but I was just seeing them better. Besides the pain in my body during zazen I saw the pain in my relationships to people."

Stan did not like to be told what to do by young whippersnappers. That didn't come up much because he'd had his own area—bookkeeping, shopping, or office. When the guest season started, Reb was in the office and Stan, head of the office, asked him to create a schedule for the office staff. Reb included Stan in the schedule and when he told Stan it was his time to work there, Stan said, "No, it's not. You're not in charge of scheduling anymore."

Stan was the heaviest smoker I ever knew. One thing that has puzzled addiction experts is how smokers almost never get urges to smoke when they sleep. But Stan would wake up and smoke a couple of times during the night. He'd smoke three cigarettes before the first morning zazen. He'd smoke during the walking kinhin between sitting periods—every one of them including every kinhin in a week-long sesshin. He went to Suzuki once because he felt bad about how much he was smoking. Suzuki said he could smoke and added, "but please don't do it around me."

Stan made sumi ink drawings with humorous Zen themes. Their settings seemed to be someplace that was a cross of Tassajara and China or Japan, often peopled with funky young or grizzled old monks, some resembling Bodhidharma. I didn't notice any females. Some had captions split into two parts for dramatic effect. One featured a monk with a large belly that read, "Simple vegetarian cuisine—agrees with the monks." Some were touching, such as one with a young monk on a path with staff in hand looking up a steep mountain and words brushed on the left side reading, "Good luck on the journey—and then on the right—ahead." One had a monk sitting with hands out imploring the age-old query, "Who is it—who sits zazen?" The cards and envelopes he put in the outgoing mail would usually have more art than words. I thought about taking photos of them for their artistry and unique penmanship but I didn't have a camera.

Suzuki had to go to the city to do a funeral for a member of the Japanese congregation. When he was ready to return, there was no one available to drive him back to Tassajara. He said he'd take a bus to Monterey. He was told they'd get him a ride, but he said no, don't, that he wanted to take the bus. Stan went into Monterey with the Dodge flatbed to do some shopping for Tassajara. Ed Brown had some personal errands and went with him. They were waiting for Suzuki when he got off the bus in the afternoon. On the way back, they got a load of sand for cement. Suzuki picked up some sand, let it run through his fingers, looked over at Ed and said, "Cook this up for breakfast." That got the three of them laughing.

Stan and I were sitting in the dining room, just the two of us talking and drinking tea. I said, "How dainty you are with your cup."

"That's one thing you never forget from being raised in a rich family," he said. "Suzuki Roshi once said to me, 'You have an awful lot of manners.'"

Stan always paraphrased what Suzuki said, putting it in his own vernacular and sometimes, to my mind adding what he felt was implied.

He once wanted to show his appreciation to Suzuki, so on a town trip he went to the Japanese market in Monterey and bought some expensive green tea. He called it "ocha with the twisted leaves." Suzuki was genuinely appreciative and invited him into his cabin to have some when the bell for service rang, so he said, "Another time."

The other time never came, but Stan remembered how pleased Suzuki was to get that tea. So he bought more and presented it to Suzuki, who received it, said a perfunctory thanks, but didn't invite Stan in. At *chosan*, morning tea with the officers, when the anja was starting to make tea, Stan pushed the tea canister he'd bought over to her to use. Suzuki growled, "No—use the bancha. Monks don't drink that tea." When chosan was over, Stan said, "I walked away looking like Robert Crumb's bent-over guy. I felt so low. But I feel in order to learn from a Zen teacher, it's good if they whack you."

Stan didn't go on hikes with Suzuki or try to be close to him. "I didn't like to be with him in crowds because everybody was always climbing all over him and I would think *give the poor man a little space.* There's a difficulty in being a respected leader with people wanting your presence all the time." Stan thought Suzuki should be left alone to rest more. "He was not a well man. My feeling is that during the war there was so much deprivation that he was malnourished."

Stan had difficulty following a lot of Suzuki's lectures. Then one day Suzuki said, "You probably had a hard time understanding what I said, but some day you will." Stan said, "That's good enough. With Zen practice you begin to understand the process is enjoyable."

Kobun and Harriet

Kobun and a student named Harriet fell in love and wanted Suzuki to marry them. The wedding was planned for July. They came to Tassajara to see him and talk about the details.

Kobun's family name was Otogawa. His father died when Kobun, born in 1938, was eight years old—seven in Western counting. His master, Hozan Koei Chino, adopted him and Kobun became Kobun Chino. His master was not pleased when Kobun went to America and did not approve of Kobun's plan to marry Harriet.

When Kobun and Harriet came to Tassajara to talk to Suzuki about their wedding, there was tension in the air. Mitsu asked me where Harriet was staying and I told her to mind her own business. In Suzuki's cabin, Kobun and Suzuki spoke in Japanese. Harriet was puzzled at Kobun's tone of voice. He turned to her and said that Suzuki had decided not to perform the wedding. Kobun and Harriet came out of Suzuki's cabin distraught. Harriet was sobbing. I talked with them while they got ready to leave and suggested they find a justice of the peace in Monterey or Salinas. I carried Harriet to the car, she was crying so hard. They got married soon thereafter in the Santa Clara courthouse with Haiku Zendo students Les and Mary Kaye as witnesses.

I couldn't understand why Suzuki would honor Kobun's master's wishes over Kobun and Harriet's. Or, maybe he had some other reason. But no matter what his reason was, it was disturbing.

Di Primas

Diane di Prima first came to Sokoji on a visit from New York City in 1964 with her handsome mate, Alan Marlowe. While they were there, Shunryu Suzuki performed their wedding ceremony. Diane's six-year-old daughter from a previous marriage, Jeanne, attended the wedding. They knew no one in San Francisco, but a lot of folks who practiced zazen at Sokoji attended the wedding and chanted the Heart Sutra. For Diane, meeting Suzuki was meeting "some rock-bottom place in myself."

"If Suzuki had been an apple picker or a welder, I would have promptly taken up either of those arts. I sat because he sat, to know his mind. It was the first time in my twenty-eight years that I had encountered another human being and felt trust. It blew my tough, sophisticated, young artist's mind."

She was a prominent Beat poet and, before being with Alan, had been hooked up with well-known writer Leroi Jones, with whom she had her second daughter, Mimi. Diane and Jones had been arrested for obscenity for their literary ventures. Diane and Alan had two kids together and spent over a year living at Millbrook, New York, with Timothy Leary, Richard Alpert, and others who participated in a lifestyle centered around exploring their minds through LSD.

While back on the East Coast, Diane had some communication with Suzuki via Richard Baker. In 1968, she and Alan moved to the Bay Area with their four children, and a few friends, one a male lover of Alan's. Diane covered the cost of the plane tickets by dressing up like a woman of wealth, checking into a fancy hotel, and charging the tickets to her room.

In San Francisco, they got involved with the Diggers, some of whom they moved across the street from in the Haight. The Diggers were anarchists who distributed free food, clothing, books, and whatever in Golden Gate Park, in their free store, and via Diane and Alan's VW bus. They got donations, of course, and were a wonderful extended family of people doing as much giving and good as they could.

There were some who had too much "us and them," and I also didn't like hearing about "ripping off the man," which I'd run into from those I thought didn't have the true Digger spirit. I knew one Digger guy who worked for the post office. He diverted Christmas gifts headed to rich folks' houses, to kids from poor, hippie families. Another bragged his Christmas tree had come from a fat capitalist pig's yard. I knew another who amassed support from collecting welfare using multiple personas. But overall, I admired them and thought all groups and individuals have their dark side.

Diane and Alan went to Tassajara for the interim after the 1968 fall practice period and were there for the New Year's Eve bash. Rick Levine, a new student in from Reed College just for the interim, remembers them rocking out in the dining room at the mochi-pounding party. Diane was a celebrity to him, having just read something she'd recently published in *Evergreen Review*.

Diane's *Memoirs of a Beatnik* was published by a French publisher in 1969. A reviewer wrote that it "blurred the lines between fiction and life, art and pornography, and history and fantasy." In City Lights Books in North Beach, I heard complaints that Don Allen's omission of di Prima's and Joanne Kyger's work from *The New American Poetry* was one of the few weaknesses of that important book. All three of them were involved with the early Zen Center.

Diane came to Tassajara as a student with her children. Many of us were familiar with her as a poet and the writer of the recently distributed *Revolutionary Letters*, published in underground newspapers, but at Tassajara we forgot all that and she blended right in. She wrote a poem while there.

Tassajara, 1969

Even Buddha is lost in this land
the immensity
takes us all with it, pulverizes, & takes us in
Bodhidharma came from the west.
Coyote met him.

Diane and the kids returned to Tassajara in 1970. Jeanne got involved in the student schedule. She often worked in the dining room. She was precocious, smart, energetic, a good worker, tall and worldly wise for her age. She told me she first took LSD at Millbrook at the age of eight, that she was required to take it multiple times, and that she wasn't ready for it and found the experiences confusing and disturbing. People thought she was years older. Diane had dedicated *Memoirs of a Beatnik* to her.

A student named Janet was setting tables for guest dinner with Diane and Jeanne and was surprised at the maturity and openness of their conversation. She said she sure couldn't have had a talk like that with her mother. Diane said to her, "I don't worry about her having sex. I just want it to be with someone who's good at it."

"Jeanne seemed older than twelve," Janet said. "She seemed so sexually ripe. She was luscious."

Back in the city, Diane wrote a poem.

Letter to Jeanne (at Tassajara)

dry heat of the Tassajara canyon
moist warmth of San Francisco summer
bright fog reflecting sunrise as you
step out of September zendo
heart of your warmth, my girl, as you step out
into your vajra pathway, glinting
like your eyes turned sideways at us
your high knowing 13-year-old

wench-smile, flicking your thin
ankles you trot toward Adventure
all sizes & shapes, O may it be various
for you as for me it was, sparkle
like dust motes at dawn in the back
of grey stones, like the shooting stars
over the Hudson, wind in the Berkshire pines
O you have landscapes dramatic like mine
never was, uncounted caves
to mate in, my scorpio, bright love
like fire light up your beauty years
on these new, jagged hills

Jack Novcich

The cabins had all been booked up so far for the guest season, the dining room tables full of hungry guests. The regulars kept coming—John Stace and his Monterey County Roughriders entourage on horseback, the Pages, Wenners, Phillipses, and the beloved old-timer Jack Novcich.

This second guest season was Jack's eightieth year and the fifty-fourth year he'd come to Tassajara. He was a meat and potatoes guy who said the food had gone downhill since the Becks got the place, and then became even worse when we got it, but he liked us and we liked him. He said when he was younger he used to come with the Watsonville Domino Club and drink and hang out with them. But we were the perfect fit for his later years. He'd bring beer for the boys and candy for the girls.

Jack came from Yugoslavia in 1906. He bought a shovel for seventy-five cents and worked for a dollar a day as a laborer building Grand Central Station. After that, he came out to San Francisco, where he said there was still plenty of work due to the devastating 1906 earthquake. For a while he worked at the Tadich Grill, which had been in business since the Gold Rush. Then he moved south to Watsonville. He worked on road crews, where he got the nickname

Dynamite Jack. In 1914, he was handling a metal pole that touched a high-power line. He woke up in the hospital to find he'd lost a good amount of his right leg and left arm. He heard about Tassajara and went there to help his wounds heal. He'd been coming for two weeks a year ever since.

From Jack, we learned that the dining room was built in the prior century and was called the Club House. He said the dorm above was used to house employees such as the Chinese cooks who smoked opium up there. He called the big oak tree at the steps where the road ends, Gossip Oak, and said it used to have one or two hammocks by it. Jack said that the road on the way down from Black Butte Summit was called Tony's Boulevard, after Tony Dourond who was in charge of building that part of the road and ran the resort for Charles Quilty for some years before Jack's time. He said Dourond also built the Tony Trail. He said the road was made public highway before it was a road—when there was just a trail leading into Tassajara.

Jack told us that until recent years, people would come to Tassajara to get their fill of partying and alcohol, or for the healing waters. He said we were the first owners who didn't push the healing aspect at all. "The guests used to come to the hot springs first thing in the morning to drink the hot healing waters. The hot spring water came out from a dozen different places and they each had a different temperature and mineral content. The one on the far downstream side was the favorite of some, especially for drinking, but I preferred what came out of the rocks near the steam room and attribute my long life to it."

We had a male student help Jack at the baths, but other than that he took care of himself. I've been with him when he got dressed. His underwear, then his prosthetic leg below the knee, then pants, then his shirt, the left arm sleeve folded above where the elbow would have been, suspenders pulled over. He kept his clothes in his old leather suitcase, which he said had immigrated to America with him.

At mealtime, he'd walk up to the dining room, select his napkin, stick it under his arm, enter, find a seat, and get his napkin out of the napkin ring. He would politely refuse help from fellow diners. I'd offer to keep his cane because it was a little awkward having it leaning on the table where a passing waiter would sometimes knock it down. He said it was cherry wood and told me not to lose it, that he'd had it since he first came to Tassajara.

After his accident, he opened Jack's Cigar Store. Jack was there every day except when he came to Tassajara. It was a little out of the way to go to San Francisco through Watsonville, unless one wished to take the scenic route through Santa Cruz up Highway One. Some students did visit Jack there and heard more stories about the old days.

Becks Back

Robert and Anna Beck were back with young Katie and younger Adam. They ran into Suzuki on their way to dinner. Suzuki raised his arms to greet the kids and with his long sleeves looked like some sort of Batman to Adam who ran behind his parents and hid—then peeked out. Suzuki crouched down low and said hi and Adam wasn't scared anymore. He was amazed at the metamorphosis of the Batman into a Hobbit.

Robert and I took a walk out to Grasshopper Flats. He said he wasn't looking for a place to build anymore. Now the deal was that they could come and stay as our guests anytime they wanted. They were always busy hustling antiques and art, so there was no danger of them taking too much advantage of that deal. "On the weekends we go to flea markets and yard sales," Robert said. "We buy junk in the mornings and sell antiques in the afternoon."

Sometimes Robert would drive in for the day. Usually, he'd get some of the remaining stuff out of his storage room in the lower barn. I was always impressed with how much he knew and noticed about the place. Once, he admired our new bridge to the baths. We stood in the middle of the bridge, looking down at the creek facing the Hogback. He pointed to a huge boulder. "It used to be further back. Must have been a hell of a creek knocked that one loose," he said. "I never thought it could be moved."

Old Lefties

Dick Wertheimer was a pro bono lawyer for Zen Center for years. He came with his wife Julia and their friends, the Brodskys. Wertheimer took care of Zen Center's incorporation when it was changed in 1968 to a corporation sole—like the Catholic Church. I engaged with them about social and political issues past and present, their lawyerly struggles with the inequities of the system, and always about the Vietnam War, which was highly disturbing to so many of us.

Lou and Blanche Hartman were also old Berkeley lefties. Their turn to eat with the guests came up and I seated them with the Wertheimers and Brodskys. They were all familiar with each other. Beginning in 1950, Lou had been the host of *This Is San Francisco* in the persona of Jim Grady. It was called *The Jim Grady Show* on KCBS radio. He was a celebrity, the "Herb Caen of the airwaves," a man-about-town, on an expense account going to restaurants and shows and reporting about them. In June 1957, he was subpoenaed to testify before the House Committee on Un-American Activities and refused to answer questions about his political beliefs. As a result, he was blacklisted by CBS. It was a traumatizing experience for him and his family.

Wertheimer was especially helpful with student immigration issues, running interference for foreign students so that they could get the right visas to stay at Tassajara. He established that Niels was already a citizen because Niels' father had spent time in America when he was young and had become a citizen. I accompanied Niels to Wertheimer's office once and, while waiting, looked at a past issue of *Life* magazine featuring American Indians. As we were leaving, I asked him if I could keep the magazine and he said, "Of course.

Anyone can have anything of mine that they want. That's the way the world should be, don't you think?"

"Absolutely," I said and turned to Niels. "I'd like his jacket. How about you?"

"I want the nice desk in his office!"

"We'll come back later with a truck," I said.

"Oh you, Zennies," he said, shaking his head.

Child Play

There were a bunch of kids that summer with parents or parent—Eliot and L Walter, Alex and Minnie di Prima (Jeanne was almost thirteen and wasn't considered a kid anymore); Monica with Jed and Maria Linde; Ejyo and Yasuhiko Katagiri with Tomoe; David, Julie, and Suzie Petchey with Pauline; Rhonda and Aaron Johansen with Toni and Tony; Aaron and Sim with Lynne Warkov who'd come to Zen Center a year after Suzuki arrived with her husband Saul. Toni and Lynne took care of a loosely structured childcare program. The kids worked in the garden and kitchen when they weren't involved doing something else. There was a kids' zazen instruction. They were seldom, however, in the zendo, but at the pool a lot, usually being observed by adults.

Rick Levine was walking by the pool and saw a girl lying face down in the water, completely passive, immobile, floating peacefully with arms outstretched, hips and legs sunken, shimmering in the light. He jumped in and dragged her out from about ten feet away from the shallow side of the pool. She wasn't breathing. It was Suzie Petchey. He carried her to poolside, lowered her head and chest, drained the water. Her mother Pauline ran over. Suzie spluttered, started breathing, and recovered pretty quickly.

I made the mistake of doing my duck talk with the kids, because after that they hounded me to do it more. When they asked me to do Donald Duck talk, in duck talk I'd tell them I was not Donald. I was David Duck. I didn't like doing it that much, but they kept asking and it improved with practice, so it got pretty good that summer—much better than Donald Duck. I got to where I could clearly enunciate Ls, Rs, and some other challenging sounds. I finally said David Duck had left Tassajara.

A group of the kids created a play called *The Day Coyote Made Man,* based on an indigenous tale. There was also a water show with mermaids and seals in pantyhose. Mainly, the kids were dispersed and on their own. The only time they were all together was at meals and the ever-popular afternoon tea which Suzuki usually attended if he was at Tassajara. And he was fun.

Lynne Warkov

I enjoyed talking to Lynne Warkov and hearing about what it had been like at Sokoji with Suzuki in those very early years. She said that Suzuki would give his talk to a group of them sitting in a circle in chairs while sipping tea from a teacup. One evening, a guy she'd never seen before had obviously gotten some idea about Zen from reading stories. He snatched Suzuki's teacup from his hand and smashed it on the floor. Suzuki made a small sigh, stood up, and walked into the kitchen. He came back with a dustpan and a broom, swept up the pieces carefully and walked back into the kitchen. They could hear the teacup pieces being put into the trash, the broom and dustpan being put away. He returned to the room, sat down, and continued his talk.

—CHAPTER SIX—

STILL 1970

The Bread Book

Ed Brown had been working in the garden since the 1969 guest season ended. He put up a little birdhouse-size altar there and when he arrived to work, he'd offer a stick of incense and he, and whoever was working with him, would bow in.

There were two garden plots, one up by the shop and the lower garden to the left of the path walking toward the pool. A lot of what they were doing was digging all the stones out. But he hadn't just been working in the garden; Ed was building a book. I knew he'd been working on one, but it was only in the back of my mind until one day a box of them showed up in the office. I picked one up. *The Tassajara Bread Book* by Edward Espe Brown. The Espe was new to me. Frances Thompson did the illustrations. Guests gobbled up the books as fast as they did the bread.

Guests had been asking how to bake bread like that since the first guest season. Ed would invite them to join him while he made it. To be involved with the whole process would mean taking breaks and coming back for the next step, the last one being eating a hot, buttered slice straight out of the oven.

By summer 1968, Ed had collected a bunch of bread recipes with the help of the kitchen staff. He photocopied them and made thirty stapled booklets with a heavy yellow paper cover. He gave one to Richard Baker who suggested he show it to Lawrence Ferlinghetti of City Lights Books, which published as well as sold books. Ferlinghetti told Ed sure—they'd publish it as is. Ed asked Ferlinghetti if he didn't intend to at least typeset it. It was messy with notes written into the margins. Ferlinghetti saw it as perfect for hippie communes and such the way it was. Ed said thank you, but then took it to Sam Bercholz at his little Shambhala Book Store on Telegraph Avenue in Berkeley. That was 1969, the same year Sam founded Shambhala Publications. Sam looked at the book for three minutes and said he'd love to publish it. He generously offered Ed 10 percent of retail sales which meant 10 percent of list price, not what it sold for. An excellent deal for Ed.

Before long we learned that the book was getting rave reviews and doing exceedingly well in the outside world. Meanwhile, Ed continued to dig out the rocks to fit together in a wall and make way for the expanding lower garden.

Me Gu

Meg Gawler went to a talk by Suzuki on a Saturday morning in 1968. She said to herself, *Oh my goodness, this man knows more than all my brilliant Brandeis professors put together. I'm going to study with him.*

Meg went back to the East Coast and gathered her stuff. She dropped out of college and gave up her passion for dance as well, "I felt that zazen, sitting perfectly still, was the ultimate dance." After spending half a year sitting at Sokoji, she was accepted for the practice period which would begin in January. She arrived at Tassajara toward the end of December of 1968 and did the initiatory tangaryo with Roovane "in the freezing cold."

Meg was twenty-one when she came to Zen Center. "I had a traumatic childhood, and a lot of trauma still to work through. The first year, I think I cried every period of zazen. The tears would just be streaming down my face, day after day."

Lou Hartman was hitting the han for zazen. It was the third round with all the students sitting quietly on their zafus in the zendo. As Suzuki approached with his jisha holding the lit stick of incense, Meg came out crying. "Like a sheepdog he guided her back," Lou said. "She'd go to one side and he'd hold his stick out and guide her back and she'd go to the other side and his stick would be over there. He kept going forward and she went back in."

Meg was hard on herself, but kind to others. When Blanche Hartman first came to Tassajara, Meg was her roommate.

"I wasn't sure it was OK for a woman over forty-five to be there," said Blanche. "Only Katherine Thanas, Pat Herreshoff and I were that age. There was a sprinkling of people in their thirties and everybody else was in their twenties. It wasn't clear they wanted someone around who looked like their mother. Meg made me feel welcome and I was totally grateful to her."

Meg was having tea with Suzuki in his garden. She noticed he was in a particularly playful mood. He showed her a small smooth stone he'd found in the creek and pointed out the eye-like design on one side. "Me," he said, "Japanese for eye." He brought out a brush and sumi ink from his cabin and drew a G on the other side of the stone. Then he held it up to her and he went, "May-gu." That's how Meg would be pronounced in Japanese.

"Suzuki Roshi's really big teaching to me," Meg said, "is that he treats me as though I am the Buddha. And he actually perceives each of us as the Buddha. That makes me think to myself, *Oh gosh, if I'm the Buddha, maybe I'd better start acting like the Buddha!*"

Herman Aihara

Loring came up to me and said that Herman Aihara, a leading spokesman for the macrobiotic diet and philosophy, was a guest at Tassajara. Loring hoped he could speak in the dining room to students. I wasn't as into it as Loring, but it would be a break in the routine. I'd met Aihara and jazz musician Gary Peacock at a macrobiotic presentation they gave, that Loring took me to, in San Francisco a few years before.

I was grateful to Loring for having turned me on to better eating habits, but macrobiotics could be a bit culty. There was a couple in the city so into it that they fed their German Shepherd a diet consisting almost entirely of brown rice. That dog had so much energy it would go bounding around in their apartment. The same thing happened to me when I went for two weeks on the macrobiotic #7 diet of nothing but brown rice and sesame salt while working for the post office. At first, I got ravenously hungry, but after a few days I just wanted more brown rice. I was full of energy and strength loading and unloading those trucks. My supervisor might have thought I was on speed.

I went to Suzuki's cabin and said a number of students wanted to hear Aihara speak. He shook his head and said, "In Japan, we'd never do anything like that. We're jealous and don't want other teachers to come and speak at our temple. But this is America and things are different, so ... OK."

Suzuki attended Aihara's talk. Afterwards, he went up to Aihara in the courtyard outside the dining room and greeted him warmly. In parting, Suzuki patted Aihara on the back and said, "Don't worry so much."

A Big Grin

The first time Jane Runk drove Suzuki to Tassajara was in the fall after the first practice period. She started talking about astrology. She didn't really know much, mainly what Bill Lane had told her about it on their bus ride to San Francisco the prior spring, but she expounded for a while. Suzuki looked at her and said, "You look so serious when you talk."

Driving along the ridge, they got out to look at the view. Suzuki came up to Jane's shoulder. As they were getting into the car, he asked her, "Do I remind you of your father?"

"No, not in the least bit."

"Really?"

"No, my father's real tall—he's 6'4."

"Oh, you mean that difference."

Jane found that studying with Suzuki was not like studying anything she'd studied before. She'd listen to his lectures and think she understood everything he was saying, and then when it was over, she couldn't remember a word he had said. Still, she felt she understood more than she could account for. She felt a warmth coming from him and an expansiveness, but didn't see quite what he'd done or she'd done to bring this about. It seemed to her he didn't have any particular teaching, instead, more a method. She didn't know quite how to define it. To her, he had a way, but for everyone it was different.

"All he tries to do is wake us up," she said. "If you're this way, he's that way, and if you're that way, he's this way."

This reminded me of something Huineng said. Suzuki greatly admired Huineng, the celebrated sixth patriarch of Chinese Zen. When Huineng was dying, he gathered his disciples together and gave them advice on how to teach. He said that there were many pairs of opposites and whatever your students came to you with would be one side of a pair. He said just respond to them with the other side. Thus, Huineng and Suzuki would try to bat that dualism away. Suzuki called dualistic thinking a one-sided understanding.

After having finished his talks on Sandokai and the Eko, Suzuki told me that next he wanted to speak on the Sixth Patriarch's Sutra. He gave it the highest praise. I looked forward to studying it with him. "Maybe next summer," he said.

Jane was driving Suzuki and Peter to Tassajara. On the way, they stopped at the Buzz Inn diner in Gilroy. Jane raved about the delights of a banana split. Later, on the winding road into Tassajara she got nauseous, stopped the car, dashed to the side and vomited. She needed a minute to recover and sat on the road feeling miserable. Suzuki came up to her and leaned over with his hand on her shoulder. She was touched that he was making this effort to console her. She looked up and saw a big grin on his face as he said, "Jane, would you like another banana split?" She couldn't help but laugh with everyone else.

A Coupling

Jane was now the ino, in charge of the zendo and ceremonies. The ino was also traditionally in charge of attendance, discipline, rules. The main rule at Tassajara was just to follow the schedule. What else? Don't steal food from the kitchen. As with the others, these rules weren't printed or posted. One just learned them.

Back in 1968, Richard Baker had suggested the six-month rule—don't get intimately involved with someone the first six months they're practicing. That was a long way from Buddha's day when a monk or nun would be permanently expelled from the sangha for sexual intercourse—including with an animal.

For two students to become an official couple at Tassajara, they had to get permission from Suzuki. Then one day in February, Jane was just falling asleep in her room in the dorm when she was awakened by hearing the door to her room open. Someone slowly stuck their head in. It was Peter. "Can I come in?" he said. "Sure," she replied.

From then on, when Peter and Jane weren't in the zendo or doing their duty, they were together in her tiny room. After a couple weeks, Paul Discoe told Peter he shouldn't be living in the women's dorm. So they moved into a nice little cabin by the lower garden. Suzuki must have been consulted, but that's not the sort of thing there were announcements about. They were so low key that this all was hardly noticeable to the rest of us and before long it seemed like they were a couple that had been together a long time.

Two Weddings

"Suzuki Roshi said to us, 'Do you think you should be getting married?' I thought, oh, he must think this is a marriage made in heaven." Carolyn was telling me how she and her husband Rick

Morton came to get married at Tassajara early in the summer of 1970. They'd arrived as a couple back in '67. "I guess he thought it was time," she said. "But I remember him telling other people not to get married."

I told Carolyn that, in the case of her and Rick, I thought he was obviously right. Seemed to me to be a perfect fit. They both were quiet and not subject to drama. Carolyn and Rick's wedding was a low-key event.

Meg Gawler and Ed Brown's courtship was rather short. "It was actually an arranged marriage," she said. "We got married a year-and-a-half after I got here. Ed and I were kind of sweethearts and we thought it might be nice to explore living together. One day, we asked Suzuki Roshi if we could see him together. We said, 'Suzuki Roshi, if it's OK with you, we'd like to live together.' He said, 'Oh, that's wonderful! I'd like to marry you as soon as possible!' We said, 'No, no! You don't understand. We hardly know each other! We're not ready to be married. We just want to live together.' He replied, 'Would June be all right?'"

Ed and Meg's wedding date was set for the summer solstice, June 21. A number of people arrived a day early and stayed in guest cabins, others drove in just for the day. Everyone was in high spirits. The ceremony was simple and elegant. They took Buddhist vows and nuptial vows. Meg's included, "In brightness and in utter blackness I vow ..." It was a joyful occasion. Then Suzuki made some comments.

Ed said, "The wedding was a grand occasion, but there were some unusually candid words in Suzuki's extemporaneous remarks at the end when he said we would have a really difficult time of it. He'd waited until we were married to tell us that."

Blanche Hartman said, "It was a very heavy wedding. I remember Suzuki Roshi saying, 'All of you are going to have to help Ed and Meg.' Okusan was crying. He said, 'It's going to be very difficult for them.'"

Suzuki said, "Both of you are going to suffer a lot." That seemed to me to be something they had in common. It was not unusual in zazen for Ed to be shaking and Meg to be crying.

After the wedding, Lou Hartman told Suzuki it was a wonderful wedding. Suzuki said to Lou, shaking his head, "Too serious."

So to lighten things up, we turned to alcohol. Meg's father arrived with crates of champagne. There was a scrumptious outdoor wedding feast. The kids were popping the tops off the champagne and filling everyone's glasses.

Jim Murphy prepared a big bowl of dark ripe cherries for the group. "My intention was to make the rounds with cherries for all. I walked up to Roshi and offered to him first, expecting him to take a few. His face lit up and he took the whole bowl from me! All I could do was gassho."

A small bandstand was created, and once again, a band named the Non Burnables came together. However, unlike the first New Year's Eve party, the Non Burnables trash can did not serve as the principle drum. Craig was a drummer and set up a little trap set that he kept down in the barn. Lew Richmond, a classical pianist, was on an electronic keyboard he had used with headphones. The two of them were the trained musicians. I joined in clumsily on guitar. Alan Marlowe improvised vocals quite freely. Peter Schneider joined in playing a kazoo. Suzuki wandered over, listened to the jumble of sound and said to Peter, "I didn't know you could do that." Peter told him it was easy and handed him the kazoo. So Suzuki sat on the band platform playing a kazoo—and wearing Bill Lambert's cowboy hat.

Everyone's memory goes blank at that point.

I met Suzuki the next morning at sunrise on his way back from the baths. He wasn't used to drinking. He shook his head and said, "Too much. Too much."

Naughty Jays

One day, as I walked across the courtyard with a tray load of bread baskets covered with a tablecloth, my entrance into the dining room was blocked by an empty basket dangling on a string before my face. I stopped to contemplate this incongruous object, then heard laughter. Looking up, I saw Dianne and Meg's smiling faces peering down from the dorm window. I knew what I was to do. A moment later, I returned with bread and butter for their basket, which they then pulled up to the window. Suddenly, a Blue Jay swooped by the basket, flying off with a slice of whole wheat bread. Luckily, the rest didn't spill. I should have thought of the Jay threat. The next load up was covered with a cloth napkin.

Life was good without the pigeons. I pictured them happy in an area with organic rice fields. But then again, maybe the Koda Brothers and their farming neighbors had ways to keep the pigeons away that didn't impinge on the organic quality of their crops. Maybe by flowing silver banners, like I'd seen in pictures of Japanese rice fields. Or bullets.

We enjoyed our songbird neighbors. So sweet—until the Jays arrived. They were squawk-birds. They came and the songbirds left. The pigeons weren't noisy and didn't run off the songbirds. I wondered if the Jays would have come at all if the pigeons were still there. We called them Blue Jays, but Sterling Bunnell called them Steller's Jays. That's too hard to say, so we kept calling them Blue Jays or just Jays. One characteristic they had in common with pigeons was an eagerness to eat anything they could get their beaks on. They were much more aggressive than the pigeons, though. Aggressive and fearless.

They'd arrive in the spring and leave in the fall. In Blue Jay season, it was risky to eat outdoors anywhere near the center of Tassajara. That's where they tended to congregate, perched on branches around the courtyard waiting for a careless student or guest. I often heard guests complain that their lunch had been vandalized. I've seen Jays swoop down and snatch an apple slice out of someone's hand. Ed had a fit when one hit a sandwich he was eating, got off with some of it, knocking the rest onto the ground. And their squawking was as irritating as their thievery.

A farmer from Greenfield said the thing to do was, when they first show up in the spring, shoot one and the rest will fly off and not return. We couldn't do that, though some of us wanted to. So we learned to live with them, and in some cases, appreciate them. Sterling did, at least. But he acknowledged that the Jays were also predators that ate the eggs and food caches of other, sweeter birds.

Suzuki brought birds into his lectures, but those were birds that went *peep, peep, peep.* Clearly, he felt affectionate toward the peepers and the singers. But like Sterling, he accepted the Jays and said, "The bird cannot disturb the mountain."

Sun Seeds

Amertat Frederick Cohn, a student of Sufi Sam, got permission to bring a film crew to Tassajara. He was making a film to be called *Sunseed* on contemporary gurus who were changing the spiritual map. He'd recently returned from filming in India. His crew got footage of us in the zendo—during zazen and at the beginning of an oryoki meal. They shot Reb carrying the kyosaku and striking a student and they interviewed some students.

A smiling Bill Shurtleff said, "Our practice at Tassajara and Suzuki Roshi's practice is not based on attainment. It's based on living totally in each moment. Some people ask, well, you know if there's nothing to attain, then why are you practicing? What's the purpose of sitting zazen, of getting up at 4:45 in the middle of winter with no heat in the morning? And, like, there's no answer to that question. But here we are, you know [laughs]. And we're doing it."

Radiant Meg Brown said, "I got into Zen without even being aware of it. It was like before I knew it, it had taken my life. I read a book, and then I came to San Francisco, and I started sitting, and that was it. I met Roshi and as soon as I could I came to Tassajara."

Alan Marlowe with customary flare said, "Everything that he does is with concentration. It comes out of zazen, out of sitting. I keep Roshi's house, and when he eats an apple, the core of the apple is about a matchstick thin. He's really eaten that apple."

Suzuki was filmed in the shade of some trees. He pointed to a Jay and said: "If we try to listen to something wonderful [laughs]—it means to ignore the bird which we are listening to now. You know, when you think Buddha said something wonderful, and I must find out what he meant, then your mind is directed to Buddha's words, so you don't hear the birds."

In a lecture that summer, he said, "There is no barrier. There is no disturbance. It is difficult to say, 'That is bird, and this is me,' because they are interrelated very closely. So it is difficult to separate the Blue Jay from me."

When I heard that, I thought I should probably be more accepting of the birds at hand.

A Monk

While Suzuki was talking in the film about not getting distracted by what's happening in the moment, Ron Browning walked up in his robes. I didn't know he'd left Japan till I saw him there. He watched and listened while maintaining a formal stance. Ron was thin, gaunt, and looked so intense. He seemed to be in some sort of an altered state.

I met Ron when I first came to Zen Center. He was from Dallas next door to Fort Worth, where I come from. In 1964, he went from a conservative family in conservative Dallas to radical Berkeley at the time of the Free Speech Movement and the beginnings of the anti-Vietnam War movement. At some point his father learned he'd applied to be a conscientious objector as an alternative to military service and disowned him. In Berkeley, Ron met Ken Spiker, his first hippie, who told Ron about the *I Ching*, LSD, and Zen. Ron read a book about Zen and was amazed reading about experiences of Zen monks. Ken told him about a Zen master in San Francisco. Ron went to Sokoji and met Suzuki. He told Suzuki that he wanted to go to Japan and become a monk. Suzuki said, "Maybe it would be better for you stay and learn our way first."

Ron and his wife Joyce started going to Sokoji early mornings. In time, they moved from Berkeley to San Francisco, a block away from Sokoji. They had jobs and were saving money to go to Japan.

One day during the Saturday morning work period, Ron was cleaning the zendo floor with a damp rag which he pushed around with his foot. Suzuki came over and without saying anything, gently took the rag from Ron, got down on the floor, cleaned it vigorously for a moment, then handed the rag back to Ron. Happily, Ron followed suit, though he couldn't do it the way Suzuki did—squatting without touching his knees to the floor. Ron remembered that in a lecture Suzuki had said to put 100 percent of your awareness into whatever you were doing. He noticed that in activity, though, Suzuki taught almost entirely without explanation, without words. Powerful teaching, he thought.

Ron would, at times, drive Suzuki to Los Altos to give talks to the group that met at Marian Derby's house. Those were special times for him, with a feeling of happiness and contentment of being with Suzuki—of serving him in that way. And learning to be more mindful—not only from him, though. Once, Mitsu came along. When they arrived there, it was warmer, and Ron pulled off his sweater and threw it in back. She said, "The sweater says ouch."

Ron and Joyce got a railroad flat across the street from Sokoji and rented rooms to other Zen students. They shared cooking and cleaning. Ron loved it. It was the beginning of a visible Zen Center community. One by one the neighboring buildings were rented by students, as well—upstairs and downstairs.

Ron and Joyce were at Tassajara for the first practice period. He did roofing and Joyce worked in the garden. For the first time he felt like his practice was going at a deeper level. After the practice period, they returned to the city. Ron was beginning to have doubts about his plan to go to Japan and was thinking that this was a really suitable place for him to practice. "What if I were to just stay here and practice and not go to a monastery in Japan?" he asked Suzuki.

"Good students are more important than monasteries and centers," Suzuki replied. He said more, but that's what Ron remembered and cogitated on. He decided Suzuki meant that he should go to Japan to become a good student. In the summer of 1968, he and Joyce were ordained by Suzuki and were off to Japan.

First, Ron went to Antaiji where zazen was emphasized and ceremonies were few and brief. Unlike most Japanese temples, it had no *danka* membership that it performed funeral and memorial services for. Instead, it was supported by lay people who practiced there and *takuhatsu*, monks begging. While he was at Antaiji, Joyce was in a nunnery.

When Kobun Chino was back in Japan, Ron and Joyce went to stay with him at his family's temple in the small town of Kamo, northwest of Tokyo. Ron picked up that the family was not pleased that Kobun was planning on returning to America.

Ron enjoyed the deep feeling of being in the centuries old temple. But he was also becoming disturbed. He reflected on karma and started to worry about harm he was causing other beings and bad karma he'd acquire as a result. He didn't understand that karma is intentional action and that, even in the most literal interpretation, he would not be held accountable in future lives for every bug he accidentally stepped on.

There wasn't a lot to do in Kobun's father's temple. They cleaned floors and meditated, and Ron's meditation took him well beyond where he'd been before. He called Suzuki up at Sokoji and asked him what to do. Suzuki said that when the way-seeking mind arises, he should go sit with the monks at Eiheiji.

Ron went to Eiheiji. He found the mammoth ancient temple to be amazing and intense. But the monks ate so fast—usually just white rice, miso soup, and pickles as fast as it could be downed.

Kobun had given Ron an English translation of the *Zuimonki*, a collection of Dogen's dharma talks recorded by his dharma heir Koun Ejo. For Ron, it was life-transforming. It was different from Suzuki's talks for American lay people. Now, Ron felt like he wasn't practicing in accordance with the way that Dogen taught. In those lectures given 800 years prior, Dogan was clear and direct about some of the criteria of practicing. Ron wanted to practice that way.

At about the same time, I was reading the *Zuimonki* at Tassajara and found it to be chillingly strict.

Ron made a phone call to Suzuki. It wasn't a calm phone call. From the insufficient diet, already thin Ron had lost a lot of weight—and the weight of the *Zuimonki* was pressing in on him. He had entered into a whole other reality. His call to Suzuki was a cry for help. "What should I do?"

To Ron, the monks weren't practicing enough zazen. He started sitting by himself in the *gaitan,* just outside the monks' hall. This did not please his elders, which was everyone else there.

Ron woke up to find himself riding on a train. He felt groggy, a little dizzy. The last thing he remembered was sitting zazen by himself in the gaitan and—in the corner of his eye—monks approaching. Then he noticed Hoitsu, Suzuki's son, was with him on the train. Hoitsu took him to Rinsoin where he ran off into the mountainous woods above the temple. He was finally found after a search, emaciated, shivering. "Japanese enter the stream with others. Americans think of My Way," Hoitsu said to deaf ears.

Joyce stayed in Japan, but now Ron was back, brought to Tassajara to recuperate. Last I'd seen him, he was serious and determined to get enlightened, healthy and focused. Now he was a wreck, frighteningly thin, bug-eyed. He obviously hadn't supplemented the Japanese monastic diet, as the Japanese monks there did.

He stood before me in robes, hands at the solar plexus in formal *shashu* squeezed in toward his ribs, shaking slightly, talking about rules. Rules? Yes. He said we're not following them. I told him I thought we had plenty of rules. I said I'd heard Paul Discoe explain the rules to a new student. He said the rules are clear: you have to wear a shirt, you can't catch fish from the creek, you can't smoke marijuana, you can't run from one place to another, and you can't walk barefoot outside. Ron ignored that and said we weren't practicing Dogen's way, and we were not following the Vinaya, the rules back in Buddha's time, hundreds of rules, with more for women. Not to eat after the sun is at the zenith, not to touch money or women. Of course, no alcohol. Possessions a monk could have were few, and stipulated. There was a prescribed length for the sleeping mat. He'd seen sake served to monks in Japan—even at Antaiji. He'd seen them eat meat and they got married, and so much more.

Ron seemed to me like someone on an acid trip and not a good one. He could not relate to others in a normal way. Standing by a tree—staring, tense, withdrawn.

Suzuki gave an evening lecture in the zendo. Ron stood rigidly in the back. Suzuki talked about how Japanese Buddhists flout the rules. He went on and on about it laughing and saying, "We're shameless," laughing at how they ate meat, got married, drank sake. It was not the usual Suzuki subtlety.

After the lecture, our friend could not be found. The next day, at chosan, Suzuki and the officers agreed it was time to go look for him. Paul Discoe came to me and said Ron had run off into the woods the night before and they wanted a few of us to go look for him. He said they chose us because we weren't judgmental and wouldn't be seen as authorities. Actually, I did have judgmental thoughts, but I wouldn't hit the poor guy over the head with them.

At about noon, six of us went out—two up the road, two upstream, and two down. Tim Aston and I went downstream, checking spots not visible from the trail. Tim took the path up to the Horse Pasture. I kept going downstream. I found Ron sitting bolt upright on a boulder below the Narrows. I had a bag lunch for him. Each of us searching for him had one. He was famished but wanted to know if it was past noon because then he'd have to wait till the next day. I assured him it was before noon, though I knew otherwise. He ate with gusto, obviously famished. I swatted a mosquito. He said I'd spend an eon in the Avici hell realm for that. More spooky talk. He wept bemoaning how we'd strayed from the true path. Then we walked back.

After Ron left Tassajara, he went into a hospital for examination. He was diagnosed with severe malnutrition with dry beriberi that can affect mental processing of information and cognitive functions. He stayed in the hospital for days recovering. His mind became clear.

He wondered if he'd misinterpreted it when Suzuki said that good students are more important than centers and monasteries. *Maybe he didn't mean I should go to Japan,* Ron thought. *The effort I made there was too much. It was over-efforting without an understanding of the foundation.*

But Ron didn't regret having burned his robes before he left Tassajara. He did it out of respect for the purity of the dharma because, he said, he couldn't maintain it, he couldn't live up to it.

Nervous Guest

A businessman who lived nearby with Mike Murphy of the Esalen Institute. He seemed like someone who'd had too much coffee. Something of him would always be moving—fingers tapping, fidgeting. He was open and friendly, but I was not surprised when he said he had a hard time when he joined us for zazen. He admired us for being able to sit still that long. But, he said, the workshops, talks, encounter groups, and atmosphere at Esalen worked better for him. I told him that from what I'd gathered, the more difficulty one had with sitting still, the more one got out of doing it.

Legions of people were going through big changes, and he was one of them. He said his life had been rotated 180 degrees. He had long been a member of the Bahá'í Faith and believed that there were many admirable aspects of Bahá'í, such as respecting other religions and teaching the equality and oneness of all humanity. But Bahá'í was so strict, and now he was living a life that went against much of their moral code—drinking, smoking pot, nude mixed-bathing at the Esalen baths, promiscuity. He was a well-known figure in Monterey County. Other guests would recognize him, and some blamed the drastic drop in the value of their portfolios on him losing his bearings due to his love affair with the Esalen scene—rather than the recession that the economy was going through.

He and I were talking in the courtyard when his attention was diverted to almost thirteen year old Jeanne who walked by. He asked me if he might be able to have her for the night.

Roovane on Guard

Most of the males at Tassajara were draft age and all of us, possibly, except for Stan, were against the Vietnam War. Some were conscientious objectors whose firefighting status at Tassajara covered their obligation. The rest of us had gotten out of the draft one way or another or hadn't dealt with it yet. A few, like Roovane, had joined the National Guard. He had to go for two weeks' service during the summer.

Roovane returned early from his first two weeks of service. I asked him how it went. In characteristic form, he said that it had been a peak experience. "Oh please, do tell," I said, and he did.

On Sundays, the guardsmen gathered before disbursing to the place of worship of their choice—Catholic, Protestant, or Jewish. Roovane, holding a zafu and little bell, said he was Zen Buddhist. He was told he could have a room for his prayers. He said he just wanted to meditate under a nearby tree. The officer said that a room would be better. Roovane said that Buddha was enlightened while meditating under a tree and that was his religious practice. The officer reluctantly said OK. Immediately, others raised their hands and said that they were Zen Buddhists, too. The officer gave up and said, "OK, you can go join him under that tree."

Roovane bid his flock get cushions, blankets, whatever they could find to sit on. Once they were all gathered by the tree he gave a zazen instruction. He had them loosen their ties and unbuckle their belts, pull their shirt tails out, and open their pants up on top so that there would be nothing restraining their lower abdomens from freely moving in and out with their breathing. "Put your strength there," he said, "in the tummy—as my teacher says." He told them to be perfectly quiet, relaxed but alert. Just sit upright with your chin in, do not move, and follow the breath. Time passed peacefully. There was a breeze to soften the heat.

The commander of the base was walking nearby and noticed the group sitting under the tree. As he approached, he saw that these guardsmen were breaking the dress code, not presenting themselves in public as befits guardsmen, and called, "A-tten-tion!"

Roovane quietly reminded the sitters, so that the commander could hear, that they were in a religious service and were not to move or make a sound. The commander loudly called out again, "Attention!" adding that they were breaking the dress code and were to immediately tuck their shirts in, button and belt their pants, tighten their ties, stand up, and get presentable!

Everyone continued sitting quietly without moving. The commander then started screaming at them. So Roovane hit the bell to end the meditation and softly told them what to do—swing side to side, stand up, fasten your belt. The commander stormed off.

There were no recriminations for Roovane or the others. He continued to do strange things that threw the officers there off balance. He reported to target practice with a teddy bear and said he didn't touch guns but would hold his teddy bear instead. He was allowed to fulfill his commitment to the guard by meditating alone in a room. Soon, he was told he could leave early and would not have to return.

Yvonne's Gift

On a hot summer day, Yvonne drove Suzuki back to Tassajara from conducting a funeral for a member of the Japanese congregation in San Francisco. She also brought Tassajara a gift—and a story to go with it.

Yvonne told how she and a few others had taken a trip to the Southwest. They had walked into the Grand Canyon and camped for a few days with the Havasupai Indians on the canyon floor. At Hotevilla, a traditional village in the third mesa of the Hopi reservation, they visited with a village elder named David Monongye whom she called Grandpa David. He was one of four Hopi elders entrusted with sharing the Hopi prophesies with the outside world, a decision made in 1946 as a result of the advent of the nuclear bomb.

I'd met Grandpa David the prior December when Bob Halpern, my sister, and I had driven to Texas. Bob Watkins told us we should not drive by there without meeting Chief David, as he called him. Watkins explained that a traditional village is one that resists outside interference—just visiting is an imposition, so keep quiet and be respectful. Driving on the Hotevilla dirt road, we asked a man working on a roof where we might find David Monongye. "If he's not out talking to white people," the man said, "he'll be at home." He gave us directions to an adobe home nearby. We knocked on the door. An old Indian man answered. Before we could say anything, he said, "Welcome. Come in. Would you like to spend the night?" His wife served us coffee and fried flat bread. David showed us an ancient map and told us about their prophecies. It was a wonderful visit.

Yvonne's time with Grandpa David was more in depth. An outsider staying there overnight was unusual and frowned on by his fellow Hotevillans, but obviously David didn't care. Yvonne and party stayed in Monongye's small earthen home with him and his wife Nora. She said they spent the first day and a half just sitting silently. "Grandpa David was very interested in the Heart Sutra," Yvonne said, "and chanting the Heart Sutra. I remember sitting for a long while with him and his saying that it's wonderful that there's the sort of resonance between the spiritual path that you're on and the path that my people are on but please honor your own path and don't try to be Indians. That struck me because I also heard don't try to be Japanese either, which Suzuki Roshi emphasized."

Not far from there, they visited Canyon de Chelly (pronounced shay) taking the White House Ruins Trail used for centuries by the Navaho. "I had a very big experience down there," she said. "Coming back out of the canyon late in the day it was as though I flew up the hill. I was in quite an altered, transcendent state. It was a kind of opening to interdependence. I stayed in a transcendent state for quite some time. But I particularly remember coming out of the canyon almost like floating I was so blissed out one might say. When I got back to Zen Center, I had a book of photos of the Navajo and Hopi lands and Canyon de Chelly and that area. I brought the book with me when I went to see Suzuki Roshi to tell him about the trip and what I'd learned and what I'd seen and what it was like. He opened the book and he brushed the pages quickly aside till he came to the picture of the trail coming out of White House Ruins and he said, 'This is where it is. This is where it happened.'

"Without my saying much at all he knew that something big had happened to me and he knew exactly where it happened. It was like some other level of communication. It was really powerful. From that point on he was very supportive of my interest in native people and the hunger I had to know about the geology, the land, the plants, and sense of place which he didn't think was weird at all."

Yvonne's gift for Tassajara was Hopi corn. With a few of us watching, she and Roovane, following the instructions of Grandpa David, had a brief Hopi corn planting ceremony. It was a hot, cloudless day. An hour or so later, some dark clouds floated over and there was an exceedingly unusual July rain.

Bill's Diary 3 SUMMER 1970

Charlotte Selver and Charles Brooks arrive at Tassajara to teach us sensory awareness.

Robert Bly comes for a day of reading poems from *The Teeth Mother Naked at Last*.

Christie Shurtleff [Bill's sister] visits Tassajara for the first time; we sleep outside on the guest dining room porch. Nice hikes down Tassajara Creek, swimming.

Cloe Scott teaches dance.

Organic John walks down the road with his sheathed knife and makes a superb salad.

The Stone

Dan Welch was snooping around in the small creek, looking for stones. His search led him to the entrance to Tassajara where the creek goes under the road in a large pipe. After he'd gone about 200 feet up creek from the gate, he spotted a stone that grabbed his attention. He took Suzuki there to show him, "thinking that it would be a wonderful addition to the collection of gnarly stones in his garden." Suzuki was pleased with it, so Dan and some others got to work to dig it out. They started digging then dug more—and more—and more. It was a huge stone, marbled. An extraordinary find. Surely too big for Suzuki's garden.

Suzuki saw the stone with more of its mass revealed and was captivated. He said it would be perfect for his headstone. No need to deal with it at the present, though. It's not going anywhere—and Suzuki had no plans that called for its use anytime soon. When that time came, the stone could be dug up and put in place at the site on the Hogback Suzuki had chosen for Trudy Dixon's ashes—and his own.

Lay Ordinations

Earlier in the summer, some parents asked if the children could sew their own rakusu for a children's ordination. Tomoe and Dainin Katagiri liked the idea, and Suzuki went along with it. The di Prima, Johansen, Walter, Petchey, Warkov and Katagiri children participated, twelve in all. Not Jeanne di Prima. She was older than the others, would be a teenager in the fall, was practicing with the adults, and would wait her turn with them.

Each child received a rakusu with the robe chant and their Buddhist names written on the back in kanji calligraphed by Suzuki. In the ceremony, he said, "What this means for all you children is that you're going to be good and brave and beautiful." Some of us thought it was a little too cute and sort of weird for little kids to get rakusus and lay ordination when they were too young to appreciate it. After the ceremony, I realized that the children had pure innocent beginner's mind and would be a tough act to follow for those of us with all our ideas, competition, and pride.

On August 25, Suzuki performed the lay ordination for those of us who'd sewed—or helped to sew—our rakusu. Now, there were thirty-six of us with this new status we could proudly wear. That wasn't the intention. We each tried our hardest in our own way to be "a person of no rank."

The rakusu, like the kesa, were worn in the zendo, but not until the end of morning zazen. Until then, they remained in their pouches neatly placed on the tatami before or beside the sitter. At the end of zazen there was a brief chant. We called it the robe chant, but it referred only to the robe of ordination, the kesa and the rakusu which was really just a miniature kesa worn around the neck with straps. We recited the robe chant in Japanese with it still in its pouch resting on our heads. It had been chanted at the end of zazen for years going back to the pre-Tassajara Sokoji days, except back then no one knew what it meant which was:

> Great robe of liberation
> A field far beyond form and emptiness
> Wearing the Tathagata's teaching
> Saving all beings.

I liked the use of the word *field* in the gatha, as these garments were indeed sewn from pieces into a pattern that represented a rice field.

When that recitation was over, we unpacked the rakusu or kesa and donned them. The rakusu were less formal than the kesa so they would be worn more, like at meetings or anytime people wanted. Priests with kesa would wear their rakusu at less formal times, as well. One morning, as we were departing study period in the dining room, we were greeted by some strong gusts of wind. Robes and rakusu were lifting up into the air in a flurry, a sight that emphasized the poor aerodynamics of our Zen apparel.

In the preparations for the 1970 lay ordination ceremony, Liz Wolf asked Suzuki what if she decided she wanted to become a Christian, later? Suzuki told her that was fine as long as she felt sincere about what she was doing at the moment. Later, Liz crossed paths with Suzuki. "Like moonlight in Tassajara Creek," he said to her. She realized that was his explanation of the Buddhist name she'd received from him at the lay ordination ceremony.

On the day after our ordination Yvonne walked down Polk Street wearing her rakusu. A woman came up to her and said, "Oh that is the cutest little bib honey. I want to get one too. Where'd you buy it?"

Brown Robe

Suzuki had a plan as to who would succeed him as abbot. He had been letting people know that he would be going to Japan in late August for a few months. He wanted to encourage more back and forth flow between Soto Zen in Japan and America. He heard more about Westerners practicing Rinzai Zen—with Nanrei Sohaku Kobori at Ryoko-in, a subtemple of Daitokuji where Ruth Fuller Sasaki and Gary Snyder had been. Also in Kyoto, Mumon Yamada at Myoshinji had a number of Western students. Richard had written in praise of both of those teachers.

Suzuki planned to seek out Soto Zen temples and monasteries that might be suitable places for Americans to practice. He wanted to visit with family, especially his son and heir Hoitsu, and meet with old friends and members of Rinsoin, his temple in Yaizu. Most importantly, he wanted to spend time with Richard and do a transmission ceremony with him.

Little by little, Suzuki had been letting people know of his plans. He told Bob Halpern and me early on, maybe because he knew we'd share the information with others. Not everyone was enthusiastic about the thought of Richard in a brown robe. At a meeting with senior students, concerns were expressed. Suzuki finally told them they'd just have to trust him on this. Beverly Horowitz said it was the only way Suzuki could get Richard to practice—to place him in the bamboo tube of such authority. Katagiri said we didn't understand what transmission meant and if that's what Suzuki wanted, we should just gassho.

Too Late

Early in 1970, Suzuki asked to see Bob Halpern and me. He said he wanted to ordain us as priests together. He said we both needed to develop patience. I thought we were more likely to be patients in a mental ward and was surprised he'd even consider ordaining us. Either he saw through our erratic behavior that there was potential, or it was part of his program to promote a certain level of chaos at Zen Center. He seemed pleased, but he didn't set a date.

At Tassajara, I asked Suzuki what was happening with our ordination and he said that Bob was too—indicating with his finger—up and down. He added he didn't want to make Bob jealous of me and resent that I'd been ordained without him. "You're too late for that Roshi," I said, "It's not me he'd be jealous of. It's Reb, who he grew up with—and you've already ordained Reb." Suzuki just made a *mea culpa* grimace.

Mission to Mexico

Alan Marlowe decided he should go to Tibet to attain enlightenment. But first he wanted to visit Mexico with his son Alex, whom he thought he might not see again for a long time.

Bob had an itching to go to Mexico to visit a mentor of his from his past, Juan Becera, who he said was wise, mischievous, and with a wonderful sense of humor. Becera lived in Barra de Navidad, a little fishing village on the West Coast. Bob wanted to bring him back to meet Suzuki. But he knew Suzuki wouldn't agree to that, so he went to Suzuki and told him Alan wanted to go to Tibet and spend the rest of his life meditating in a cave to attain the rainbow body.

He knew Suzuki wouldn't like that either. Bob suggested to Suzuki that he go with Alan to Mexico and talk him out of going to Tibet during the trip. Suzuki agreed. Bob's friend and fellow Zen student Mike Gilmore went along.

First, they went to Mazatlan on the West Coast. Alan decided it was a good place for him and Alex. Bob and Mike continued south. It was dark when they arrived, as close as they could get by road to Barra de Navidad. Mike slept in the VW bus. But Bob was eager to see his old friend, and walked the two-kilometer path into the village with the help of a flashlight. He descended the path onto a beach and walked along it close enough to the water so that the village dogs wouldn't get riled up. When he came upon a figure in the dark, it was Juan Becera.

Bob and Mike stayed for a few days. Becera agreed to go back with them to meet Suzuki. Reb had met Becera when he visited Bob in Barra de Navidad in '66. He could vouch for Becera to Suzuki. But then Becera decided Suzuki should come visit him instead. Oh well, it was a good idea.

Bob went back to the City Center, happy he'd seen his first teacher. Alan decided to return to Tassajara. Mission accomplished.

Bob's Decision

Bob was living on the same floor of the City Center as Suzuki and Okusan. Most who wanted to see Suzuki would thoughtfully ask for an appointment with his jisha or Yvonne, his unofficial secretary and advisor. That might take time. Bob preferred the ambush approach, instead. He'd bring a gift to Okusan, ask to use the toilet, and then open the wrong door saying, "Oh, excuse me, Roshi," knowing he was incapable of saying *I'm busy*—except to his wife.

This time, Bob had something serious to say to Suzuki, so he made an appointment, but he didn't want to wait in line, so he told Yvonne it was an emergency. That got him in right away. He told Suzuki to please forget about ordaining him as a priest. Bob said that he'd probably just strut around in his robes for a couple of weeks and then lose interest in the priest trip. Suzuki accepted Bob's decision.

Sweet HOOM

The guest season was over and I was in from Tassajara for a week to see my sister, and of course, Bob. My first evening back, Bob and I went to see *Joe*, a film basically about killing hippies. Afterwards, Bob and I were walking back to the City Center, through the seedy Tenderloin section of town when a few young HOOM (pronounced home) members approached. HOOM was the Holy Order of Mans, a sort of mystical Christian group that began in '68 around a certain Earl Wilbur Blighton, who went by the honorific "Right Rev." They had a house near Duboce Circle. They wore black with clerical collars and were basically nice people.

Bob said hi. They stopped to talk. The HOOMsters were all smiling, a female smiling especially blissfully. Bob asked her what she was so happy about. She said that she was at peace, beyond desire and anger.

"Oh, is that so?" he said and hauled off and slapped her on the face so hard that she fell down. But right away, I could tell by Bob's reaction that he thought he'd gone too far this time. Before he could apologize, she called out, "Thank you! Thank you! You have shown me that I'm not beyond anger!" He helped her up. She was crying and continued to thank him over and over. We walked back in silence.

Rinpoche Returns

"You're drunk!" Suzuki had scolded Bob back in '69, for drinking too much beer at the Hagiwara home, where he had driven Suzuki to do a family service. Bob thought his practice at that time was to drink with their host. He had the on switch but not the off switch—even though he was no drinker.

I'd gathered that alcohol is often part of the scene with Japanese priests. I knew there were some austere lineages and priests who didn't drink, but Japanese priests were known for their drinking. Most people in the Zen Center didn't know about that, and only on rare occasion would we see Suzuki or Katagiri drink alcohol. Suzuki would soon fall asleep, and Katagiri would get emotional. At a banquet with the Japanese congregation that included bottles of whiskey placed on the tables, Katagiri came up to me, sat in my lap, hugged me, and said, "I love you, David."

Suzuki was used to priests, even revered roshis, drinking at times to excess. He didn't like it, but he didn't judge. He pretty much disregarded Chogyam Trungpa's seemingly constant alcohol consumption.

A former Zen Center student named Henry Schaeffer escorted Trungpa into the City Center. The dining room was packed for his talk, during which he continued to drink a clear liquid from a clear glass. Suzuki sat up front with the students. There were questions. Leland Smithson asked, "If you put a mirror in a box will it reflect darkness?" Trungpa said, "You put the mirror in the box. You figure it out."

Then someone asked why he drank and smoked, and he tossed it aside. A guest student named David Schneider asked whether Trungpa shouldn't protect himself by avoiding bad habits, much as we protect our eyes with sunglasses. Trungpa said, "There's nothing to protect."

After Trungpa's talk, Suzuki greeted him in the hall and Trungpa said, "Hi, Roshi, I'm drunk." Walking to his room, Suzuki said to Bob Halpern, "He's such a good teacher. If only people could see how he's teaching them." At another time, when asked about Trungpa's drinking, he said, "He drinks because he suffers."

On another occasion, Trungpa dropped by with Henry unannounced. Suzuki came down from his room and sat with them at a table in the dining room. Trungpa asked Suzuki, "What's the difference between dharma and prajna?" Suzuki said, "They're the same." But Trungpa then said they're different. Suzuki excused himself, saying he had to go check a reference book. He came back and said yes, you're right, they are different. Henry thought this was an example of Trungpa teaching Suzuki. I thought they were teaching

Henry the two sides to everything—in this case, the different and the same.

No Hope

If Trungpa was in town, Bob would spend as much time with him as he could. On one occasion, Bob asked me to come with him to a warehouse where Trungpa was giving a talk. Over fifty people sat and waited, mainly young, a lot of long hairs. Trungpa was quite late, which I gathered was the norm for him except at the Zen Center where that wouldn't have worked well. He spent a long while just looking around and smiling, occasionally taking a sip from a glass. He spoke with a soft, yet penetrating, voice. He said the practice was to be awake, to be fully with the moment, not to take any trip away from simply being present. "Please don't go on any trips," he said and then repeated, "Please don't go on any trips." There was an imploring quality to his voice. He repeated that many times with such earnestness it seemed he was about to cry. Suzuki would occasionally say the same thing. Bob and I nodded knowingly to each other.

Allen Ginsberg came in. Trungpa commented on how we could see him now that he was clean-shaven. Turned out Trungpa had been with Ginsberg before the talk and had chided him about his beard, so Ginsberg got rid of it. That's why he was late. He carried a harmonium. Trungpa bid him to play us something. Accompanying himself, Ginsberg sang a poem with a tag line of "and all the hills echoed" which he repeated a number of times. I recognized it as a line from a William Blake poem. When he was through, the room was silent. Everyone was looking at Trungpa. He gave Allen the finger, and said, "Fuck you." Not like any dharma talk I'd ever been to.

Afterwards, Bob took me to an apartment where Trungpa was staying and we sat up with him drinking and smoking and talking. I told Trungpa I'd loved his book, *Born in Tibet*. Bob said he'd read it in '66 when it came out, and then stocked it in his Satori Shop in L.A. Bob said that Frank with the big Adam's apple, who'd studied with Trungpa in Scotland, had given the book to Suzuki the year before Suzuki and Trungpa met. When Bob paid one of his uninvited visits to Suzuki, the book was in Suzuki's hand.

Trungpa said that after he left Tibet he never heard of his teacher again, and he felt so sad and alone, but when he met Suzuki he felt that he had found a true friend. He said he liked being around Bob and me because we reminded him of Suzuki. He said our problem was we were too serious.

There was the time that I went to pee and Trungpa joined me. We peed together into the same toilet. Not many men in my culture would feel comfortable doing that, and I hadn't done it since I was a little kid with my father. I'd look at the mole on my father's penis as we peed. I don't recall anything about Trungpa's organ, but I do recall going on about how lucky we were to meet great dharma teachers and that, where I'd come from, memorizing the capitals of the states was what we were taught. He said, "Memorizing the capitals of the states is the dharma."

His grasp of English was impressive. He spoke with an English accent. He was born and raised in Tibet, which he escaped in 1959. He lived and studied in India till 1963, when he went to Oxford. He'd only been in America for a year, but he imitated my Texas accent, which wasn't that strong.

Trungpa said in his talk, "There's no hope, you know." I brought that up and said that Bob and I had a comment on that, and Bob immediately joined me in singing *There's No Hope for Us All*, which we'd sung over and over many times driving together. We only did one pass with Trungpa that night. I'd say it was well-received, in that he did not shoot us the bird or say fuck you.

One night, Bob excused himself, saying he had to find someone "to retire to Rinpoche's room with him for the night." I knew Trungpa had slept with one woman who was there, and asked, "What about her?" Bob said, "Well, you know, it's hard to beat new ones."

Before long, a woman from the Zen Center came up to me and asked if I could tell her husband she was spending the night with Rinpoche. I said, gulp, "Sure." They lived at the City Center where I was headed. I got back late and tapped on their door. He opened it bleary-eyed. I told him his wife wasn't feeling well and would be staying at the apartment where Trungpa was staying. The next day, she came up to me and was angry, asking why I lied to her husband. "I told you to tell him I was staying with Rinpoche and you told him I was sick, and he was really worried about me." I told her I was sorry, but that I just couldn't bring myself to tell her husband she was going to sleep with another man. "He's not just any other man," she said. "He's our teacher."

Friendly Persuasion

Once the guest season ended and the closed signs were posted at Jamesburg and our gate, Tassajara would become even more quiet and seem somewhat empty, unlike the spring interim when we'd be busy getting ready for the guest season. There was plenty to do in the fall interim, too, but it still felt, by comparison, lazy and free.

On a four-and-nine day, Dianne and I went to the Narrows, and it was just the two of us for a good hour till a couple of back packers arrived. It wasn't practice period yet so no one cared enough to stop them. They were surprised to learn they might have been sent away.

Every now and then during practice period we'd get someone at the gate who would have their minds made up that they should be at Tassajara. One long-haired guy told me he'd come there to meet god. I told him that god was everywhere and that he could just as easily meet god say on a walk to the Wind Caves. The trail leading to them and ultimately Church Creek Ranch, was opposite the Horse Pasture trailhead. That worked.

During sesshin, we were seriously shut, when a persistent dreadlocked fellow insisted that he wouldn't be in the way. Just wanted to soak in the hot water. I told him that there were three basic times at Tassajara: there was the guest season, when we were open to guests, and at that time, and in the interims, we were flexible. I said, "That's like when you're hanging out with friends drinking a little beer." For the practice periods, I told him, we were more selective. "It's really just for us, but if someone shows up, we'll usually be friendly, let them walk up or down creek, maybe offer them some tea. That's like when you're getting stoned with some friends on some good pot and don't want anyone to bring you down—but you can be flexible." "But we're in sesshin now," I said. "That's seven days straight of zazen, Zen meditation, from before sunrise to late at night. That's like an acid trip. We've got the set and the setting under control, and we don't want any distraction at all, even from friends." He nodded. I walked him to his VW Bug and we bowed in parting.

Sometimes I'd fail. One poor lost soul had tried to convince me he should be able to stay during a practice period and, when nothing I said worked, I took him to Katagiri. He sat with Katagiri for a while and on his way out said he'd met a real compassionate Zen master, and then looking at me he added, "Not like that uptight, bureaucrat asshole I talked to, first."

California Traders

Tatsugami was back, and another ninety-day practice period with him at the helm was smoothly cruising along. Those who couldn't adjust to all Tatsugami's forms and ceremonies didn't return.

Katagiri was again reluctantly translating for him in lectures, and morning tea, but Dan, now the director, gave Katagiri frequent breaks by translating in meetings. Peter was working on *Wind Bells* and editing Suzuki lectures. Jane was the ino, in charge of the doanryo and zendo. Paul Discoe was assistant director; Maggie Kress was the treasurer; and Frances Thompson was the tenzo, head cook. Ed Brown was doing stone work, this time creating a foundation for a new abbot's cabin. Niels, now with mighty work leader power, was using me as a gofer to do odds and ends and anything he didn't want to do like research or make lists. And now he actually had the authority to berate me. The smoothest cruiser of us all, though, was the shuso, head monk, Silas Hoadley. He was the sixth shuso, but was generally regarded as the dharma flag-bearer among Suzuki's students. And he was mellow, a pleasure to relate to—socially or dharmicly.

Out of curiosity, I visited Silas at his warehouse one day back in '66 and learned a few things about him. He attended Andover and Yale. While in school, he imported guitars from Mexico, ran a cap and gown rental, and played poker. When he was in the navy, his ship ferried officers' wives and children between San Francisco and Okinawa, where he came upon the glassblowers. After the navy, Silas made a living importing hand-blown glass jars from Okinawa. His pieces were in Tiffany's and all over the country. The name of his business was California Traders.

Stan was there. He spent most of that time smoking and talking to Joe, who shared the space with Silas. Stan went back to his desk and I went over to Joe's section and introduced myself. I asked Joe how he liked sharing space with Silas, and he said Silas is probably the best person in the world to share anything with. I asked him where'd he come from. I hardly ever met anyone originally from San Francisco. Joe said he came to the US after the war. I couldn't help but notice the tattooed numbers on his arm. "Oh my god," I said.

"Oh, this," Joe said. "It's a little tattoo I got—at Auschwitz."

He said there were many concentration camps, but that Auschwitz was the only one that tattooed prisoners. He said the lucky ones got tattoos. That meant they'd be forced labor rather than go to the gas chambers and ovens. He said that before the Red Army liberated them, most of the prisoners were evacuated on a death march. Those too weak or sick were left behind. The fact that he was so weak was his second good fortune. Joe's third good fortune was that when he stood in line to get food the Russian soldiers were dishing out, his friend standing next to him knocked the plate out of his hands. Joe ate what he could recover from the ground. His friend told him that was all he needed. Joe said that many got terribly sick or died from eating too much at first.

Silas sold California Traders to Joe for less than it was worth. He gave a big chunk of that money toward the purchase of Tassajara. He gave a salesman who'd worked for him enough money to travel around the world. He didn't need so much anymore. He didn't need the business. He'd invested his life in Zen Center.

Chanting in English

Since the spring practice period, Peter had been working on the *Wind Bell* and on translating the gathas, the brief chants for the baths, toilet, face-washing, going to bed. He didn't know much Japanese but he had my character study of these gathas and consulted with Katagiri and Suzuki. He was also working on creating a chantable version of the Heart Sutra in English. The old Sokoji chant cards had the basic English meaning of the words above the kanji. Allen Ginsberg chanted them and it sounded great when he did it. But Peter had something else in mind. So he had that sort of translation Suzuki did, a rudimentary character study of the Heart Sutra I'd done, and a translation by D.T. Suzuki from his *Manual of Zen Buddhism*, published in 1935.

Peter was a poet and wanted to make the Heart Sutra flow like the old Sino-Japanese did. Ryogen Yoshimura, a priest who had joined us and was, with a relieved Katagiri's blessing, translating excellently for Tatsugami, was a scholar and spoke good English. He helped Peter craft the words for chanting. Peter showed the finished product to Tatsugami, who immediately wanted to use it. So it was included in the morning service and became the only English we chanted, except for the English meal chant done at breakfast. Yoshimura taught doans how to hit the big taiko drum instead of the mokugyo with this English Heart Sutra. It was powerful. That was done during morning service for a while and then just on special occasions.

Marian Derby AUGUST

Shunryu Suzuki gave Marian Derby an inscribed copy of the newly released *Zen Mind, Beginner's Mind: Informal Talks on Zen Meditation and Practice*. In doing so, Suzuki was giving Marian a gift she originally had given him.

Six years earlier, Marian had a good life in a good home in a good neighborhood with a good income and five good children. But she was dissatisfied. In the fall of 1964, she went to Esalen Institute for a weekend seminar on meditation. The high point for her was Gary Snyder instructing her in Zen meditation. Back home in Los Altos, she dreamed of going to Japan to find a Zen master. Then in February of '65, she saw a notice in the local newspaper that a Rev. Suzuki, a Zen priest from a Zen temple in San Francisco, would be coming to nearby Palo Alto once a week for a class in Zen meditation. She wondered why Gary Snyder hadn't mentioned there was a Zen priest in San Francisco.

She became a regular at Suzuki's 5:45 a.m. meditation and talk. One morning in July 1965, she invited him to her home for breakfast before driving him back to Sokoji. He marveled at her spacious living room, and right away she knew what he had in mind. She said she had children who'd be a distraction. Suzuki said that would just strengthen people's zazen.

Marian added coffee, cinnamon rolls, and open discussion to their Thursday morning zazen and lecture schedule. She had a reel-to-reel tape recorder, and, with Suzuki's permission, started to record and transcribe his lectures so people could read them. Suzuki gave Marian permission to compile the lectures into a book. When a draft was ready, Suzuki suggested she show it to Richard Baker. She gave him a copy of her draft in March '67 with the title, *Beginner's Mind*. A year later, Richard asked Trudy Dixon if she'd take on this project.

Trudy had worked for a few years with Richard on *Wind Bells*. She was ill with breast cancer, but agreed to do it. Marian gave Trudy copies of all the lectures she'd transcribed, many more than the thirteen she included in her draft. She also brought Trudy all the tapes. Trudy and Richard decided to have the lectures transcribed again so that Trudy could start fresh. In August, Trudy gave Richard the completed draft of the book which she, with Suzuki's and Richard's involvement, had brought to fruition. Richard took the manuscript with him to Japan, doing some final work on the ship. In Tokyo, he found a publisher, Weatherhill, whose founder, Meredith Weatherby, invited Richard to stay in his Tokyo home. He also insisted the word "Zen" be in the title.

Now, a copy of that book was in Marian's hands. She felt some satisfaction, but it was tempered by her sorrow that Trudy had not lived to see her work published. Whatever pride Marian felt, she shared with Trudy, who she so admired. "She taught us how to live," said Marian, "and she taught us how to die."

Two years before, Marian had been dissatisfied with her life and practice and decided the problem was her environment. She told Suzuki she wanted to move to Tassajara. Suzuki was OK with that—he wanted to ordain her as a priest. But he tried to dissuade her from giving her home away. Marian was adamant. She donated her home with its zendo to Zen Center, which sold it to Les Kaye, using the money to help pay off the City Center mortgage. Les had a family, a career with IBM, and was a dependable presence at Haiku Zendo, who Marian knew would take good care of it. Her ex-husband took their two teenage daughters, who were still living at home. Fellow Suzuki student and close friend, Bill Smith, picked Marian up and drove her to Tassajara, with three boxes of possessions she'd not given away.

Marian had been at Tassajara for a year when Tatsugami arrived for his first practice period. After a couple months practicing with him, Marian was satisfied with him, but she was dissatisfied with her practice, her Zen life. She'd read somewhere that a Zen monk should have three teachers. Suzuki was her first. She asked Suzuki if Tatsugami could be her second. Suzuki agreed. She met with Tatsugami in the abbot's cabin. It was March 12, 1970, her 47th birthday. She asked him if she could become his disciple and he said that since she'd asked on her birthday, he could not refuse. This instilled new enthusiasm in Marian.

Before Tatsugami left to go back to Japan for the summer, he told Marian the wonderful news that he'd be bringing robes for her ordination when he returned in September. He added that after the fall practice period, she would study Japanese in San Francisco before going to Japan to enter a nunnery. This shocking news plunged Marian into despair. She just wanted to be Tatsugami's disciple at Tassajara—but she said nothing about her doubts before he left. She was in a quandary. Her mind was rushing with thoughts.

Marian became obsessed with the Bodhisattva's vow to save all sentient beings. She decided the closest she could come would be to save one hundred sentient beings who each in turn would save a hundred, and eventually that process would save them all.

Marian felt she had too much responsibility at Tassajara and then was asked to take on more. She crashed, mentally and emotionally exhausted, and retreated to her room in the upper barn. She didn't come out for zazen, for work, or for meals. The kitchen sent trays of food to her. That was quite a trek. I'd deliver a meal to her now and then and sit with her on the deck of her room overlooking the creek. It became easier to visit her when she decided to stop talking. But she had a journal she wrote in.

Weeks passed. Marian settled into her role as Tassajara's eccentric hermit. Suzuki let her be. The officers left her alone. Her mental disturbances gradually subsided, and her sense of self, what she came to see as an idea of self, vanished.

When Tatsugami arrived, he learned that his ordainee-to-be was incommunicado and entrenched. She did have dokusan with him, in which she remained silent, and he uttered one word in Japanese. She went back to her room and he left her alone. In mid-November, Tatsugami asked to see Marian. He told her it was time to go, and she accepted it as the next step in her practice. On November 20, Bill Smith picked her up and took her to Big Sur. He walked with her and her boxes on a trail in the Big Sur woods to an abandoned structure with two walls and a roof. He left her there alone and, for the time being, satisfied. She was sure that she had found her third teacher—her formless self, her own spacious mind.

Party Down

There was a party at the end of the practice period, Tatsugami started it off with the toast: "I like zazen, sex, and alcohol—in that order. Now, enjoy the party!"

Dianne was not at that practice period. A female student and I took Tatsugami's encouragement and, after the meal and enough to drink, slipped out. We had to hide in high grass from the prying flashlights of two authority figures who almost stumbled onto us. Finally, they gave up, returned to the party, and we continued our innocent stroll out to Grasshopper Flats.

Moving On

Since arriving at Tassajara, I'd happily welcomed new arrivals and sadly bade farewell to those leaving. They were arriving for different intended stays and departing for a limited or indefinite time or forever. Some stayed longer and seemed more permanent, but I could see that none of us were permanent. Some were just gone from Tassajara. Others were gone from Zen Center. It wasn't bad, though. People have to move on when the time comes. Marian was gone. Emma Bragdon and Tim Buckley got married and were living together in San Francisco. Suzuki had wanted Tim to become a priest, but he said he had to become a man—have a family and make a living.

I was grateful to Tim for something he left behind—the spring 1969 *Wind Bell*. It was unlike any *Wind Bell* before, had no news. It was like a book, totally dedicated to a presentation of Suzuki's fall 1968 lectures on the Lotus Sutra. Tim had worked with Suzuki on editing and arranging and summarizing them. I'd had such a problem listening to those lectures, but after reading that *Wind Bell*, I wondered what my problem had been. Good job, Tim.

Phillip Wilson left Tassajara during the summer of 1968. He lived across the street from Sokoji for some months, but there was no role for him. He didn't feel comfortable living there and his behavior was erratic and sometimes disturbing. He moved north to Sonoma County to join his wife J.J.

Bob Shuman had left during the spring practice period, because he didn't feel comfortable with Tatsugami's way of doing things. But he was dissatisfied with Suzuki, too. He said he couldn't have a close enough relationship with Suzuki, who was always sick or somewhere else or too busy to see him. He went to L.A. to study with Sasaki.

I remembered Bob for his innocent sincerity. I also couldn't forget the pre-sunrise zazen we had up at Black Butte Summit with a sunrise Easter service conducted by Brother David. After the service, Bob turned to me and said, "That's the first time I've seen a sunrise." When he lived in the City Center, he returned from looking for a job and said maybe he should be a chicken strangler. *Why on earth would you want to do that?!* He said someone was going to do it, so maybe it should be a Buddhist. I envisioned Bob saying to each chicken before strangling it, "Become a Buddha."

Alan Winter was the first of us to live and practice zazen at Tassajara, but he'd left and moved to Jamesburg before Zen Center had bought Tassajara. After a year as a cook in the Merchant Marine, he'd returned to sit at Sokoji. Suzuki told Alan that Ed needed his friend, and so Alan went back to Tassajara in 1968 and worked with Ed in the kitchen, mainly as the baker. Then he hurt his back lifting heavy pots, and he walked out over a closed road after a heavy snow. He moved across the street from Sokoji and supported himself by baking bread in the oven of his apartment. He called it "Fresh Bread Fred." Alan returned to Tassajara a couple of months later.

In the 1969 guest season, Sterling Bunnell came down with his wife, Kathy, their kids, and Kathy's sister, Anne Stackpole. When the guest season was over, Alan hooked up with Anne and they lived in a teepee in Big Sur on some land where former Beck employees, Bill and Kathy Parker, were caretakers. Alan returned to Tassajara in 1970 to make the cake for Ed and Meg's wedding.

Then, he and Anne moved to Slocan Valley in British Columbia and became landed immigrants. Alan got a job as a baker in Nelson.

Tim Burkett, who got the Zen group going in Palo Alto back in 1964, left after the first practice period was over and returned for the spring '68 practice period when Phillip Wilson was shuso. Suzuki made him Kobun Chino's attendant and told him Kobun would teach him many things about ritual. "Kobun invited me to his cabin many evenings," Tim said. "He whipped up ceremonial tea which we drank together and he never taught me any ritual." Tim quit formal Zen practice after that and moved to Los Gatos with his wife Linda. There was too much ritual and Japanese for him and neither of them, who'd been students of Suzuki's for so long, wanted to be under the authority of Richard Baker. The last time he saw Suzuki, Suzuki asked him if he had any students, acknowledging Tim's understanding without any ceremony. Tim was grateful to his teacher and the sangha, but he was not attached to them.

Stan Leaves

Stan White was turned around by something Suzuki said in a lecture that he thought was right on. In a dokusan, he repeated it back to Suzuki. Suzuki shook his head. "No?" Stan said, puzzled, "But you said—" Suzuki cut him off with, "When I said it, it was true. When you said it, it was false."

In another dokusan, Stan told Suzuki, "Here I am at Tassajara, fifty-five years old." And he expressed concern about his future, adding, "What am I going to do?" Suzuki told him not to worry, that he'd get ordained. Stan was delighted and asked when. Suzuki said, "When we're ready."

Eventually, Stan decided he wasn't ready. He went to Boston because his mother was seriously hurt in an automobile accident. When he returned, he met with Suzuki in the city. Suzuki asked him how he was doing. Stan said he was fine but that he'd had enough and wasn't going back to Tassajara. He'd brought his belongings with him when he left. Suzuki asked him how he liked

Tatsugami. Stan said he thought Tatsugami was great, but the scene was too competitive. He knew that some sort of order was necessary, but he didn't want to get caught up in the "who's going to be head dishwasher game." After six years of Zen, he was ready for a change and moved to Mexico.

Bill Departs FROM HIS DIARY THAT YEAR

Jan. 1, 1970. As the new decade begins, I am age twenty-eight, living at Tassajara Zen Mountain Center in the Santa Lucia Mountains south of the Carmel Valley, California. I am single, having never been married. Occupation: Zen monk, practicing meditation.

Sept. Picking carrots in Salinas. No bugs, many crooked. Chemical farming.

Dec. 16. I leave Tassajara to go to Japan, with no plans of returning for a long time. I plan to finish my Tassajara Cookbook (to be published by Shambhala) then leave for Japan by my birthday (April 28). Suzuki Roshi wants to open a place like Tassajara in Japan for Japanese and foreign visitors. He wants me to go over in advance to learn Japanese and help him with the project. I also would like to be a translator at Tassajara when I return. Tassajara friends: Roovane, Meg Brown, Angie Runyon, Steve Brown, Alan Marlowe, David Chadwick, Maja Dremaine, Marian Derby, Lew Musto, Debbie Madison, Barbara Meyer Rifkin.

Main memories of Tassajara: The beauty and power and joyous mystery of meditation; in great effort there is great happiness (the stronger you hit the bell, the bigger the sound); the beauty of wild nature and the uninsulated life in the mountains; the terrible winter cold; sometimes too much loneliness. I wanted to be head cook (tenzo), but a woman (Frances) is given the job; I don't want to work under her. I don't have many friends at Tassajara. I want to get away for a little adventure while continuing my practice of meditation.

Dec. 28. At Zen Center in San Francisco, after hearing about Nanao in the desert, I throw away all my work on the Tassajara Cookbook. This frees me to go to Japan.

Dec. 31. Vivid memories of this day taking peyote with Christie, hiking in the misty Berkeley hills, then dropping in to see Fellini's amazing film *Satyricon*. It is a perfect manifestation of my mind, and of form is emptiness, emptiness is form. There is no art, only Mind which art manifests/reflects with various degrees of brilliance. At Zen Center that evening Suzuki Roshi scolds us for something. At Christie's I hold forth on the theme of "you cannot cut the sky with a sword" as it applies to the experience of personal criticism.

More Bill Memories

Bill might have thrown away the cookbook he was planning to publish, but I had a copy of *The Tassajara Food Trip*, which he made the year before. It had a whole bunch of recipes from the Tassajara kitchen typed up, and a lengthy introduction in which he describes an oryoki meal in the zendo, and equates the quality of one's state of mind, spiritual attainment, and health with the quality and balance of one's diet. He describes our grain and cooked vegetable-based diet as closely related to the food eaten by most traditional societies, specifically Jesus' diet as related in *The Essene Gospel of John*. Bill made concessions to the sweet tooth and included some modest sweet snacks and desserts.

He also included two signs from the kitchen wall. One was, "Love is not only the most important ingredient, it is the only ingredient which really matters." And he wrote, "There is a small altar on the wall. Nearby in italic calligraphy is written: 'Handle the silence with care.'" Bill's attitude toward wise eating and health is summarized by a quote from Hippocrates: "Thy food Shall be thy medicine." Such lines as "The total consciousness or 'vibrations' of the cook are transmitted to the food he prepares and to those who eat it," might seem awfully idealistic but Dogen wrote the same thing with different words.

Bill was an exemplary zazen practitioner and worker on any task, especially stones. He was work leader twice. He wrote in his diary that he would have stayed if he could have been tenzo, but I suspect the officers thought that might be like having a born-again fundamentalist teach a course in comparative religion. I assumed that in whatever future Bill was heading, that he would continue to combine religion, meditation, health, food, and evangelizing in some form. Possibly, I thought, he'd turn the Eightfold Path into the Ninefold Path, the ninth of course being Right Diet.

Before he left, I asked Bill what comes to mind when he thinks of his time at Tassajara. "Two memories stand out," he said. "Once after a lecture you said to Suzuki Roshi, 'I've been listening to your lectures as best I can for all these years, and I like it, but I don't get it. Could you just say it in one sentence?' Everyone burst out laughing, but Suzuki Roshi did answer it. He said, 'Everything changes.' It's the same thing that Henry Ford had carved in stone above his headquarters in Dearborn Michigan—'Of all things only one is sure—that everything changes.' It was such a beautiful statement on Suzuki Roshi's part in terms of my understanding of what Zen is all about.

"The other memory is that at the end of a summer sesshin in shosan, Dan Welch walked the full length of the zendo—and there was this loud silence. He looked at Suzuki Roshi and finally said, 'Suzuki Roshi, listen! Quick! Crickets!' and then, all of a sudden, our ears shifted into a new gear and we could hear all these crickets chirping all over the place. It was the strangest sensation because before that it seemed like everything was absolutely silent."

"Suzuki Roshi," he went on, "attracted a great variety of students to a difficult practice. It was cold, hard, the most unlikely people you'd ever expect like Lucille Harris, Stanley White, you, Bob Halpern, but not me or Dan—austere monastic types who like rarified atmosphere—that's something unique, the way he attracted the unlikely ones."

Christmas Eve

As usual, during the winter interim, Tassajara was sparsely populated. On the day before Christmas, Roovane suggested they do something special in honor of Jesus. Those few who remained for this darkest and coldest of times happened to be a perfect group for Loring to dig into a secret pouch and cook up a powerful batch of hash cookies. They were set out on a platter as the afternoon tea treat. As the railroad bell tolled, students gathered in the dining room, sipped tea and ate their cookie. The afternoon went by slowly. Loring and Roovane prepared dinner. The others spent a good deal of it at the baths. The bell for evening service rang.

"We chanted the Heart Sutra like it had never been chanted before," Roovane reported. "Bob Halpern was there. Little, thin Anna, on whom the birds who would rest. It was like Tibetan chanting. We were just there and giving it our best energy, I think that service more than anything at Tassajara changed my consciousness."

The word did not get out about the verboten festivities at Christmas Eve, since those who attended knew whom to share with and whom not to share with. When I asked Halpern how it went for him, he rolled his eyes and uttered like a man in a trance, "Cosmic."

—CHAPTER SEVEN—

1971

Universal Recommendation

Tatsugami was back for his third practice period, or *ango*, as he called it. Peter was now the shuso sitting on the altar, not in lotus, but with one leg dangling over the edge as he'd injured his knee.

Tatsugami was giving lectures on the *Fukanzazengi*, Dogen's *Universal Recommendation for Zazen*. He said that at Eiheiji the monks chant the Fukanzazengi during evening zazen, so he thought it would be good for us to do the same. There were two zazen periods at night before bedtime—as long as Tatsugami wasn't giving a talk. The Fukanzazengi was not easy to chant, as it wasn't in the old Chinese bare-bones style like the Heart Sutra, which can be chanted in a steady beat. The Fukanzazengi was in formal Buddhist Japanese from Dogen's day, which has a lot of connecting words that lead to an uneven beat. The Sandokai chant was like that, too, and we'd gotten it down, but the Fukanzazengi was much longer. It took up more than half the period to chant it while holding up a chant card. It seemed to me he'd thrown an obstacle course into evening zazen.

To add another hurdle, the woman who sat next to me in the zendo chanted a half beat ahead of everyone else. It was so irritating. Outside of the zendo, I asked her if possibly she could chant with the rest of us. She said it was too slow. I pointed out that she was not speeding it up, just chanting a syllable ahead of everyone else at the same speed. She just repeated that she was trying to speed it up. I told her it wasn't speeding up anything, and anyway, that's not her job. The doan with the kokyo position for that day introduces and sets the pace. "They should go faster," she replied. I talked to Jane, still the ino. I asked her if she'd speak to this student about it. Jane declined, suggesting I figure out how to deal with it.

To make the most of it, I studied the Fukanzazengi in the original—with patient and generous assistance from Ryogen Yoshimura. That made the chanting more cerebral, in that, now, I was getting flashes of meaning accompanying the sounds—with a preview of what was to come from the off-beat chanter next to me.

The only translation I had was from *The Three Pillars of Zen*. He titled it *Universal Rules of Zazen*. But we settled on the softer *Universal Recommendations for Zazen*. Of all the precious gems in that text the one that grabbed me most was on what to do about thinking in zazen. It read, "Think of not-thinking. How do you think of not-thinking? Non thinking. This in itself is the essential art of zazen." We liked it better without the "of" as in "Think not thinking." Then, how do that? Non thinking.

My father once said to me, "Thought is god." I knew he didn't mean the objects of thought. Just thought itself—like at rest. I remember looking at my hand, seeing it as thought. Then, I'd move the fingers and see that as thinking. Hmm. Thinking. Not thinking. Non thinking. Hmm. I saw those words, whatever they meant, as the heart of Dogen's universal recommendation. Regardless of how they were translated, it seemed the ultimate example of *easier said than done*.

Ryogen Yoshimura

When I went to Yoshimura with questions, he knew so much and imparted it so clearly. I appreciated how generous he was with his time.

He was tall and handsome and looked strong and healthy, but he told me he'd had health problems all his life, that he'd graduated from college with top honors while spending a lot of the time in the hospital with tuberculosis. He had read more English literature than I had. One of his favorite writers was Henry Miller.

I went to see Yoshimura one morning after breakfast. When I arrived at his door, he was chanting in his room. I waited outside till he was through and knocked on the door. He invited me in, removed his yellow kesa, folded it, and put it in a drawer. Next to it was a folded brown kesa. I asked him if there was any difference between the yellow and brown kesa. He said the brown robe meant he could be abbot of a temple and teach. He said that his father was a big shot priest in Hokkaido and that he'd received the brown kesa from the abbot of Eiheiji, skipping a bunch of intermediate steps and ceremonies. He said it was just connections, didn't mean anything, and he didn't wear it. Intermediate ceremonies? I told him the way we saw it was there's being ordained as a priest, then being a shuso for a practice period, then transmission, and that's it. From what he said, I gathered that there were ten levels below the brown robe and two steps with the brown robe. I feigned horror. He laughed and said it wouldn't be necessary for us to duplicate the system they have in Japan, and that even there, monks don't have to go through each step like climbing a ladder. He wondered, though, about our use of the word "priest" for an ordainee who hadn't at least been a shuso. He thought novice would be more accurate. I said a lot of people weren't comfortable with the word priest, but didn't like monk or novice either.

"We don't really know what we are," I said. "Suzuki said we're neither priest nor lay. Sometimes he distinguishes one from the other. He's used disciples for ordained priests and students for the rest of us, but then he'll call us all students. He called Trudy Dixon, a lay woman, 'oh my disciple' in her funeral."

"It will take time for the dust to settle," he said.

I asked Yoshimura what he was chanting when I arrived. He said that was his lineage from Keizan Jokin down to his master. Tatsugami added the names of the buddhas and ancestors to be chanted after the Sandokai. It was a long list. First, there were the six mythical buddhas before Shakyamuni Buddha, then Shakyamuni, then Mahakasyapa, his dharma heir according to Mahayana Buddhism, and then down the line to Bodhidharma in China, to the Sixth Patriarch, to Dogen in Japan, stopping at Keizan Jokin. After each name was the honorific *Daiosho,* great priest. So it started with Bibashi Butsu Daiosho and ended with Keizan Jokin Daiosho.

Yoshimura said the lineage branched out at Keizan so that at a training temple where there would be monks from different lineages, it wouldn't be proper to keep chanting the names after Keizan, that each monk did that privately after the service. He said that it was Keizan who popularized Soto Zen, bringing it to the farmers and workers. Keizan founded Sojiji in Yokohama, Soto Zen's other great root monastery after Eiheiji. He said that Dogen was the father of Soto Zen and Keizan the mother, and that Keizan ordained and promoted women as teachers. I always learned so much when I spent time with Yoshimura.

Attention to Details

Reb said Tatsugami taught the craft of chanting and ceremony, and that Suzuki worked with that, teaching the subtlety and nuance. Tatsugami emphasized Dogen's teaching of *Memmitsu no Kafu.* The characters literally were "tightly woven family wind," which meant "way of careful attention to details."

Tatsugami had never been in a mixed monastic setting before. Mainly, he adapted well to it. But he did bring his assumptions. At first, he wouldn't let women hit the mokugyo to provide the drumbeat for the chants. At times, it could get going pretty fast. He said women were too weak to keep up. That lasted until Louise stood up to him and said she was strong and bigger than he was.

Tatsugami extended his participation with students to spending nights with his anja. She was open about it, said he certainly hadn't taken advantage of her, and that he was more of a man than any of us guys. Overall, they were discreet, and no one paid much attention or seemed bothered by it.

We had a little clandestine group that met a few times during this practice period. After firewatch the night before a four-and-nine-day, one of us would sneak into the kitchen and walk-in cooler to fill our shopping list. The next morning, after the single day-off morning zazen, we'd exit the zendo before morning service started. The tenken just checked zazen attendance, not service, and the four-and-nine-day vibe was lax to begin with. At the downstream end of Tassajara Lane, below the lower barn, Ken Sawyer had his VW bus parked with the side door open. One by one, we'd arrive: Ken, Dianne, Jerry Fuller, Tim Aston, Steve Brown, and me.

Ken's VW had a double burner camping stove and two frying pans. One was for the scrambled eggs, the other for pancakes or French toast. We had our own maple syrup. Two thermoses held enough coffee for our mugs. We had a vow of secrecy. No one else knew and no one ever caught us. They were all in the zendo being good Zen students, following the schedule.

Girl Next Door

The first three cabins from the bridge on the creek side of Tassajara Lane were divided into two sides, each with a front and back room. I lived at the far rear of the third cabin. There was a toilet, sink, and storage area in the far back. The toilet was blocked from view on the right side by a redwood wall as was a stack of deep shelves on the left, but there was a wide opening which I felt was not good aesthetics.

Using a treadle sewing machine, I made long curtains from heavy white cotton that I hung in the opening. The front room had bunk beds. The back room had two tatamis on the floor. During guest season, we'd double up but during practice period, Tommy Dorsey was up front and I was in back. In my spare time, I built a bed from scrap wood on which an old tatami sat within a four-inch fir border on three sides and a twelve inch wide board at the head with a shelf above. The enclosure under the tatami was for storage. I had a pillow and slept in an arctic sleeping bag on the bare tatami. The room also had a small table and a chair.

I followed Suzuki's admonition of rising as soon as I heard the wake-up bell. I'd pee, wash my hands and face, brush my teeth, put on my robe, and go to the front room where Tommy, already in his robe, would have a cup of hot chocolate and a wee cookie on a little table waiting for me. We would drink our hot chocolate, nibble on the cookies, and sit quietly until the clack of the han urged us to get to the zendo.

Tommy kept his room immaculate. He'd sweep mine and tend to the back toilet area, as well, including after I'd done it. He put a vase on the shelf by the sink big enough for a flower or attractive stem and leaves. He did the same for both of our rooms. He'd also rake in front and on the side of the cabin. Tommy worked slowly and methodically. If I seemed to be rushing through something he might say, "You'll get it done just as fast if you slow down."

Sometimes he'd tell me salacious stories of his drag queen days when he was Tommy Dee—"So beautiful you won't believe it" and "The boy that looks like the girl next door." He had a couple of photos and indeed was quite attractive as the girl next door. He started off dancing in night clubs in San Francisco's North Beach in the fifties, and then he and his manager, Mickey, and a couple of other chums involved with his act went on tour. Tommy made extra money selling sex, especially after a show. They'd also make money as small-time grifters, gambling, tricking and wooing drunk male customers out of their money. He said that Alaska was a particularly lucrative market for them.

Tommy had shared an apartment with comedian Lenny Bruce, who introduced him to the joys of shooting heroin, which he continued using habitually for four years. He said twice in New York City he'd been assumed dead from an overdose, his limp body driven to a bridge to be dumped into the East River. He woke up both times before sleeping with the fishes. He said he shot a lot more speed than heroin, and kept up that lifestyle choice for thirteen years. I never shot anything, but I'd taken too much speed when I lived in Mexico in 1965, and the thought of shooting speed all those years made me cringe.

Tommy had been a doorman at the Condor Club in North Beach, famed for Carol Doda's topless show, the first in America. It was the second most popular tourist attraction in San Francisco after the Golden Gate Bridge, so he had a busy demanding job with frequent insults and challenges. Nothing ruffled him. He liked Doda, said she was an artist who studied at the San Francisco Art Institute. Tommy and his gang got a place in the Haight-Ashbury and their tastes turned to psychedelics.

In his room at Tassajara he had a photo on the wall of a benign looking man with very short white hair on his head and face. He had that picture a long time before he found out it was Ramana Maharshi. He still didn't know much of anything about him. Back at the commune in the Haight, Tommy would take LSD and gaze at the photo. When he met Suzuki for the first time, he looked at Suzuki's face and saw the same glow he'd seen with Ramana Maharshi's face. That was all he needed to keep coming.

In 1968, Tommy showed up at Sokoji. He had long hair and came across as fuzzy. I could hardly understand him when he talked. He was the epitome of a drug burnout. He seemed to be a hopeless case, but he was nice and went to zazen. Soon, he moved out of his commune and was living across the street from Sokoji. In 1971, he was clear. He was steady. He was thoughtful. He was a model of steadfastness. Everyone respected him. Dr. Wenner said that watching Tommy evolve in the last three years had changed his mind about what he had thought of as the irreversible damage done by years of hard drugs.

One day, a couple of Hells Angels rode their motorcycles into Tassajara. They were just curious, but as much as I like to relate to everyone, I felt a little nervous and that's not a good sign. I told them I'd get someone to show them around, went to the kitchen where Tommy was the *fukuten*, assistant to the tenzo, and told Frances, the tenzo, that there was a special circumstance Tommy was needed for. She objected, but I just pulled him out, introduced him to our guests, and all was well. I wanted them to feel comfortable and I knew Tommy would be the best host for them.

All they wanted was water and coffee, so I brought that to them at a redwood table in the courtyard. I noticed, then, a bottom patch on their distinctive Hells Angels jackets that read "San Francisco." They were the cool ones, could be found in the Haight and at concerts and blended in fine—as long as you weren't taunting them, as I saw a fellow do at the Human Be-in. They were off to the side minding their own business and he came up and started screaming vulgar insults at them and they knocked the crap out of him. Tommy spent an hour together with our visitors, walked them out, and all was copasetic.

Tommy said that back in his dancing days, as he got older, he came to perform at seedier and grubbier places. One night, he was getting ready to perform in a lowlife dive in the Tenderloin section of San Francisco. He was at rock bottom and so was the venue. "The sort of place," he said, "where I'd see a guy pissing on the floor by the wall backstage." The audience was a dozen drunk, hooting men. The floor smelled of stale beer. The band, a piano, horn, and drum kit, was pathetic. Just before he went out, his manager Mickey told him to do his best, that his parents were in the audience. Tommy hadn't seen them in many years. All he could do was go out and perform his act.

At intermission, he went down to join his conservative Catholic parents, his father a retired navy officer. All dolled up in a flimsy dress and thick makeup, sweating from the heat of the lights, probably not smelling so good, he sat down, smiled, and said hello. His mother shook her head and said, "You know, Tommy, this isn't a very nice place."

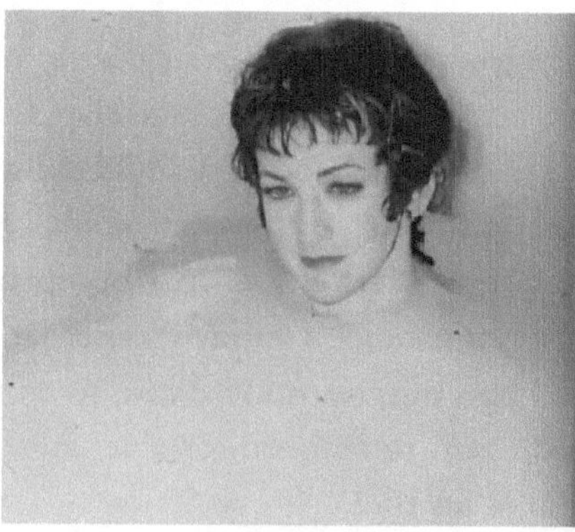

The Freezer

We had no working freezer. Silas had gotten rid of an old bulky rectangular one right off when we got the place. He said it would use too much electricity and it didn't seem like we'd need to freeze anything anyway.

We could have added to the guest season income, though, if we had a little ice cream store. When people came to Tassajara, they'd worry they couldn't do without meat. But it became clear after a while that what they really missed was ice cream—and Coca-Cola—but mainly ice cream. I'd hear students and guests say they'd love to have an ice cream cone about now. Then, one four-and-nine day a couple of years back, Ed Brown drove out early in the morning and returned with an ice cream maker, chunky salt, a bag of ice, cartons of whole milk, and one of whipping cream. We had a wonderful afternoon watching it turn into ice cream, which we enjoyed more than any ice cream we'd ever eaten. After that, once or twice a year there would be an ice cream day.

Robert Beck still kept some stuff he wanted to hold on to, in the front right room in the lower barn. Mainly furniture. Periodically, he'd come and take some of it. One day in 1971, he told me we could have what was left, which included an old square freezer. I was work leader that summer. In an officers' meeting we talked about what to keep and what to give to Goodwill in Salinas. We decided against keeping the freezer. Electricity was too precious, and we needed what we had to keep the walk-in cooler cool.

We'd been warned not to let heavy trucks use the bridge over the small creek. So we loaded the pickup at the lower barn and transferred a load to the six-ton Dodge, which was sitting in the intersection above the zendo. The next item to go was that freezer. There were four of us and it was heavy. We figured five hundred pounds. We got it as far as behind the pickup when the bell to end work and get ready to go to noon service rang.

I said, "OK, let's get this up there so I can get going over the mountain right away after lunch." My fellow students shook their heads saying we could finish at the beginning of afternoon work period—and we needed two more guys anyway. I called out, "We can do it!" as they walked off and left me standing there alone with the freezer.

The pickup bed was about three feet up. I scratched my head. And then Niels happened by. "David Chadowick! What are you doing?"

"I wanted to get this freezer up there on the truck, but everyone stopped working when the bell rang."

"Well why don't you load it?" he said.

"Gee, Niels, sure. And then I'll move the mountain."

"You could do it by yourself. You don't need anybody. You just need leverage. I'd do it for you and let you watch, but I'd rather follow the schedule." And he walked off.

Hmm. Maybe I could do it, I thought. I knew if I didn't, I'd be the victim of his ridicule. I found I could tilt the freezer. I did so and pushed a board under the slightly raised side. Rocked it another direction and slipped a brick under the other side. Just kept doing that sort of thing and it got higher and higher, till it was even with the bed and I pushed it in, right side, left side, right side, left side. It took almost an hour for it to go three feet up and four feet forward. Then, I drove it up to the Dodge, which had a flatbed about a foot higher, and applied the same technique to load the fridge in it.

I was standing on the bed of the Dodge next to the freezer when everyone walked out of the zendo after lunch. I waved to my co-workers who had deserted me. Got some nods and a wave back—but nods and waves as if they didn't see anything unusual. Niels walked up and I proudly extended my arm, palm open, toward the freezer sitting on the truck bed. He berated me for being so slow. It was another moment of glory fizzled.

Alan's Improv

Alan Marlowe was tired of Tatsugami and Tatsugami's seemingly endless formalities and additions to what had been a simple, straightforward practice. He particularly was irritated by the Sanpachi Nenju ceremony, the sole purpose of which, it seemed, was to say that the following day is a four-and-nine day. Sanpachi Nenju was literally "three eight chant."

On three-and-eight days, work would end an hour early. We'd go to the baths, then meet outside the zendo. We were to wear the white tabi socks which Alan said were too prissy. I thought that was awfully inconsistent of Alan considering his own attention to ceremonial detail with Suzuki. He just didn't want to do what Tatsugami was initiating.

Alan stopped attending Tatsugami's lectures, which were happening every other night. Instead, he studied, sitting upright in his chair at a small desk, a lit kerosene lamp to each side, window open to the cold, facing the path in front of the dorm by the bridge, defiant in white T-shirt and shaven head even though Tatsugami said that only monks should shave their heads. Behind Alan, his massive library of books.

During the third and final round of the han, Tatsugami would walk from his cabin to the zendo, behind him Lew Richmond, his jisha, holding a stick of burning incense. Tatsugami would go right past Alan in his illuminated obviousness. He paid no attention to Alan's boycott which continued for the entire practice period.

We were having a rehearsal for the shosan ceremony, wherein each student asks the teacher a question. People were seated on their cushions, Tatsugami on the altar, not yet in his ceremonial robes. Those who were next to ask their questions stood in a line in front of Tatsugami. When it was their turn, the student would walk forward hands in gassho, drop down on their knees on a zabuton, call out "Docho Roshi!" Tatsugami would answer, "Hai!" The student would then just say, "Thank you very much," skipping the question and answer, stand, make a standing bow, and slowly return to their seat with hands in shashu, joined at the solar plexus. When it was Alan's turn, he called out, "Docho Roshi!" in his best theatrical voice. Tatsugami responded, "Hai!" Alan paused, and then with enormous volume and force, screamed out, "Pigggg fuckerrrrrrrrrrrrrr!"—loud enough to seem to reverberate beyond our valley, almost uproot trees on the slopes, frighten birds to fly off, rodents to descend into their burrows. Tatsugami turned to Katagiri, who was sitting next to him and muttered, "Nani?" (What?). Katagiri shook his head as if to say, it's nothing. The ceremony rehearsal continued with all of us much more awake, some perturbed with Alan, some grateful.

Throwing Away

Tatsugami's lectures might have been long and often boring, but we learned a great deal from them in time, especially when Ryogen Yoshimura did the translating. In retrospect, I realized he got through to me in ways I didn't expect. Points he made would crop up in my thoughts and I'd nod and go, *Thanks, Tats.* For instance:

> In the *Fukanzazengi,* Dogen Zenji asks: "How do you think the unthinkable?" Dogen himself answers, saying that you should throw away everything. This means that you should go directly forward, without looking backwards or forwards, towards the left or towards the right. What will happen if you plunge into doing something, eliminating everything? Dogen Zenji states that no matter what you are doing, throwing away everything should be the basic attitude towards life.

Six Paramitas

Paul Shippee returned to Tassajara in early January, a few days before the practice period started, so he'd have plenty of free time to read. He had always been attracted to books that helped him delve into what everything was all about. College was all about science, but even then he'd been attracted to a book called *Hinduism and*

Buddhism by A.K. Coomaraswamy. He still had that book on his bookshelf at Tassajara.

His first year in San Francisco, 1959, he'd read Kerouac's *On the Road* and *The Dharma Bums*. After he was introduced to zazen at Sokoji, he asked Gary Snyder, newly returned from Japan, for advice. Snyder told him don't just sit—read about Buddhism. He suggested Paul start with *Buddhism: Its Essence and Development* by Edward Conze.

At Tassajara, Paul read books from the library about Tibetan Buddhism. He was reading *The Life and Teachings of Naropa* when his cabinmate Van returned and said he'd brought a tape of a lecture Chogyam Trungpa had given. He asked Paul if he'd like to hear it. Paul said he wasn't interested.

He'd recently gone to a talk by Trungpa at the City Center in the Buddha Hall. It was so crowded, he had to sit in the back by the doorway. After the talk there were questions and Paul's hand went up. Trungpa called on him. The question and answer weren't important. The talk didn't interest him that much either. But the way Trungpa answered his question struck him. He felt an intimacy, like an old friend was speaking to him. He wasn't looking for a new teacher, though, and didn't feel a need to hear another Trungpa talk.

Paul continued his readings about Tibetan Buddhism during the morning study periods and breaks. He and Van had adjoining rooms with a shared toilet and sink in the back. One day, toward the end of the practice period, on the way to the toilet Paul passed by Van's desk with that Trungpa tape on top and noticed the word *paramitas*. He looked closer. It was a Trungpa lecture on the six paramitas. Paul had read several books about the paramitas that intrigued him. They weren't good reading, but they left him wanting to know more. He knew what they were at least superficially—the six perfections or transcendent virtues, the heart of a Bodhisattva's practice—*dana*-giving, *sila*-morality, *ksanti*-patience, *virya*-effort, *dhyana*-meditation, *prajna*-wisdom—wisdom enshrined in the voluminous Prajna Paramita Sutra and the heart of it which we chanted every day.

"I'm going to listen to that tape," he said aloud. He borrowed a battery-operated tape recorder and the next morning during study he started listening to it. There was a tap on his shoulder. He stopped the tape recorder and looked around, and there was the tenken saying, "You need to be in the study hall."

"I'm studying here today," Paul said.

"No, you can't do that, you have to go to the study hall."

Paul said, "Well, I have to listen to a tape. That's what I'm studying. I can't listen to the tape in the study hall."

"It doesn't matter. You have to go to study hall."

Paul looked up at him and said strongly, "Look, I'm not going. Leave me alone." The tenken left and Paul returned to Trungpa's lecture.

The next time they saw each other, Van asked Paul how he liked Trungpa's lecture. Paul said, "I was blown away. The way he explained the six paramitas was crystal clear to me. It was like he had learned the American idiom. He knew how to talk to us. The way he explained the six paramitas was something I felt like I could actually relate to as a practice and understanding and really make it mine."

Paul was in a dilemma. He'd been considering becoming a priest so he could give back to the Zen community the gifts he'd been given. But now he was thinking of doing something different. He sat down and wrote Trungpa a letter asking if it was OK for a Zen student to become his student.

The seven-day sesshin with Tatsugami was over and the closing ceremony was coming up. Paul was packing his belongings. He never got an answer from Trungpa, but he knew Trungpa was back in the Bay Area. He decided he'd go find him. Trungpa had been staying in the Bay Area with Paul's friend Henry Schaeffer. The next practice period wouldn't be till mid-September.

He thought about how wonderful the practice at Tassajara had been. He was disappointed in how cold and distant so many people were, but he'd not come to socialize. He came to meditate, and meditate he had. He remembered the sunlight that had awakened him and Suzuki's response with no fuss or philosophy. "He just told me that a bird singing wakes him up," Paul mused.

He thought back to his original encounter with Suzuki—watching him sit so still, then laugh so openly, so full of humanity. Paul could see that going to Suzuki's lecture that night had set him firmly on the path. He thought, "Whatever that man had, I had been looking for that all my life—and I didn't really know it. I found it when I saw him. When I landed on the cushion, I found my way. I dropped out of everything I was doing and landed in the lap of Suzuki Roshi."

As Paul drove his truck out the gate, he felt a great sadness and didn't know why. And then it fell on him like rain, and he intuitively knew he would not return to Tassajara.

New Kitchen MARCH

The large, wonderful stone-walled kitchen was finally finished and in use. A long, wide sycamore slab in the center of the room provided a generous amount of workspace. The Wolf gas range now had a partner. The griddle top had been moved there, as well. Both old gas refrigerators were in a corner. Ed Brown had designed shelving and worked with Paul Discoe on the design and needs of the various areas. There was a generous space for washing pots and pans and another with a sink on the other side just for washing vegetables. There was plenty of room now for guest and student meals to be prepared, bread baked, pots and pans washed and set on drying racks. There was an altar at the end of the workbench, a small, high table-desk with a stool, even a little area for student snack food, once forbidden. The shack we'd been preparing meals out of was now a good-sized pantry and the county health inspector wouldn't have to say once again, "Let's not go to the kitchen."

Tatsugami had told us there should be no flesh of animals in a Buddhist temple and finally we heeded him. So from this new kitchen there would be no meat or fish prepared and served. For the first time, we were vegetarian for guests as well as students—lacto-ovo vegetarian with dairy and eggs included in the diet.

The kitchen done, Paul and Ruthie left for Japan in March 1971. Paul had learned they were going a half year earlier when someone said Suzuki brought it up in a meeting. In Japan, he'd study Zen and temple carpentry. Before he left, he and Niels finished the area adjoining the kitchen and the zendo where they created an alcove with a library above. Then, the meal servers could carry food straight from the kitchen to the zendo without getting wet if it rained.

I would no longer hear Paul and Niels arguing up there as I walked by. They were both sure of themselves and neither would back down. I didn't know what they were arguing about, but it also didn't matter. They produced a beautiful kitchen and library.

Meanwhile, Marc Alexander worked silently beside them toward the end of the job. He came to Zen Center soft-spoken, focused, and good at detail. At break time he could be found doing fine woodwork up in the shop where he made a superb hardwood chest of drawers. He did a few finished pieces that were pure works of art. One was a foot-and-a-half long, twisted branch of madrone, that had five squared sides finely finished. He handed me a curious piece he'd done from a manzanita burl. It must have started off roughly shaped like a softball but it had no roundness left to it. There were a number of flat sides all about the same size. I asked a geometry teacher what that would be called. He said it depended on the number of sides. Since we didn't know, he said it was a polyhedron.

Blanche and Lew's teenage daughter Trudy, happy to be in the new kitchen, did not miss the old one or some of the other aspects of summer practice there. "We prepared three meals in that old kitchen with those two little fridges, and three hot stoves. It was stifling. The evening gruel made with leftovers that we served was awful. We sat in the zendo in junky thin gray robes drenched in sweat. At the end of the summer there was a sesshin. During some of the kinhin intervals between zazen periods, Cheryl and I would go down to the creek, take off our robes, go in naked, and get back to the zendo in time."

Moon Food

In 1968, Joanna Bull had gone to bed at Woodstock, New York, in the home of Albert Grossman, Bob Dylan's manager. Lying there, she saw a man in knickers and a plaid worker's shirt standing on the other side of the door to the room—a door that was closed. She had never looked through a door before, didn't think it was possible. She got out of bed, and as she approached the door, he disappeared.

The following morning, she told Albert's wife, Sally, what she saw. Sally said that was Knickers, who built this home back in the early nineteenth century. She added that Albert's father slept in that room with a gun by the bed. Joanna couldn't see what a gun would have helped, and anyway, Knickers wasn't hostile. Just standing there, on the other side of the door. As a result of this experience, "It occurred to me," she said, "that there could be ways that we perceive what we don't understand at all in this great, amazing, miraculous thing that we're swimming around in."

She went to a nearby bookstore and got *In Search of the Miraculous* by P.D. Ouspensky. She thought, *That's what I must be looking for,* but upon reading it, decided it was not. She thought it odd that he wrote that we were food for the moon. She was going to visit her family in Chicago, went to a travel agent to get a ticket, and in the course of their conversation, told him about her search. He said, "Don't waste your time, just read Zen." So she went back to the bookstore and got Alan Watts's *The Spirit of Zen.*

"I was living in this little cabin in the woods when I started to read about Zen Buddhism and I ran out into the snow and leaped about in joy, pure joy. I kept reading. And I started to sit." Right away, she had figured out that to get to the bottom of her search, she needed to meditate.

Joanna heard about Shunryu Suzuki and the San Francisco Zen Center with its Tassajara monastery. She wrote Suzuki a letter that fervently told him why she wanted to come and what it meant to her. She got no reply. So she took a bus across the country. She didn't want to fly. It was a pilgrimage. Arriving in San Francisco, she went from the bus station to Sokoji and met Suzuki. He hadn't seen her letter. "He was extremely preoccupied, almost as if I was barely there, didn't have much to say to me and I left it at that." There was no room in the apartments across the street, so she went to the Berkeley Zen Center, and from there would go to Sokoji for lectures and the Saturday program.

After six months, Joanna was with a group of students on their way to Tassajara. "It was treacherous going up and down that road, but it's part of the adventure. We were met by wonderful people with some hot soup and bread, and they were so loving and caring and welcoming to us."

The next morning she met Tommy Dorsey. He asked her why she'd come, and she said, "To get enlightened, of course." Tommy laughed and said, "Well, you'll get over that."

Joanna started off in the kitchen but that didn't work out, so by mutual agreement, she was moved to the garden. She planted pine trees with Frances on the mountainside. "And when the guests were there, I made sure that the cabins were all ready for them, that everything was clean, and that there were sweet flowers for everybody."

"One day working in the garden with Frances, when she was across the garden, maybe seventy-five feet away, all of a sudden, I was inside her mind. There was no distance between her mind and mine. I was just there and she was there and there was no space between us."

Joanna didn't have a lot of friends, but she loved Dianne and Ruthie, who she planted trees with. But Stan, she said, was always mean to her. She didn't know why, but she let it go. He was older than she was, but she was older than most people there, and had become a pretty solid person before she first heard about Zen. She'd been married to Donald Levine, a sociologist well-known for his Ethiopian scholarship. They lived for years in Ethiopia and were close with Haile Selassie, the emperor who became, for reasons unknown to him, a sort of patron saint of the Rastafarians.

At the end of the fall 1969 practice period, she sat the Rohatsu Sesshin. "I was sitting in the zendo and the pain in my legs was just absolutely terrible. I sat with it and sat with it and sat with it. At a certain point, sitting with all that stuff, I suddenly thought to myself, *There is nothing left of me but the pain in my legs.* And the second I said that, the pain in my legs disappeared."

In the shosan ceremony on the last day of sesshin, Joanne told Suzuki what happened to her and he said, "You're further along than you think you are."

"I learned," she said, "that Suzuki's attitude toward some special experience was. *That was nice, now go back and sit*—which I also knew did not mean just to sit."

Joanna was lying on her tatami in her room in the dorm above the dining room "and the moon was blasting in. I had the most uncanny feeling. It was as if it was going to devour me. I thought, *Well, it looks like maybe Ouspensky knew what he was talking about, but this is not something that I'm here to get into and explore. It's not my path.*" So she turned over and went to sleep.

"I didn't need to be close to Suzuki Roshi. He kept saying, 'Just follow the practice,' so I stayed out of the political and social stuff and kept to the deeper dharmic level. I was content with that."

The next practice period was the first one led by Tatsugami, and Joanna felt like she'd gone from heaven to hell. But she was determined to focus on practice and not her preferences. "I wasn't comfortable with him. I didn't have the same feeling with him or for him as I did with Suzuki. I was not a happy camper as I sat in the zendo, but I sat there and did the practice. I got up and did everything I was supposed to do. When he left, I said to him sincerely and spontaneously that I was grateful."

Joanna stayed until the summer of '71 when she left to begin the path of becoming a psychoanalyst.

"At my last meeting with Suzuki Roshi in dokusan, I expressed great gratitude and thanked him for the teachings, and as he smiled at me benevolently his face broke up into pieces, turned into this mass of moving particles, was completely shifting and changing.

I just watched it and thought that this was telling me something about what reality was. That's how I learned that the table in front of me may look solid, but it really isn't."

Emma Bragdon

After graduating from high school, Emma Bragdon spent a year abroad before attending college. She went to Germany where she studied ceramic sculpture. She met a young student of psychology, Jorg, in Munich who introduced her to meditation. Within a few minutes she had a blissful experience and right away she knew that meditation would become the cornerstone of her life.

Jorg introduced her to his teacher, the psychotherapist Karlfried Graf Durckheim, author of *Hara: The Vital Center of Man,* also a Zen teacher of meditation who ran a retreat center in Germany.

Upon returning to America, Emma discovered that her mother's sister, Aunt Harriet, was involved with the Rochester Zen Center, indeed, had been part of Chester and Doris Carlson's meditation group, responsible for inviting Philip Kapleau there as their teacher. Sitting with them in Rochester was her first formal experience of zazen—along with the formality and rules. Inspired, she started a small meditation group at Bard College, during her first year there as a student.

A couple years later she moved to California after being invited to be a teaching assistant in ceramic sculpture at the University of California, and studying at Davis and in Berkeley. She visited the Berkeley Zen Center, began siting zazen there, and met personally with Mel Weitsman. She was questioning her next steps in life, so Mel suggested she go to Tassajara for a weekend.

Shortly after arriving at Tassajara, Emma didn't want to leave. She felt like it was the home she'd been looking for all her life. So, in the summer of 1967 she went to Tassajara for a long stay. She got right into the practice, completed a five-day tangaryo, and was happy being with like-minded people during a practice period. A high point for her was when she was asked to be an attendant for Anagarika and Li Gotami Govinda. She felt that Lama Govinda, as he was called, was a living example of the embodiment of wisdom and compassion.

Emma had some extradonary experiences while at Tassajara. One day during early morning study, a student stood up to make an announcement and suddenly she could see right through him as if his body had vanished into thin air. She could see the tables and chairs behind him. And then he appeared to her again. It was a glimpse of the world of light that took her briefly out of Plato's cave. One night, on her way to her cabin after evening zazen, she was struck by a deafening roar that was unlike any normal sound. She felt like her whole body had become an eardrum and heard dimensions of sound previously unknown to her. She was frightened, but knew she had to deal with the fear. She also knew she needed help to learn how to manage these powerful, non-ordinary experiences that were initially disorienting.

After leaving Tassajara, she was encouraged to try LSD once, by a close friend whom she trusted. She reconnected to a source of profound wisdom that felt very familiar. Truth seemed so obvious, she wondered, *Why can't all people just see it?* Coming down from the trip was a disturbing return to the small world of fears and doubts, of daily concerns. She wondered how the two could be balanced—or does our innate wisdom have to be suppressed so we can function in normal reality?

Emma felt like her continuing zazen practice, going to Suzuki's lectures, meeting other priests, the Zen Center community, and the books she was reading—such as Carlos Castaneda's—were helping her to balance the two worlds, the ordinary and the extraordinary. But she also sought more help. Why had she been shaking uncontrollably in zazen—Was it unresolved emotional issues? She turned to a Neo-Reichian therapist and uncovered deeply held emotions of grief, and anger, and suppressed trauma. The release was important for her to reclaim her full emotional self so she continued the therapy and meditation at the same time.

About 1969, she met Harry Roberts, a Yurok Indian shaman. She became his student. Tim Buckley also became a student of Harry at the same time. When Tim and Emma married in October 1970, Katagiri married them at Richard Hieb's property on a bluff overlooking the Russian River's entry into the Pacific Ocean. Later that day, Harry Roberts performed a private marriage ceremony for them as well. In 1963, Richard Hieb had offered some of his land to Zen Center for their country retreat. He was a well-known potter who had studied with Hamada in Japan. The wedding party was held in his outdoor pottery studio surrounded by his native plant garden.

There were many who came for the wedding from the Berkeley Zen Center, the City Center, and Tassajara. A band played and people danced. Harry Roberts smoked salmon above alder chips he'd specially selected and brought in. A feast was spread out on Hieb's pottery tables.

Emma's blueblood family, as she called them, came from the East Coast, including her father and her mother, Marge. Emma had taught meditation to her mother and Marge had been at Tassajara as a student in the summer of 1969. It was a happy time for Emma. All her worlds came together.

After being married Emma and Tim lived in an apartment in Noe Valley in San Francisco. He did carpentry. She did bookkeeping for Alaya Stitchery, a business which arose out of the Zen Center community, selling zafus, zabutons, and loose clothing for sitting zazen. They continued their Zen practice. When she became pregnant, she began practicing hatha yoga in preparation for natural childbirth.

An Unexpected Death

Peter and Jane went to the East Coast and were living on Chappaquiddick Island near the famous bridge. Peter was working on editing the Sandokai lectures Suzuki had given at Tassajara the previous summer—maybe for a book. Suzuki was happy for them to be there because there were good friends of Zen Center in New England, especially those Yvonne called "the East Coast ladies," who were well established in those parts and not inclined to move west.

Suzuki hadn't been to Tassajara for almost a year. He was in Japan the last part of 1970, and then he'd had his gall bladder removed in mid-March and it took him three months to recover. He'd been giving lectures in the city for a month. On July 7, 1971, as he was about to leave the city for Tassajara, there was tragic news. Marge Bragdon had unexpectedly died.

Emma and Tim were soon on a plane to Vermont. Peter and Jane received a call from Yvonne, took a ferry to the mainland, and hitchhiked to Vermont from there. The family asked Suzuki to come spend time with them and do the funeral. Jay later told Peter how comforting Suzuki's presence was.

June McKnight invited Peter and Jane to stay nearby her on her property, and they did. First, in a large barn made over as a holiday house, and then in Emma's mother's house, adjacent to June's property.

At Tassajara, we had a service for Marge Bragdon. There was one at the City Center, as well. I remembered her from an earlier summer when she'd come and practiced with us, not just as a mother of a student.

On July 20th, Suzuki arrived at Tassajara. That evening, he gave a lecture. In it he said:

> If you lose your friend, then you feel very lonely
> because you think as long as your friend is alive,

> she is with you, which is material or physical. But after your friend dies, she changes into a spiritual being, leaving her physical body behind. People may call it soul or spirit, but that is not our understanding. We don't know the other side which is not possible to understand. But even though we do not understand, we cannot deny things which are not understandable by our small mind.

Inner Sound

After the practice period, Bob Walter and Alan Rabold left Tassajara to do sesshins with other teachers. They sat a weeklong sesshin with Maezumi in L.A. and then did one with Chinese Zen master Hsuan Hua at his Gold Mountain Monastery in San Francisco. Monks there gave them the idea to do a hundred-day sesshin, which they did at Fil Lewitt's Big River Farm in Mendocino. The general attitude at Zen Center was that this was not Suzuki Roshi's way. That was true. Suzuki encouraged daily sitting and said one or two sesshin a year was enough.

"I returned to the City Center in early June," Bob told me, "and said I wanted to talk to Suzuki Roshi. I was told I was not a real student, so I was way down on the list." And the list was long. Suzuki had just recovered from his gall bladder operation of mid-March and another flu.

"I was working in the building," Bob said, "and had to go to the Suzukis' apartment and ask some question. Suzuki stuck his head out after I had rung the bell and said, 'Just a minute.' Then he returned and asked with visible excitement, 'How was it?' I said, 'I'll tell you when I see you,' and bowed. When I did see him and tell him about it, he was totally supportive.

"I told him about the inner sound that I was experiencing, and he said that yes that was enlightenment and I'd taken good care of myself and now I had to take care of everything. I said, 'What do you mean by that?' and he picked up a pencil on his table and said, 'You have to take care of this,' and he picked up something else and said, 'and this,' and he kept picking up things and saying that. My interpretation was that he was saying you have to take care of all sentient beings."

Now, Bob was back at Tassajara. Suzuki was there, too. Bob saw that Suzuki was giving everything he had and could feel a sense of urgency. Bob wanted to go to L.A. for a week to join Soen Nakagawa in a sesshin. He went to see Suzuki about leaving for the sesshin with the idea in mind that there's nothing Suzuki could do to stop him. Suzuki said, "The reason you're not going to the sesshin is that you're my student now and when I die you can be Soen's student." Bob walked out stunned. No way was he going to that sesshin. He felt good about it.

Katagiri Agrees

Tatsugami thought that he would be the abbot of Tassajara for life, but he wasn't invited back after his third tour in the spring of 1971. It wasn't because he wasn't appreciated. It wasn't planned, rather just the result of an unexpected unfolding of events.

Katagiri had resigned from Zen Center and planned to move to Monterey to live with a few students in a large house there. It was an unexpected blow to Suzuki, and to so many of us who considered him one of our teachers, someone we could count on. But we'd taken him for granted. Suzuki had, too. Mitsu said Katagiri's resignation was so upsetting to her husband, she was afraid it would kill him. But Katagiri wanted to establish his own lineage, not just serve Suzuki's.

At a board meeting at Tassajara, each member, including me, told Katagiri how important he was to each of us as a teacher and friend, and asked him to please stay with us. Then, Suzuki asked him to lead the fall practice period instead of Tatsugami. He said he'd write Tatsugami and uninvite him. Katagiri accepted on the condition that

Suzuki help him lead it. Suzuki agreed. In the span of one minute, Tatsugami was gone and Katagiri was back—at least for a while.

When Paul and Ruthie's son Benjamin was just a little baby, Paul took a photo of Suzuki holding him while standing next to Tatsugami. Looking at the photo Suzuki said, "I'm the mother and he's the father." Paul liked Tatsugami and thought he did what Suzuki wanted him to do. The way he saw it, Suzuki set the whole thing up with himself playing the female role and Tatsugami the male role. "But you know," Paul added, "Japanese women control everything anyway."

Carpenter Bees

When the Becks owned Tassajara, they gave kids badminton racquets and paid them a nickel for every carpenter bee they killed. We screened the large creek-side opening in the loft of the lower barn while preparing it to house short-term students in the summer. The next day, the floor under the screened-in opening was strewn with dead carpenter bees that couldn't get out.

I was standing on the bridge over the small creek when my eye was caught by the post on the corner of the deck outside the dining room. I went down and examined it. It was only a 4 x 4 and it had a lot of responsibility for keeping that deck up. I looked at the other supports for the deck. They seemed awfully minimal. So I decided to take this on. I was the work leader, which meant I had nothing in particular to do, and it was interim. I wanted to get it done before the guest season.

The next day, I put up signs to stay off the deck while it was being worked on. I set a couple of long 2 x 4s to hold up the back corner of the deck before the 4x4 post was removed which I did using a Sawzall. When I removed the corner post, it felt so light. I put one end on a stone and stepped on it hard in the middle. It broke in two revealing five carpenter bee holes almost the size of my little finger running down its length.

A few days later, the deck to the dining room was supported by a ten-foot long, 8 x 8 corner post I'd found in our scrap wood stash. It sat in a concrete footing bolted to a steel fixture called a concrete sleeve. Another post was replaced, 1 x 4s were nailed between the posts for shear strength. Below the deck under the near side of the dining room was a supporting stone wall built on the slope to the small creek. I placed a beam behind an opening in that wall and ran from it a couple of cables to ensure the deck couldn't pull away from the building.

Finished. Secure. Still, I had disturbing thoughts of all the times that deck had been full of guests and students.

A Shining

Ron Leyva sat sesshins with Yasutani, Soen, and Maezumi for a few years before he came to Tassajara in the summer of '70 and washed guest dishes. He returned in January for the winter-spring practice period and stayed for the interim and guest season. He was a swarthy, solid, quiet young guy.

Ron stopped me on the path between the dorm and the kitchen one afternoon. He said something had happened. He had to tell someone and decided on me.

"OK."

"Now, I'm a matter of fact type guy, wouldn't you say?"

"Yep."

"Well, something happened last night that I wouldn't blame you for not believing."

"Try me."

He was jikido, zendo cleaner for the day, who slept there the night before and lit the place up in the morning. Every once in a while, a jikido would oversleep and that's what Ron thought had happened when he was awakened by light shining through the zendo windows. Thinking someone else was putting the lanterns out for him, he jumped out of his sleeping bag, slipped on his pants, rushed out the doorway, turned toward the path and stopped abruptly.

The light was not coming from lanterns. It came from across the path by the han and densho bell not twenty feet away. What he saw was a brightness with oval form hovering a few feet above the ground. It was about the size of a human body, but there was no body, just light, that illuminated the surrounding area. In the immediate vicinity he could see details in the bricks, stones, wood, leaves. He could see his hands and feet. He knew he wasn't dreaming. He stood and looked on. He said it was not normal earthly light. He was not afraid, sensed a benign presence, a bright, silent presence that after a while began to dim. Details faded. It dimmed and dimmed until Ron was standing in total darkness.

"What did you do, then?" I asked after a pause that I needed to take it in.

"I went back into the zendo and looked at the alarm clock. It was still too early to do anything, so I went back to sleep."

The Librarian

On the trip to Texas the prior December, we stopped in Jerome, Arizona, a once populous copper mining town promoted as a historic ghost town for tourists. I bought a picture postcard with "Jerome" printed in large script over a photo of some nineteenth-century buildings and sent it to Jerome Peterson at the City Center with the message "Greetings from Jerome to Jerome."

When I was first around Zen Center, Jerome was a fixture at the scene, a quiet one. I'd walk there in the early morning darkness and he'd be standing reading a paperback under a light in the Bush and Laguna corner entry-way alcove to the Toyo Market. Before entering the zendo, almost everyone quickly slid their sandals off and put them on the rack. Jerome untied the strings on his shiny black shoes.

One morning at Sokoji, I had to leave before service. I had use of Tim Buckley's Volvo. Jerome asked if I could drive him home. Sure. He lived at the little Crown Hotel right by the Mission Dolores. He managed it, and had since 1962, the year he arrived in San Francisco and found the Zen Center. He started work at seven in the morning.

As an eager new student, I naturally asked him about Suzuki and Zen Center and Zen. He sure didn't try to encourage me. He said he'd watch people come and go, that after two years ninety percent would leave, not enough happening there to keep their interest. That was a bummer. I asked him why he stayed, and he said there was enough there to hold his interest. He said he felt at home as soon as he arrived on a Sunday in time for Suzuki's lecture and Della and Betty were handing out apples at the door, gifts from a farmer in the Japanese American congregation. He said that he felt more comfortable doing zazen than anything he'd ever done, that it just seemed natural.

I didn't see him socializing ever. He just came and went from Sokoji without a word. But he was easy to talk with—no airs, direct. I asked if he had any advice for me as a new student.

"Buddha, dharma, sangha," he said.

"What's buddha?"

"Big mind."

"What's dharma?"

"Look into it."

"OK. Can you tell me anything about Suzuki Roshi?"

He said Suzuki was into graphology, that he had people write their name down in a book when they came for dokusan. I asked, "Don't you just think he was trying to remember their names?"

"He wanted to see what their writing looked like."

"So what's his teaching?"

"Beginner's Mind."

"Anything else?"

"Stick around."

"You mean if I stick around I'll find out?'

"His teaching is *stick around.*"

"I see," I said. "Don't give up too quick. Yes. In a lecture he said, 'Give me two years.' Like practice with him for two years before giving up." Jerome was quiet. "Come on. Just a little bit more."

"At first, Suzuki seemed just like a regular person, nothing out of the ordinary."

"And now?" I asked.

"He's not pretentious."

Neither was Jerome. He was another Minnesotan, tall, gangly, awkward at times. He would periodically grimace and stretch his arms out like Ed Norton on *The Honeymooners.* I saw little kids in Lily Alley behind the City Center run away when they saw Jerome coming toward them. I called him Zen Center's Frankenstein. He was a misfit who hadn't felt at home anywhere till he came to Zen Center. Even there, he was eccentric and somewhat discriminated against in subtle ways as happens in any group. He'd lumber slowly around—but he showed up on time.

In 1970, Jerome finally made it to live at Tassajara. He was the librarian, as he'd been at the City Center. He'd in fact been a librarian in El Paso before going to California. At Tassajara, he helped newer students figure out what to read. He was generous with his time. His matter-of-fact way of speaking and lack of pomp were endearing. He didn't try to be close to Suzuki. He didn't have that hungry, driven vibe a lot of people had.

In the diminutive Tassajara library one day I reminded him what he said back in '66 about how people come and go and said there were a lot of them staying now.

"Tassajara," he said.

"And then the City Center," I added. "You said there wasn't enough for them to get involved with. Now there's lots."

"Hippies and Baker," he said.

"Baker with a little help from his friends," I said. "He was in Japan when the Page Street building was bought."

"He got the ball rolling."

Some of the oldest students bemoaned the loss of intimacy with Suzuki as a result of Zen Center's expansion. They missed the days when they could have breakfast with him and Mitsu. Suzuki himself said Zen Center had gotten too big. Jerome said Suzuki started saying that when we got the new building in '69. I asked him how he felt about losing the good old days. "When they're gone," he said, "you continue without them."

One day, I went into the Tassajara library to return a book. "Jerome, I'm a slow reader," I said. "Save me the trouble and just tell me what's it all about."

"I have a peculiar way of looking at Buddhism," he said. "It's the development of identity—on a personal basis—whatever your identity is. It's never solved but always there—you're always seeking. Some people don't know this. But that's what you're really trying to do."

I'd never heard it said that way. But "Who am I?" is the original koan, going way back in India, where there were gurus who said just keep asking that.

Books and Books

There were plenty of copies of *Zen Mind, Beginner's Mind* in the cabins and for sale in the office. *The Three Pillars of Zen* by Philip Kapleau was also always around. The books in students' rooms and hands, though, were not limited to Zen.

Chogyam Trungpa's *Meditation in Action* was very popular, as were works on Tibetan Buddhism such as *The Life of Milarepa: Tibet's Great Yogi. Magic and Mystery in Tibet* by Alexandra David-Neel, published in 1929, was fascinating, and so was she. People liked Lobsang Rampa's *The Third Eye*, but took it as fascinating fiction—even though he didn't. Some were turned on to Bubba Free John's *The Knee of Listening*, and others praised Yogananda's classic *The Autobiography of a Yogi.*

There were probably more books lying around by Gary Snyder than anyone else—his *Cold Mountain Poems* and *Earth House Hold,* among others. Snyder's *Smokey the Bear Sutra* poster was on the wall in the office. It proclaimed, "those who recite this sutra ... will enter the age of harmony of man and nature ... will always have ripened blackberries to eat and a sunny spot under a pine tree."

Early in 1971, a book came out named *The Recorded Sayings of Layman Pang*, translated by Ruth Fuller Sasaki, Yoshitaka Iriya, and Dana Fraser. It was popular reading at Zen Center. Pang was a layman but he, his wife, and daughter had practice stricter than most monks. Layman Pang lived in the eighth and ninth centuries. The stories and sayings were such a relief after some of the more complicated dharma we'd been consuming. "Ordinary mind is the Buddha." "My miraculous power: drawing water, chopping wood."

The previous summer, Dana Fraser had spent a week at Tassajara as a student and given a talk about his experience studying Zen in Japan. He said what they called a Zen man in Japan we called a gentleman. I eagerly listened to what he had to say about his time in Japan. He'd gone in 1964 and spent a year at a Rinzai temple named Shokokuji in Kyoto. The meals there consisted of white rice, pickles, overcooked vegetables from the garden, and thin miso soup. The monks in the temple did takuhatsu begging and would eat well from food offerings on those excursions, but Dana wasn't a monk and didn't join them so he was expected to supplement his diet when he went out for Japanese lessons. But he didn't and got weak, became jaundiced. To avoid an early death, he moved out of the temple and only went there to do sesshin and work on koans and drink tea with the abbot, Kajitani Sonin.

Dana had a hard time. He said that Irmgard Schloegl, a German woman with an English passport, had been a great help to him that year. She was involved with Ruth Fuller Sasaki at Daitokuji. Dana worked with Sasaki on translating until she died. Then he worked with Yoshitaka Iriya to bring Layman Pang to completion and get it published. While at Tassajara, Dana heard Suzuki give a lecture and visited with him. He said, "Suzuki Roshi was a spiritual friend. My roshi was the same. We met for tea, we talked about the weather."

Jacob Needleman was a professor of philosophy at San Francisco State. His book, *The New Religions*, had come out the prior year. He'd come to Tassajara the first summer and was back again in '71. I told him we had a copy of his book in our library and that there were some in students' private libraries. I said that Tassajara was crawling with Harvard grads like him, and that Richard seemed to be partial to them. But since Richard was in Japan, he'd get no preferential treatment.

There was a chapter in his book on the San Francisco Zen Center, and a section of that chapter on Tassajara. He noted that Suzuki's Zen Center brought something unexpected to the Western Zen scene in that when people came anticipating drama, koans, existential warfare, they were told just to sit. Needleman called Zen Mountain Center "the center of gravity of Zen practice in America, and, perhaps, the whole Western world," and added that the practice there was "not a flight from society but to society." He wrote, "The power of thought itself is wretchedly inept without exposure to a spiritual discipline," and quoted Shunryu Suzuki as saying, "When we say kill the thinking mind, we mean to be free from its authority."

In 1970, a student named Jonathan Altman brought us a box made from heavy card stock. It was about twelve inches square. "From Bindu to Ojas" was written across each edge of the cover so that all four faced a colorful mandala on the face. It was signed "Namaste, Ram Dass." The cover was side-bound with cord ties. Inside was a tall book with the same title, *From Bindu to Ojas*. Jonathan said from bindu to ojas meant from subtle seed to vital essence. It was printed on fine rice paper and hand-stitched with heavy thread for binding. There were two other thin books inside—*Cookbook for a Sacred Life* and *Painted Cakes Do Not Satisfy Hunger*. There were loose sheets with mandalas and spiritual images, and an LP record with Hindu chanting.

In the summer of 1971 we received a pre-publication copy of a book made from those ingredients. It was called *Be Here Now*, scheduled to be published in October. It was published by the Lama

Foundation of which Jonathan Altman had been a co-founder. The book told Richard Alpert's journey from psychology to LSD to finding his guru, Neem Karoli Baba, in India. Following was a free-flowing, hand-lettered eclectic guide to a spiritual life decorated with drawings and aphorisms. There was a section on Tassajara with photos of Suzuki and Baker. An amazing trippy book.

Not everyone who wrote about us had a sense of the Perennial Philosophy or was complimentary about our precious baby monastery. Back in '67, a couple came in one afternoon, looked around, and talked to me. Later, I came across a small pocketbook they'd put out on the evils of meditation groups, which mentioned that before falling into the clutches of the Zen cult, I'd been with the left-wing radical Students for a Democratic Society. I proudly placed the book with the few others I kept.

In '71, some guests left a book behind in their room: *New Gods in America*, by Peter Rowley. It had a chapter in it on Tassajara. After reading a bit, I realized it was written by an ornery guest who'd come a couple years before. What he wrote about Tassajara was three pages of nasty. It's "called Zen Mountain Center but it's not on a mountain." It's an "ex-health resort-camp. I was reminded of a mixture of Tobacco Road, hippiedom, and Zen. Which element was triumphing seemed uncertain. The road was torturous, the accommodations were overpriced." He wrote he was mocked for paying so much by a person in the office. "The baths smelled like excrement, the mountainsides were parched, there were thick swarms of flies. The electricity didn't work so people had to use kerosene lamps."

How about this excerpt? "Have some more spaghetti and meatballs, said the young Zen student mockingly to my wife, lifting some limp cold strands with a fork from the side of the jar. Opposite us another student was flirting with a very young girl about nine years old who had long flaxen hair." I never realized before how snide and evil we were.

Here's how deep he dug with Amy and Lew Richmond, who supposedly used the word "Zen" in a novel way: "'We have come closer together since starting Zen,' said Amy, who had expressive eyes. Lewis said, 'We will probably stay in Zen for the rest of our lives, but it is uncertain. This is a new thing we are developing here.'"

Rowley's only positive comment was for Stan White. "Having just passed by the trash dump fifty yards from the camp, I was approached by the Zen master, a tiny smiling man, and the guest master, Stan White, a charming middle-aged man. 'Master Suzuki can see you after all today,' Stan told me. We agreed on a different price. Master Suzuki Roshi was an elderly man who used a Japanese fan, sometimes rubbed a white pebble between his fingers, and who once killed a fly and then brushed it gently away with his hand."

Master Suzuki? Never heard that one used by us. I also don't recall Suzuki using a fan, but maybe. Rowley's interview concludes with, "'What is the purpose of Zen?' I asked. The Zen master shrugged his shoulders, spreading both palms up, and smiled."

One reviewer called Rowley's work, "a fatuous book" that "obviously has no scholarly merit," and "It has no logic, no charm, no pathos, and no understanding." But some of us at Tassajara got a kick out of reading it out loud and grooving on its creepiness.

The Rainmaker

Roovane said he mainly had silent dokusans with Suzuki. "We'd just sit together. He might ask how I was doing and then—just sitting." He tried new approaches in meditation, said he'd spent a long time meditating on the space between his thumbs, and then on his spine.

Roovane had a friend at Tassajara named Annie who was into watching birds. She told him if you sit very quietly the birds will come and be your friend. So every day after lunch, he started going out near the compost pile and sitting on a big rock to wait for the birds to sit on him. For weeks, he tried to see how still he could become. The birds got close but never perched on him. Still, he said, it was a terrific experience in which he sat so still he became a stone.

That summer was extra hot and dry. The plants needed more water, even the drought resistant ones on the hillsides. Roovane could see the trees were thirsty. "So I started playing with an idea, and I set up a time, and I said two days from now at three o'clock in the afternoon it's going to rain. I started working on it. I meditated on it and meditated on it and meditated on it. Then, at about two o'clock on the appointed day, there was a roll of thunder. I thought, this is impossible—it never rains in the summertime. But there was a thunderstorm in the afternoon. I just went, wow! I went wild! And I went right away for dokusan. I was so excited. I thought, this is it, I'm enlightened.

"So I told Roshi what had happened, the whole story of what I'd done, that I'd meditated on rain and created a rainstorm to water the vegetables. And he started to hit me and yell at me and he was real angry. He hit me many times and he said that what I did was absolutely wrong. He said if it rains here, it doesn't rain somewhere else and how do I know where the rain should be? He said it was very selfish practice. I knew I had powers before that—everyone has powers, different powers, and I was tempted to do things after that, but I never did."

"Another time he hit me was because I did something wise-ass. Suzuki Roshi started hitting me and said I had to get rid of the black snake. He was hitting me and hitting me with his stick—he was really hurting me."

Roovane's parents came to Tassajara. Suzuki invited them to breakfast one morning. Roovane was excited about the opportunity. "I never had breakfast with him alone. My parents were freaked out about their good Jewish boy in this monastery, and how now he'll never get married. Then they met Roshi, and stayed a week, and agreed with me. My father even sat in the zendo."

Of course Roovane would bond with the most far out people who drove or walked into Tassajara—a weathered couple with tattered clothes who'd been living in the woods surviving on wild plants, a wild-eyed visitor with news that the Beatles would be waiting for us on their secret island, a convincing crusader for the wonders of bamboo. There were rumors of a hunting cult whose goal was to eat the still-throbbing heart and raw warm liver of a deer that they'd just downed. Roovane got all excited about that and went out looking for them in vain.

There were three fellows we referred to as The Sheets. They came in a few times for the day dressed in white sheets that they wore like Indian sari. They'd go to the Narrows and the baths. They ate only raw food, which they brought with them. Roovane would join them as much as he could. We all found them an interesting variation in the flow and ebb of guests.

One day they arrived in a helicopter, hovering over the garden, waving to Roovane, and then landing in the parking area above the front gate where there was barely enough room to do so. One of them had just inherited a bunch of money and they were on a mission to see how fast they could spend it. Roovane flew off with them and returned in a few days with tales about what they'd done, including going to Las Vegas and the Grand Canyon, staying in fancy places, passing out money, buying gifts for friends and strangers. Roovane brought back a large stone Buddha which he placed in the bath house. Then, he went back to work in the garden.

Bad Boys

Four young drunk cowboys came in on horseback whooping it up and shooting their guns in the air. One took his horse down the steps into the swimming pool. Two of them went into the women's side of the baths—without their horses. When I caught up with them, I told them they had to check their guns in at the office, or ride on. They said they were on their way to go camping and boar hunting in the woods and did ride on.

Five days later they came back and were drunk again. Marc Alexander went up to them and told them to keep moving. And they did.

There were also some scruffy, shifty looking dudes who came in during guest season in what must have been an old UPS truck. They said they just wanted to look around. We kept an eye on them, but not well enough. Not long after they drove off, a guest who went beyond the gate to fetch something from his car reported things stolen from it. A quick check revealed that all the unlocked cars had been gone through and some locked ones broken into. I dashed to the office and called the sheriff. The thieves hadn't thought out their getaway route thoroughly. The sheriff was waiting for them at the other end of the road.

The Refugee

I was talking to Maggie Kress when a guy came in desperate for sanctuary. He was hiding, he said, from what he feared was a Scientology hit squad. He said he was on their enemies list. He held on to me saying, "You've got to help me, please!"

As work leader, I knew well we could always use more help. So I told him he could stay for a few days if he followed the student schedule and worked with us. Maggie was Suzuki's anja. Suzuki was in the city, and she wanted someone to help her take the tatamis and bedding and stuff out of his cabin, so she could air them out and clean it thoroughly inside. She asked if the new and desperate guy could help her. Sure.

Then Maggie made a big operation out of it. It went on for three days. On the fourth day, she asked if the guy escaping the Scientologists could help her just one more day. I told her he left. She said she'd heard all about his scary problem and hoped he was OK. She asked why he left so soon, and I said that he'd arranged to lay low at a friend's home and had gotten a ride out to Jamesburg. I said I didn't tell him his ride out was with a couple of guys from Scientology headquarters who came after I called them and turned him in for a reward. Maggie was horrified till I told her I was kidding. He'd calmed down, thanked us for the sanctuary, and headed out into the dangerous world to hide in the shadows.

Big Norm

As soon as the practice period was over, student housing was consolidated to free up the guest cabins for the two-week preparatory interim and guest season. Allen Klein, a wise-cracking New Yorker who called me Chatty Chadwick, moved in with Tommy, up front, and Norm Randolph was with me in back. They were both agreeable fellows, Norm tall and muscular. A big guy but not overweight. Also a sweetie pie.

I felt bad that I had a raised bed and Norm only had a tatami on the floor. I said I'd make him a bed, too, but he declined, saying in his humorous manner that his bed was just as soft as mine, which was not soft at all. Anyway, he went on, I was a revered senior and it was only appropriate that his bed be lower. I told him he had an excellent attitude and would be rewarded—"if not in this lifetime, then in the next." A well-worn line.

He called me Dave. Nobody calls me Dave. I find it irritating to be called Dave. But when Norm called me Dave, it seemed fine, as if we were actors on a stage and that was my role.

During oryoki meals in the zendo, Norm would fill each bowl so high, there'd be as much, brown rice, for example, above the top of the bowl as below inside it. I'd worry there'd be an avalanche. Many of us, mainly the guys, took seconds, but Norm would finish his seconds so quickly he could signal the server for thirds. "Norm you sure eat a lot," I said to him back in our room changing into work clothes.

"I'm a big guy, Dave," he said.

"Yes, Norm, but you eat a whole lot of food for a big guy after taking that into account."

"I work hard," he said. "I need a lot of fuel for this body."

"You do work hard."

Norm loved hard work, the harder the better. He was the trash and recycling guy. He'd drive the old Chevy pickup from the shop to Tassajara Lane above the kitchen. He'd get the kitchen's trash and recycling and organic waste. He'd take the latter out toward Grasshopper Flats to the screened-in compost bins, pour it on, add a layer of dirt, a layer of leaves, and another layer of dirt. He'd make stops at the baths, the shop, across the road in front of the dorm, down by the pool, and end up at the trash and recycling area below the lower barn at the tail end of our usable land.

We didn't eat or drink much out of cans or bottles, but there'd still be bottles and cans from the kitchen and people's private stashes, enough for him to smash the glass inside a fifty-five gallon drum and flatten the hard steel cans on a tree stump with a sledgehammer. Sometimes he'd burn the burnables in a designated vegetation free area at Grasshopper Flats. The small amount of actual trash we couldn't process in one way or another, we collected in the drums to be taken to a landfill in Salinas on the same run with the drums of recyclables. Norm loved this job. But mainly he loved smashing the bottles and cans. Sometimes in the room before going to the work meeting, he'd say, "There are some bottles and cans down there that haven't been smashed, Dave. Maybe I should do that first."

"Sure, Norm."

Norm also liked to split wood. He'd split the crotch and stump pieces that were all twisty and close to impossible to take apart. But his favorite was busting up stones or cement. There was a large cement slab on the side of Pine Room One not far from the office. It had housed a large generator back before the Becks had Tassajara. We wanted to build a storage room there for sheets, towels, soap, etc. for the cabin cleaners. But that slab had to go. It was eight feet long, four feet wide, and a good foot-and-a-half thick. It had thick rusted iron bolts sticking out where the generator had been fixed to it.

We were planning on renting a jackhammer to do the job. I asked Norm if he'd ever operated a jackhammer. He looked at it, and said he'd do it with a sledgehammer. I said "No, that's impossible, Norm." "Ah Dave, come on. Give me a chance." I couldn't refuse him. Norm was a happy guy in those days it took him to bust that slab into little pieces. We had to replace a couple of sledgehammer handles in the process.

I was a little worried what Norm might do to anyone who gave us trouble at Tassajara. After all, he told me that he would dream of smashing heads. When those Hells Angels came, he hung out within eyesight of them as if he were ready to deal with them if he had to. Oh yeah—those drunk cowboys who had terrorized the place. While I was informing them they had to check their guns at the office or ride on out, Norm walked up and asked if I needed any help. I think a look at him encouraged them to move on. I was glad because I was wondering if I could save them if he got unleashed. When they came riding back in, I was taking a nap. Norm heard them and went out to deal with them without waking me up. Maybe, fortunately, strong but not at all tall Marc Alexander had shooed them off with a few words before Norm could get there. Maybe his potential to do harm to troublemakers was all in my imagination because he really was a gentle giant.

On nights I'd get to bed on time, Norm and I would sometimes talk for a while before going to sleep. At first he was hesitant because we were supposed to be silent from evening zazen until breakfast was over. I told him I gave him dispensation from that rule because every word we spoke was in service of the dharma. "Then I will choose my words judiciously," he said.

In one of those brief conversations, before we drifted off to well-appreciated sleep, Norm told me his parents drummed into him that he should eat a lot. "My parents were very old," he said. "They had been trying to have a child for years and years, but my mother kept having miscarriages. She had nine miscarriages before I was born. They were always afraid I was going to die. They were so protective. At dinner, if I didn't eat all the food on my plate after taking seconds, my mother would say, 'You should eat all your food, Normie. You're looking a little sickly.' So I'd eat it all and then she'd say, 'Now you're looking healthy, Normie.' Maybe that's why I eat so much."

After he revealed that unique family history, we lay awake for a while. I broke the silence. "Norm, you know how when we talk about Buddhism, sometimes you say that your practice is to escape the wheel of rebirth and that your love of smashing things is an extension of that desire."

"Yes, Dave."

"I think maybe those miscarriages your mother had were you refusing to be born." We went to sleep that night without another word being spoken.

I noticed we tended to fall asleep and wake up at about the same time, as if we had synced up in that way. One night, as we were each sinking into the realm between waking and sleep, I began to speak. "Norm—you do not hate life. You love life. You just want to smash the illusory self. You are destined to become a Buddha."

After a minute he said, "Dave, that was a little spooky."

We disappeared into deep sleep soon after that, but first Norm explained that he found my words spooky because it seemed as if I'd spoken to him in his own voice.

The Uninvited

One night when Norm was jikido and sleeping in the zendo, I was awakened by the sound of someone entering the room through the side screen door. I was sleeping on my right side facing the wall and rolled over. In the dark, I could make out a slim female form in a robe. Then the robe fell to the floor. There was just enough moonlight glowing in the room to reveal that she wore nothing else. I had a summer sleeping bag that was open. Before she could slip into it, I was out of it, got my robe on, and walked to the office in the dark. I lit a kerosene lamp there and picked up a magazine someone had left on the table. I read till I got sleepy and returned to my room which was empty. I did not bring this up with anyone including the uninvited guest and she didn't broach the topic with me, either.

The Invited

I didn't stay in my room every night. Dianne had one side of a divided cabin to herself. We both fit snugly on her single tatami and slept just fine there even though its width was less than that of the two of us. A few times we went to our clandestine tryst spot—Suzuki's cabin—but only when he wasn't there.

She'd at times join me and a guitar walking downstream on a warm night before a day off. The guitar belonged to a generous fellow student who kept it in the lower barn. Others might follow or meet us there, and sometimes guests we'd gotten to know would join us. We might possibly indulge in substances forbidden to students in addition to it being forbidden for students to be up that late.

Once, I heard through one of my spies that Claude Dalenberg had brought a rumor up at a board meeting—a rumor that I was doing all that. Nobody wanted to pursue it, one comment being, "Well, we all have some skeletons in the closet."

Black Widows

One sunny day, a guy walked into the office and said he'd just released five thousand black widow spiders at Grasshopper Flats. Before panic could spread, Sterling Bunnell stepped in. He said not to worry, that in the first place it's highly unlikely he'd have five thousand black widows in a jar, but even if he did, and released them, that the area can support only so many, and the population would soon revert to the normal balance.

It was always good to have Sterling around. He was especially helpful with how we dealt with unwanted guests that weren't human. The garden, for instance, had gophers. A few years back, Sterling brought in two long gopher snakes to deal with that problem. He must have forgotten to tell them to stay in the garden, though, because a guest came into the office holding one of them and said his room was already occupied. Luckily, it was a guest who knew his snakes and how to handle them because they look somewhat like rattlesnakes without rattles.

That wouldn't have stopped Sterling, though. Once I told him I was going to the lower barn to look for a rattler that was there, and he eagerly came along. I was shocked to see him stick his hand under a cabinet and feel around for it. He found it. We put it in a trash can, drove it up the road beyond the watershed of our creek, and watched it slide down into the woods below. Thanks to Sterling's tutelage, I confidently caught a few rattlesnakes at Tassajara after that. Unlike Sterling, though, I wouldn't pick them up and stroke them. I'd guide them into an open trash can on its side, right it, put the top on securely, and drive them out.

Two Mothers

Kathy Cook and Silas got married and she became Kathy Hoadley. She came to Tassajara when she was pregnant. Silas was busy with Zen Center business in the city and would follow later.

At Tassajara, Suzuki told Kathy, "You should stay here." She felt the implication was to stay, and have the baby, and forget about Silas.

After she gave birth, she returned to Tassajara. She heard Suzuki say that if one person in a family were to practice, the whole family would benefit. Kathy had been thriving up to then at Tassajara. Everything had been working for her. Now, with a baby, by herself, that was no longer the case.

"Whatever valuable positive things I gained as a single woman at Tassajara," she said, "were totally lost in the situation of being a wife and mother. I had a serious nervous breakdown after Amber's birth—poor girl, her early infancy must have been terrifying. And I really hadn't recovered when Suzuki Roshi wanted Silas at Tassajara. That environment was about the opposite of what I needed to regain my balance and I got worse there. I remember Suzuki Roshi saying to me 'Get a clear picture of your illness and accept it.'"

Kathy felt she lost the relationship she had with Suzuki. She didn't have time to be with him or to be involved with zendo activities. "Silas was important to Zen Center, and Suzuki Roshi said to me, 'I need Silas to be shuso at Tassajara, and your family life will have to be sacrificed.' That did not sit well with me. I felt like I was being asked to be a Japanese priest's wife, but since Suzuki Roshi had asked me, I felt like I should try to do that. But it didn't work at all. I was in cabin sixteen nearest the pool with Amber and was with her all day. I couldn't do any work. I couldn't go to the zendo. Silas firmly believed that nobody should help me with childcare because they were there to practice. I basically flipped out. The stress was more than I could handle. I didn't feel that Suzuki Roshi supported me at all anymore, or didn't support me to do anything but take care of the baby. That was extremely difficult. I felt like if I'd talked to Okusan, she'd have just rubber-stamped what Roshi said. I kept trying to fit into that role, but I was just dying in it. There was absolutely no one to turn to.

"Suzuki Roshi said to me, 'Just don't lose your own way.' I remember him saying that in the midst of all the anxiety that was going on. I suppose the first one through makes a space by being there if they do it well or badly. The next one makes a little bit more and on and on.

"Suzuki Roshi got it that men and women wanted to practice together in the same community, and he got it that couples wanted to live together without being married, and he gave that his blessing as long as they were responsible to the community that they were a part of. He was very forward-thinking in that regard. But to make the next step of how we would integrate mothers and children, I don't think he ever went there. We didn't even know what the problems were. It never occurred to me to talk to Suzuki Roshi about my situation because he'd asked me to sacrifice."

Kathy did get help taking care of baby Amber from Ruthie Discoe, but clearly it wasn't enough. Shortly after Silas's time as shuso was over, Kathy committed herself to an institution for treatment. As a result, Silas, with the help of some students, took care of Amber without Kathy until she returned. Gary Snyder's wife Masa had a baby who was in the hospital, so she became Amber's wet nurse.

Ruthie Discoe didn't have the same experience at all. She was there as a spouse, not a student. She participated in zendo activities when she chose. Even when she was hugely pregnant, she kept on working energetically in the garden or on the grounds. Once she had the baby, she carried him in a Snugli and went back to work. Paul helped out as well.

"Suzuki Roshi was very supportive of my being pregnant at Tassajara," she said, "and supportive of having Benjamin at Tassajara after he was born. I thought it was a great privilege being pregnant there. All I was worried about was getting enough protein. I didn't even want to leave there to have the baby, but I had to.

"Ben was born in November and we came home from the hospital during the Rohatsu Sesshin where everyone is silent. People would come into the cabin to see Ben and nobody said anything. Tatsugami Roshi came over and, flouting the rule, started talking to Ben."

Oodles of Noodles

At morning tea, Suzuki was discussing the menu with senior students. He turned to Janet Sturgeon and said, "I heard you used to make udon noodles for Tatsugami Roshi."

"Yes, I learned to make them by hand," she said. "The officers came one-by-one for the noodle dinners with him on four-and-nine days."

"I want to see what they're like," Suzuki said. "Can you make them for me?"

Early afternoon, Janet was in the kitchen making noodles. Suzuki dropped by. He watched a little, then got out his own bowl, flour, and eggs. He seemed to her like a kid stirring up the dough. At one point, he picked up a huge wad of dough and threw it on a breadboard on the floor. Then he took off his zoris and walked around on it, looking at Janet as he was doing so with an ecstatic expression on his face.

Mitsu came in and wanted him to leave, but he wouldn't. She tried to take over his task, but he didn't let her, so she started making her own. For a while, the three of them were making noodles together. Then others noticed and joined in. Some people worked the flour into dough on the long sycamore worktable, others kneaded away on bread boards on the tile floor. Suzuki kept adding more flour—while cooling breezes came through the screened windows.

The dinner crew arrived. The head cook adjusted the dinner menu. In the big new kitchen there was room for all. As the noodling continued, vegetables were cut, pots were washed, cups of tea were passed around. Suzuki kept adding more flour and water.

"Who's running Tassajara?" asked one of the officers sticking his head in. "We have a guest season going on."

"You go run it!" laughed Suzuki.

As the dough was being rolled out thin and cut into strips, Mitsu, who had left, returned, fuming. Suzuki waved goodbye, all smiles, as she dragged him out the door. What had started as a meal for the Suzukis and a few students, ended up as dinner for sixty students—with seconds and thirds—two nights in a row.

Noah's Pal

Ever since 1967, when Nancy Lay departed and left her canine friend behind, Noah seemed to get confused from not having one main person to relate to. He slept in my room with me for months and then one evening he didn't show and went to someone else for a while. He was an orphan with too many parents.

The happiest I ever saw Noah was when a big shaggy dog came wandering into Tassajara from the woods one day. They got along so well that we gave in and relaxed the one dog rule. Noah and that dog shared a passion—killing wild animals. They'd go running into the woods and we could hear them barking in the distance and knew what that meant. Sometimes they came back smelling of skunk, sometimes painted in blood. Once they stayed out for a couple of days, came back and slept and lay around for a few days.

Some people felt responsible and wanted them fenced in, saying it's not right for a Buddhist monastery to bring a reign of terror to the realm. Then one day Noah returned sad and alone. He'd still go out occasionally by himself.

Mountains and Rivers

Carl Bielefeldt began practicing with Suzuki at the old Sokoji in the mid-sixties. In 1966, he graduated from San Francisco State College with a BA in philosophy. In '67, after a stint at Tassajara, he and Suzuki student Fred Stoeber went to Japan and studied at the International Division of Waseda University in Tokyo for a couple years. Carl and a secretary at the school named Fumiko got married. In '70, Carl, Fumiko, and Fred went to San Francisco and lived on Waller Street close to the City Center, and practiced there. After a while, Fred moved north and built a cabin on the coast in Sonoma County.

At the time, Carl was working on his master's degree in Asian Studies at UC Berkeley. He met with Suzuki and told him he was looking for a subject for his thesis. Suzuki suggested Dogen's "Sansuikyo," a fascicle in Dogen's *Shobogenzo*. Suzuki said he'd give lectures on it if he had an English translation. So Carl got out his *Shobogenzo* and looked into what Dogen had to say. He reported back to Suzuki that it was way over his head. Suzuki said, "Yes it's a very difficult, interesting text."

"The language," Carl said, "is so hard to understand."

"It's not the language. It's the thought," Suzuki said. "This isn't just poetry, it's the philosophy that makes it make sense."

Carl asked Suzuki if he didn't think it was ridiculous for him to be "translating something so deep and rich?" Suzuki said yes, and told him to get on with it.

In the summer of 1971, Carl spent time at Tassajara working with Suzuki on the translation of what he was now calling *The Mountains and Waters Sutra*. He found it "much nicer than digging the latrines for the hill cabins which I had done the summer before."

Crayfish

John Phillips and his wife came in with the Pages and Wenners from Monterey. Phillips was head of the prestigious Hopkins Marine Station in Pacific Grove which was connected to Stanford University. He had astonished the scientific community when he first suggested that DDT and other chemicals might be harming marine life—plants, fish, birds, and mammals as well. He and his undergraduate students had been doing research on the effects of DDT.

Biologists had been wondering why some Brown Pelican eggshells were tending to be so thin that they didn't hold together. Phillips's work showed that DDT was the culprit. In 1969, he sent an open letter to Governor Ronald Reagan calling for DDT to be banned. It was signed by sixty other marine scientists. The California legislature was debating whether to ban it or not. That was just one of the deleterious effects that they linked to that pesticide. It was also one of many chemicals humans were introducing into the environment that concerned Phillips and other scientists. Phillips's work covered a gamut of pollutants. He did research on PCBs, by-products of plastic manufacturing, and found high levels of PCBs and other contaminants not only in Arctic mammals but in mothers' milk in California. He told me that formula might be a better choice.

We walked through our lush upper and lower organic gardens and ate some tomatoes we didn't have to wash. Phillips said that the worst part of his work was being personally attacked by lobbyists and legislators supported by manufacturers of the substances he was investigating. "All I was trying to do was save some pelicans," he said. Quite an understatement.

I showed him a small can with an inch of pesticide remaining in it, left over from the prior owners, and said I didn't want to dump it in the ground. He said not to worry about it, that there were twenty thousand gallons of that stuff going into the earth every day in Salinas Valley alone. I assumed he was exaggerating. He painted a scary picture of an exponentially expanding number and volume of inorganic substances we're adding to the land, sea, air, flora and fauna. He said there would be disastrous long-term consequences. I told him I read Rachel Carson's *Silent Spring* when I was a senior in high school and wondered if it had had some beneficial effect. "A little," he said shaking his head.

Still, Phillips could forget these threats to the health of the biosphere and enjoy his vacation. I found him walking up the bank from the creek above the swimming pool, a bucket in his hand. It was full of crayfish he caught in the water there. He was delighted, and said they were the most delectable crustacean—better than shrimp. He was looking forward to cooking them behind the Pine Room, where he was staying and sharing them with his friends—and me, if I cared to join them. I told him as a kid I caught crayfish, or crawdads, as they were also called, in a little creek near our house and gave them to our maid. We white folks didn't know what to do with them, but she did.

Walking back to his room, we ran into Suzuki. I introduced them, explaining a little about what Phillips did. Suzuki said that was very important work and thanked him for his efforts. Phillips praised the way Suzuki and his students were maintaining and running Tassajara. Then he praised our crayfish and held up the bucket full of them. Suzuki looked down at the bucket and gasped, then emitted a pained "Ohhhh" in genuine sadness and, after an awkward goodbye, walked on.

Our policy at Tassajara was that the critters in the creek, heck—all living beings at Tassajara—were under our protection. Guests or hikers could go fishing elsewhere but not on our property. Same as hunters. It wasn't posted anywhere, and it didn't come up much. I figured I'd let him know before he left. Didn't want to spoil his dinner.

Phillips said he was sorry he'd bummed Suzuki out. I told him not to worry, that Suzuki wouldn't hold it against him, that his wife fed him small amounts of meat and fish at the temple in the city. And we served moderate amounts of meat and fish to our guests until this year. Anyway, I told him, Suzuki would surely eat those same crayfish in a restaurant without thinking about it. He'd say we had to kill vegetables, too. As with many of us, his liberal food philosophy broke down when he ran into the stark reality of the slaughterhouse.

Later, I asked Phillips what he thought about the work of the growing environmental movement. I mentioned how many of our guests and students had been involved with environmental activism. The year before twenty million people worldwide had been involved in the first Earth Day.

"It's too late," he said.

A Sunflower

In 1970, flowing, red-haired Annie Schliffer had just finished college, hiked in mountains, and experimented with psychedelics, with which she had great insights, but found to be a dead end. She checked out communes which were either into drugs or rock music, or both. Hitchhiking, she was picked up by Fil Lewitt, founder of Big River Farm in Mendocino. He talked to her about zazen, practice, and Tassajara. That's all she needed to hear. A day later, she was hiking into Tassajara. The sun was going down, so she camped out. She enjoyed the sunset and then was welcomed to the woods by a full lunar eclipse.

She fell in love with Tassajara and zazen, chanting, the kitchen, garden, cleaning, the beauty and rigor of the practice. It was everything that she had been looking for. She was allowed to stay until the guest season was over. She went to Berkeley to put in her time with the Berkley Zen Center until she could return to Tassajara. She was back for the 1970-71 interim, then the spring practice period, and stayed for the summer.

Annie worked in the garden and then in the kitchen with Tommy who teased her about the food trip Roovane had gotten her into—eating only certain fruits and vegetables. She found Tommy to be a saint disguised as a tenzo.

She studied tea ceremony with Mitsu and was embarrassed at the mistakes she made nervously serving Mitsu's husband Shunryu who smiled and was quiet.

Annie marveled at the clear starlit sky at night. On a day off she might climb to the top of Flag Rock and practice chanting. Walking down creek she'd sit on a rock until a dipper would alight on her legs. On a picnic with fellow students, Suzuki or Katagiri, she felt the kindness, compassion, and wisdom of her teachers.

She shuddered in horror one day when Van put vases with poison oak cuttings in front of his adjoining cabin. She was highly allergic.

The summer days were sweltering and the zendo was still hot in the evenings, but she ignored the heat and soaked up Suzuki's lectures. Then there was the cool stream afterwards where the teachings could sink in and be digested.

Annie lived by the lower garden and sometimes would go out and gaze at a sunflower opening. While she was sitting in front of a large sunflower one day, Suzuki approached the garden with a guest. The guest was intrigued and came over to see what she was up to. Then she noticed the guest was Alan Watts. Watts explained that meditating on a flower was an ancient practice. He called it what seemed to Annie to be an awfully erudite name. Inside, she laughed, thinking she was simply enjoying the unfolding of a flower. *Why define it? Just do it!* she thought. She offered her stool to Watts, but he politely declined and walked on. Suzuki let Watts wander on into the garden, joined Annie and they shared a moment absorbed in a sunflower.

Anja Maggie

Maggie Kress was Suzuki's anja. She asked if she could attend his lectures and clean the cabin at some other time, but he told her no, that she was getting teaching from him all the time. So she put a tape recorder outside a zendo window. But when she went to check the tapes, they were blank. So she cheated, quickly cleaning and straightening up his cabin and then putting a chair outside the zendo and listening through a window screen. "They were very intense lectures," she said, "fiercely focused, and he was full of energy."

Being around Suzuki so much, Maggie felt that he never lost a moment of attention and awareness. "He was completely engaged in his life and the life around him and connected in feeling and thought to the people around him and everything around him all the time. It was a very calm, strong energy."

Maggie would get to Suzuki's cabin about the time the wakeup bell was going around. He was always awake when she arrived. She would go in and set his robes out while he was in his little bathroom. He'd go to zazen, and she'd clean his cabin. Later in the day, she'd iron his robes.

One day before Suzuki went to take a bath, he asked her to dig a little ditch in his garden. He came back an hour later and she'd dug a mammoth ditch. He looked at it, laughed, shook his head and said, "Not like that, not so big, you're a runaway horse—you just nudge them a bit and they fly off."

Sometimes, Suzuki would still have his beautiful delicate silk robes on while working in the garden. He would go outside to look at the garden, do a little something, then something else. Niels, Suzuki's jisha, would show up to work with him and Suzuki would forget what he was wearing. Maggie would remind him to go inside and change and he'd ignore her. But if Mitsu was there she'd get upset saying he shouldn't be working at all, and he'd ignore her until he'd give up. Sometimes, he'd ask Maggie and Niels to stand on guard and whistle when Mitsu was approaching.

Once, Maggie set out Suzuki's futon at night going in a different direction than usual. He didn't say anything except "Good night. Thank you." The next morning after zazen, he spoke briefly in the zendo saying, "When you hear the wake-up bell, you should jump out of bed right away. You shouldn't lie there. Otherwise, how could you ever face death which comes suddenly? But don't jump out of bed the way I did this morning. I knocked over my kerosene lamp." He'd gotten up in the dark as usual, run into the unexpected wall in front of him, and knocked over the lamp. By the time Maggie entered, he'd cleaned it all up.

Suzuki had been talking about attachment to things in a lecture. Maggie listened to it from outside and hustled back to his cabin so he wouldn't know she'd heard it. But he might have guessed she'd been there by the question she asked. "Roshi if you drop the cup and it breaks, to me that's no big deal but if you fall down and are broken then that's something terrible." He said, "There's no difference between me and the cup. You don't understand what I've been trying to teach you. You don't realize the sameness between me and everything else around." Maggie told him she didn't understand that and would never understand it.

Suzuki spoke with Niels in the garden one day while they were working and said he and Maggie should get married. He told Niels he wished more of his students could be celibate but most of them can't, so it's best to get married. (He didn't suggest that to Dianne and me and a few others who weren't married.) Maggie suspected Suzuki was saying that because their affair was causing too much of a commotion in the community. They were both rather volatile creatures. Maggie came up to me with excited eyes and said, "David! Niels and I are going to be married! We want to get married here! Isn't that exciting!?"

I reflected on something that had occurred one night the summer before when she was head of the office. After evening zazen, I was walking toward the baths to take a late forbidden dip when Maggie called out from the office. She told me to sit down and wait. A moment later, she was back with two glasses. From behind the office counter she brought out a bottle. "Look what some guests left in their room! Vodka from Russia! Look how much is still in the bottle! Let me show you how they drink it in Moscow."

She poured two full glasses. "Now you drink it all straight down." So we did. Wow. I sat back in my chair while a warm rush came over my whole body. But before I could even adjust, she poured two more glasses saying, "We have to drink two. They never drink just one." I protested, saying that's too much, but she said that's how they do it so we should too. So we did. I was reeling. I told her I had to get into a hot plunge.

We blew out the lamp when we heard the firewatch clackers and waited in the dark till they'd come back from closing the baths. Then we staggered down to the baths. After cooking a while in the plunge, I began to feel amorous. "No, no," she said, "I can't. Niels is my boyfriend, and I must be true to him." "Oh yeah," I said. "I forgot about that." We got dressed and stood on the bridge a moment in the moonlight. "Don't let me do this again," she said. "I forget what it does to me." I assured her I'd remember that. We both threw up on the way back to our respective cabins.

Suzuki Departs

Yvonne came to pick the Suzukis up and take them to the city. When she arrived, he was working in his garden. Maggie said he'd been there all morning. Mitsu kept insisting he stop working and get ready to go. After his whirlwind of lectures and work, he finally stopped. Ready to go, he stood gazing at his garden. Maggie saw him then as drained of energy, tired and weak. As he got into Yvonne's car, a bunch of us crowding around in gassho, Maggie had a strong feeling that he wouldn't return, and she began weeping as she said goodbye.

His Cabin

I sneaked into Suzuki's little cabin. There was still a hint of the heavenly aroma from the sachet of herbs Mitsu would put with his robes, and the lingering influence of a particular brand of temple incense. The cast iron stove sat empty and cold, no firewood neatly stacked, no newspaper and kindling in a cardboard box, but still a hatchet lying on the firebrick the stove sat on. Memory brought back the pleasing mix of odor from the split oak and ashes—or could that smell be embedded in the pores of the room? All combined to create the characteristic fragrance of that cabin. I bowed to a small Buddha statue on the altar table I'd inexpertly made with Paul Discoe's advice in our first spring at Tassajara. I sniffed it and could still faintly smell the linseed oil. Suzuki's bedding was folded up and stored on a high shelf in the narrow back room with its toilet and sink, nestled in with the stacked cardboard boxes and scrolls waiting for their turn to be opened and hung.

In the main room on three walls were two-by-four windowsills at shoulder height. These cabins were built in the 1920s, so the redwood was dark and thick—full dimension. A breeze wafted through the screens. Sheet-rock painted off-white inset between the dense old growth posts and two-by-fours. In the corner, an indigo *furoshiki* cloth covered a tray. I lifted a corner of it to peek under at a celadon ceramic tea pot and mongrel mix of cups, a canister with bancha green tea and a stack of institutional paper napkins cut in two with scissors. Books in Japanese and English filled three shelves. I picked one—*Born in Tibet*, by Chogyam Trungpa. I sat on a zabuton and opened the book at random to read, "We have to leave behind the smallest traces of worldly ambition and prepare to live the life of the wandering yogi, owning nothing, holding to nothing."

When will Suzuki Roshi return? I wondered. *Will he really come back to help Katagiri Sensei lead the fall practice period?* I put the book down, reclined on the tatami, and fell asleep.

Katagiri Chooses

The interim was coming to an end. Some students were leaving and others arriving for the '71 fall practice period. Soon the tangaryo initiation would start. Five days for newbies. Those who'd already done a tangaryo would sit the first day, a practice I assumed that was not done in Japanese temples.

Suzuki was too ill to return to Tassajara anytime soon. In a meeting in the city, Katagiri was asked whom he would like to have for his jisha and anja. He looked at the list of those who would be attending, and said he wanted Bob Walter to be his jisha and Bonnie Miller to be his anja. There was discomfort with his choices. I wondered how they expressed their reservations to him. Maybe like me in school, Bob and Bonnie got C's in citizenship. Anyway, he was asked to please choose again. He inquired if he could choose anyone he wanted. Of course, he was told. He said then that he'd like Bob Walter to be his jisha and Bonnie Miller to be his anja.

Fifty students sat quietly on their zafus, ready for the first day of tangaryo to begin. As the whacks of the third round of the han entered the rolldown, Katagiri entered the zendo to offer a stick of incense held by his jisha Bob Walter. Bonnie Miller wasn't in the zendo, though. As anja, she was cleaning Katagiri's cabin. They'd all three sit most of the first day of tangaryo—beyond the call of duty.

Home Leavers

For me and a few others, what we called the priest's ordination came in September at the City Center. Suzuki was too sick to officiate, so Katagiri did it for him. There were four of us including Ed Brown,

Lew Richmond, Angie Runyon, and me. Craig Boyan was going to be a fifth, but that didn't happen. He'd been torn between Suzuki and Zen practice and the community of the late Meher Baba of Sufism Reoriented. Craig finally decided—the day before our ordination—to go that more devotional route. He was out sobbing in the hall while we were in the Buddha Hall for rehearsal with Katagiri.

Katagiri didn't feel comfortable about the arrangement and at the rehearsal said maybe we should wait to get ordained when Richard Baker came back from Japan. It was a sad, serious time, and no one wanted to force their own wishes. No one but me.

"Absolutely not," I said. "We're getting ordained here tomorrow as planned." I said the wheels were already turning, people were arriving from out of town. "Everything's prepared and Suzuki wanted to ordain us and you doing the ceremony for him is the only way to complete what he started, what he wanted. He didn't call it off just because he can't be there." Katagiri didn't want to argue, either.

The next day, after our ordination, the four of us went upstairs to Suzuki's room to greet him. We stood together at the foot of his bed. None of us were celebrating. He was so weak. He cheered us up by being pleased to see us, wrapped in our newly received black robes, the koromo with long drooping sleeves and the large rectangular kesa with its rice-field pattern.

There was a reception downstairs waiting, but I had to be alone for a while. I went to the rooftop garden with its view of San Francisco and cried.

That night Reb talked to me about the importance of what I was embarking on. He emphasized that it was a serious responsibility and priests should conduct themselves with dignity, sincerity, and be role models. I just nodded and waited for him to stop and said thanks. He might as well have been talking to the wall.

Sad News OCTOBER 10

Chosan, morning tea, with Katagiri in the abbot's cabin was over. Departing, I stepped down into my zoris. The bell for work meeting had rung. I headed that way on the dusty road still in my robes. Dianne was sitting on the steps to the dorm putting on some boots. I went over and sat down next to her and tried to say something. The words wouldn't come. I was breathing heavily. "What's wrong?" she said.

"Suzuki Roshi ... has ... cancer," I finally got out, and started to cry. She moaned and we leaned on each other.

Dan, the director, had received a call the day before. Suzuki had met with the disciples and some others in his bedroom and let them know. First, he told them he didn't have hepatitis as previously thought, so he wasn't contagious. He didn't have to be on a special diet either because he had cancer. He said that as if it were good news. He said he hoped to live another two years, which his doctor said was the most he had left. It was obvious to anyone who'd been around him since August that he was declining. There was a sense all year that he wouldn't be with us long. He'd been dropping disturbing hints in lectures, even when he was well. Hints like, "Things teach best when they are dying."

Dan announced the sad news at the work meeting. Anyone who wanted some time to be alone should feel free to take it. The meeting was over. In the air was a dark cloud of gloom that rained down the feelings and sounds of sorrow and heartbreak.

I went to the office and called Fred Kimball, the psychic in L.A. that I'd visited a few times. He answered the phone with "Fred Kimball, here. How can I help you?"

With only a quick "Fred. David," I went straight to a question. Fred wouldn't remember Suzuki's name Shunryu. He probably wouldn't remember I studied with a teacher named Suzuki. But to hide the subject of my question deeper and make absolutely sure he wouldn't know who I was asking about, I used the seldom heard part of Suzuki's name, the part his master Gyokujun So'on had added—Shogaku. He was Shogaku Shunryu.

"Fred," I said. "Tell me about Shogaku."

Without hesitating, Fred said, "This man can no longer be your teacher."

Moon Faced

Eido Shimano, founder of New York Zen Studies Society, visited Suzuki. "Suzuki Roshi's talk with me was unforgettable," he said. "First, in a very comfortable way, with equanimity and tranquility, he said, 'Cancer and I are now good friends.' Also, he brought up the famous Zen koan when the head monk asked an ill Basso how he was and Basso's answer was 'Sun-faced Buddha, Moon-faced Buddha.'

"Our talk was amazingly enough not at all serious. Death was approaching. He knew he would die. We knew he would die. But despite all the intense sadness, he was almost cheerful. I can't understand it. It really meant something to me. It really surprised me. That was a big comfort to me. Then someone knocked at the door, and Richard Baker came in with two or three others. He didn't say anything. Just the way Suzuki Roshi looked at him—his face and eyes—I thought, my goodness, this is called compassion."

At Richard's request, Eido gave a talk in the Buddha Hall that evening. The subject was Sun Faced Buddha, Moon Faced Buddha. Buddha feeling good, Buddha not feeling so good.

I'd come to the city for a meeting and spoke to Eido that night after his talk. He was still moved by his time with Suzuki earlier that day. He said he'd always been an arrogant person and that Suzuki's total humility had touched him deeply. "He was very natural. He put formality aside. That was impressive, because I was brought up in the Rinzai establishment where formality was very important. And coming here to America and meeting Suzuki Roshi, he gave me a natural warm welcome, without formality."

One thing that surprised and somewhat bothered me was that Eido said he visited Suzuki in the city before the trip to Tassajara in 1968, and talked to him about a woman student of his who applied to go to Tassajara and received no answer. Suzuki said that he let the students take care of everything. So she didn't get in. I told Eido that her application was probably just lost, and she should have tried again. We were accepting everyone back then and the fact that she came from his group would surely have qualified her. He said he'd tell her because she really felt bad about that. I said she'd be welcome to reapply.

"I learned a great deal from Suzuki Roshi," he said. "So in that sense I consider Suzuki Roshi not only as one of the great patriarchs of Zen in America, but also, I consider myself as one of his hidden students. Nothing was drastic. So penetrating. So gentle. Like soft spring rain penetrates the earth, saturating it. That's how I see his teaching style. Soft gentle spring rain."

When Eido returned to New York he spoke of Suzuki's profound effect on him in a lecture and said, "He is a true roshi."

A Reunion NOVEMBER

Shunryu Suzuki's son and now the abbot of Rinsoin, Hoitsu, Suzuki's daughter and oldest child Yasuko, as well as a temple member named Gen'ichi Amano, all flew in from Japan and stayed at the City Center. I hadn't seen Richard Baker since he dropped by my cabin in Carmel Valley two years previously. Then, he was rather loose and friendly. Now, he was serious, somber. I could feel the weight of responsibility he'd returned to. There was a ceremony coming up, a mountain seat ceremony, in which Suzuki would step down from the mountain and Richard would step up. Everything would be different for him, for us. But now, there was only the fact that Suzuki was dying.

When I visited Suzuki for the last time, after he had shooed off my moping, he asked what my position was at Tassajara. I said I was the assistant director and he acted impressed. He asked if I would stay and spend time with his visitors.

We met in his bedroom, me using my humorously poor Japanese. I learned that Amano had long been Shunryu's *gishin* at Rinsoin. Hoitsu said that as a gishin, Amano was responsible like a father for Shunryu and now Hoitsu. Hoitsu called him father. I said, "Oh—he's Suzuki Roshi's godfather." They liked that word.

The three of them came to Tassajara for an overnight. They had tea with Katagiri and attended Bill Kwong's shuso ceremony, which astounded them. It seemed to me they saw everything in terms of something their father, and for Amano, his temple godson, had created. A proper ceremony with students in robes asking dharma questions. The questions and answers were from the heart, weren't memorized. And Tassajara itself so impressive—as was the City Center. It was almost like a dream. I'd gathered from Japanese priests that in Japan, Suzuki had done nothing like what they had witnessed. He was just a temple priest. He didn't give talks and he didn't even have disciples. Amano told me he would let the congregation back home know what he had witnessed. He said they would be proud of Shunryu-san, as he called him, and would come to understand why he came to America.

I escorted our guests to the flat on the Hogback that Shunryu had chosen as an ashes site for Trudy—and for himself. We stood there quietly for a moment. Later, Richard Baker told me it was not quite appropriate for me to show Hoitsu the ashes site for his ailing father. I disagreed but kept it to myself. Suzuki hadn't died but already there were the beginnings of closure.

Mountain Seat

Amano was ready to return to Japan, but Suzuki asked him to stay to witness the Mountain Seat Ceremony where Richard would become the new abbot. The ceremony was much more abbreviated than such a momentous occasion would be in Japan, where it could stretch out for days. But still our guests were overwhelmed by the authenticity of it. There was enough of the familiar for them to relate to, to appreciate, to be amazed again that what they had thought of as being purely Japanese was happening in America. There were low and high bells and the deep taiko drum—all familiar. There was a procession with fancy robes for Baker and Suzuki—as it should be. There was English and there was Japanese. Among the hundreds who attended, were a few dozen Japanese Americans.

Shunryu, shockingly shriveled with skin turned dark yellow-brown, entered, holding a staff with rings affixed to the top, supported by Hoitsu on one side and Mitsu on the other. At the altar, he managed to spread out his zagu and bow deeply, his forehead touching the spot it had touched so often, darkened by decades of sweat. He was helped to a ceremonial seat.

Next followed the presentation of the robe symbolically from Shunryu to Richard. A vast chorus chanted the Heart Sutra intoned by Kobun. There was the Declaration of Official Appointment by Silas Hoadley, President-Treasurer of Zen Center.

Richard recited a Gatha facing the Mountain Altar:

> This Mountain Seat, climbed many times before,
> Is the Everywhere Bodhimandala.
> With the help of my Master and everyone here
> In the ten directions and the three times
> I will climb this mind-seal altar.
> Do not wonder about it at all.

Then, Ascending the Mountain Altar:

> I offer this incense penetrating everywhere for all beings in the six worlds, for Trudy Dixon, for Mr. Chester Carlson, for all who have given in every way to make this sangha real. May their passage be free from hindrance.
>
> I want to offer a special incense for my teacher, the Tozan Seido Roshi of Zen Center, Mahabodhisattva Zendo, and Tassajara Zenshinji, Katagiri Dainin-roshi. Every day he shows us Dogen's Way.
>
> This piece of incense
> Which I have had for a long long time
> I offer with no-hand
> To my Master, to my friend, Suzuki Shunryu-daiosho

The founder of these temples.
There is no measure of what you have done.
Walking with you in Buddha's gentle rain
Our robes are soaked through,
But on the lotus leaves
Not a drop remains.

Then there was mondo, questions from some dharma siblings testing the abbot's understanding.

Bill Kwong, a priest of Mill Valley, whose transmission Suzuki was too ill to complete, stood before Richard and called out: "Chief Priest!"

Richard responded: "Is it host or guest?"

Bill shouted: "Iiiiiiiic!"

Richard: "Show me your true nature without shouting." To which Bill gasshoed and returned to his seat.

The ceremony over, Hoitsu and Mitsu helped Shunryu stand from his ceremonial seat. Half way out, he paused, looked to those assembled on the left, rolled the staff between his hands, jangling it twice. He looked to the right and jangled his staff twice again. There was a collective gasp as all were struck by a veritable bolt of lightning. The three moved on through a thunderstorm of tears. Shunryu's piercing goodbye to us all.

Two Calls

Larry Hansen came to Sokoji in 1965. He was living at Tassajara before the first practice period. "We did a lot of digging," he said, "moving rocks, felling trees for roof beams for the kitchen. Looking after the bees."

Larry said Katagiri came along on a logging trip to the woods up the road and they had to take the chain saw away from him out of fear he was going to cut off his legs. Larry was a carpenter and one of the crew that worked on building the new kitchen. Suzuki performed a marriage ceremony for him and his mate Laurie Cohen. In '69, they moved to Quadra Island, British Columbia, to help build a studio for Molly Jones's mother.

Larry visited Suzuki in 1970. He told Suzuki they were sitting regularly on Quadra Island, even did sesshins. He said they needed someone in robes and asked if he should become a priest. Suzuki said, "I'm not going to create any more big shots," and suggested Larry come back to Zen Center. Larry said he couldn't, so Suzuki said he'd send someone to help. Larry had mentioned to Silas they needed a priest for sesshin and when Silas came to lead a sesshin in the summer of '71, Larry told him he must be the person Suzuki said he'd send. That surprised Silas who said he hadn't talked to Suzuki about it.

Silas returned to Quadra Island for the '71 Rohatsu sesshin being held in an old, abandoned farmhouse in remote woods. It was snowing hard and had been for a while. It became evident that if they didn't leave soon and find another place to sit, they'd be snowed in. They decided to stay put and agreed they could be flown out in a helicopter after the sesshin if they were trapped.

At Tassajara, during the first period of zazen on the morning of the fourth day of the Rohatsu sesshin, the phone rang in the office, rang on the other side of the wall behind the altar. Dan Welch shot up and walked quickly but quietly down the aisle. In the kitchen, Dianne, helping to make breakfast, heard the ringing, too. She ran right over. Reb was on the other end. He said he wanted to speak to Katagiri. Right away, she knew what the call was about. Before she could answer, Dan arrived and she handed him the phone.

We could hear the muffled tones of his voice. Tension rose. A couple of minutes later, he was standing in the aisle behind me. He announced that Shunryu Suzuki had died that morning during the first period of the Rohatsu sesshin at the City Center. Dan returned to his cushion. Katagiri and shuso Bill Kwong, facing out on the altar platform, continued sitting silently. The rest of us did the same amidst intermittent groans and sobbing.

Later that morning, I stood up from sitting and walked out of the zendo. I went to my room and lay down on my bed. I thought about the timing of Suzuki's death. Those in sesshin at the City Center and Tassajara continued to sit quietly—except for students working in the kitchen—and me in my cabin. I picked up a paperback, *Never Cry Wolf,* and a few hours later, having read the whole book straight through, returned to my seat in the zendo.

Three feet of snow engulfed the farmhouse on Quadra Island as eleven brave souls persevered still and silent in the cold nighttime air. "And then," Larry said, "we heard some noise from out of the darkness of the wilderness. It kept getting closer and closer. It was this big Timberjack—a logging truck with four independently driven wheels about eight feet in diameter—it's for getting logs out of the bush, a vehicle that can get through that snow. There was a guy on this thing with this big bright light shining at our door and this voice came out of the darkness and said, 'Is a Hindu there?'"

Yvonne at the City Center had called Larry's wife Laurie, who'd gotten through to an old logger who had the only phone within miles. He sent his son who was told to find some Buddhists meditating at the Stroberg Lake farmhouse. He knew there was a guy named Larry, and a guy named Silas, who somehow became the Hindu. The son told them Suzuki Roshi had passed away. He didn't actually say Suzuki Roshi, but they knew what he meant. Silas rode back with him to his father's place to call the Zen Center. A couple hours later, the Timberjack brought Silas back. As it slowly turned around and rumbled off into the night, they continued sitting, sitting with each other and those at the City Center and Tassajara. On the eighth day, they couldn't leave, so they kept sitting until late in the afternoon when a snowplow pushed through and their sesshin was over.

At Tassajara, Katagiri led us sitting all night long the final night. Dan and I sat next to each other as the officers sat together. During that all-night sitting, I could feel the two of us lifting beyond the thought stream and mundane concerns, forgetting everything including the life and death of our beloved teacher.

Hauled Off

After Suzuki died, his ordained disciples moved his body to the dokusan and meeting room that adjoined the Suzuki's apartment in the building. They offered incense and chanted the Heart Sutra in Japanese and English. Then, the one hundred and fifteen students in the sesshin came one-by-one and offered incense. Others who'd gotten word came from outside and paid their respects. In the late afternoon, Suzuki's disciples carried his body down to the street, placed it inside the waiting Japanese funeral home vehicle, and bowed as it was driven off to be embalmed and prepared for the funeral. Richard explained that it was being handled in a way that Mitsu and the Japanese congregation at Sokoji were used to, were comfortable with.

I wasn't pleased to hear about the way his body had been taken away so soon. There were various cultures, including in parts of America, with traditions of sitting with someone's body for some time after they died. This is done in the Jewish tradition, which holds that the spirit remains with the body for a few days. That practice can be found in Japan and all over Asia, all over the world. When the great yogi Yogananda died, his body was kept untreated in state for forty days at Forest Lawn in L.A. Years before, Dianne had gone to be with her dying father and stayed with him until she could feel his spirit depart. There were people who knew how to prepare bodies for lying in state—cleaning and plugging the orifices so they wouldn't drain. Yvonne had mentioned this practice to me.

I assumed Richard didn't think all that mattered. He indicated to me he didn't believe in life after death. I told him I was incapable of not believing in life after death, and reincarnation as well, that my father said the same thing I'd later hear from Suzuki, that nothing dies. And my mother believed in reincarnation. "That's the best reason," Richard said.

Zen students were divided on this issue. I'd hear that Buddhism didn't believe in soul or spirit so there was nothing to pass on. I'd respond, that was true and on that level Buddhism didn't believe in a body, either. No eyes, no ears, no nose, no tongue, no body, no mind. "Anyway," I'd add, "what passes on is karma."

I really wasn't all that disturbed about Suzuki's body being carted off so quickly, though, because I knew one thing for sure, and that was that Suzuki would not have been concerned, was fine in whatever state or non-state he transitioned into.

The Funeral

Eight days after Shunryu Suzuki died, there was only one person at Tassajara. Every road-worthy Tassajara vehicle had left for Suzuki's funeral to be held at 2 p.m. at the City Center.

Bob Halpern had been living in Boulder where Trungpa had set his roots. Bob flew out and visited with Suzuki a month before on Trungpa's behalf. Now he was back with Trungpa for the funeral. He and I stood in a corner of the front hall speaking little while watching people arrive. Big Phillip with a rakusu but not robes. Hadn't seen him in a few years. The three loyal women who'd met Suzuki the first week he'd come—Jean Ross from Carmel, Betty Warren from Sausalito, and Della Goertz who'd moved next door. A dizzying flow of dharma siblings and friends.

The densho bell downstairs was starting to toll in tandem with the taiko drum—long spaces between their mournful deep echoing sounds. I went to sit with the ordained disciples.

What was once Shunryu Suzuki was in a casket in the Buddha Hall patiently waiting for the ceremony to begin. I'd already peeked inside. He, not really he anymore, looked presentable.

A section of the Buddha Hall had chairs for the many Japanese Americans from Sokoji. Otohiro, Suzuki's youngest offspring, sat with his wife, Mitsuyo, and year old son, Kazuto.

Trungpa arrived early with Sam Bercholz and sat down next to Robert Beck. Robert didn't know who Trungpa was, but found him fascinating to talk with, and noted the distinctiveness of his khaki outfit which had the look of a sort of British military uniform. There were other priests arriving in different styles and colors of robes, older students, newer students, former students, poets, artists, scholars, neighbors, some whom I knew as Tassajara guests.

The Buddha Hall was packed. Those from Sokoji's congregation were in chairs, many students on zafus. Overflow crowded the front hall, courtyard, and dining room. The ceremony was led by Rempo Niwa, in red robes and a fancy headpiece. Niwa was Suzuki's venerable teacher Kishizawa Ian's dharma heir and director of Eiheiji Betsuin in Tokyo. Assisting him were Dainin Katagiri, whom I'd never seen in fancy ceremonial robes, and Sokoji's new abbot, Daigyo Moriyama.

A good deal of the ceremony was in Japanese, mostly by Rempo Niwa, which allowed for a meditative state to surround those who didn't understand. We were told that Suzuki had been bestowed a high rank by Shinso Iwamoto, primate of the Soto Zen school. There was a lot of chanting—the mantric Daihishin Dharani evoking Avalokiteshvara and compassion which we recited at Tassajara, the Sandokai and the Heart Sutra twice each. Yvonne read condolences from afar, including from Weatherhill, the First Zen Institute, Eido Shimano, Phillip Kapleau, and Huston and Kendra Smith.

Richard and Hoitsu Suzuki offered incense for all of Suzuki's disciples and students. Then Richard spoke briefly. I'd only heard him give lectures a few times, and I was impressed with how well he expressed himself.

> Suzuki Roshi brought us Buddha, himself, and an understanding of Buddha which included us. He brought us Dharma, such a thorough understanding and living of the teaching that grasses, trees, flowers, tables did actually teach us. He brought us Sangha, the traditional ancient Buddhist community, giving us a full sense of how to live through Buddhist tradition, to learn from his own Japanese culture, and to include our own culture through which Buddhism must find its expression.

Niwa and then others walked by Suzuki's open coffin to pay their respects. There was a little subdued sobbing, but so far, the ceremony had been fairly quiet and somber. Trungpa approached the coffin and stood there for a moment weeping. Then, he let out a grieving howl and flung a white Tibetan scarf over the casket. It slipped down. Heaving in agony, he picked it up and laid it like a ribbon over the casket and Suzuki's corpse. Mitsu, who'd been composed up till then broke into tears. As people began to offer incense and walk by the casket, she went upstairs and returned with Suzuki's favorite walking stick, took Trungpa aside in a small room off the hall, and presented it to him.

The funeral was over. Beverages and sweets were served in the dining room. The somberness of the occasion gave way to mingling, socializing. Dianne was talking to Bill Wenner. I said hello to Fred Streng. Trungpa came over. I introduced them to each other. Trungpa lit up and said, "I read your book on emptiness Dr. Streng, and I found it very full." Trungpa said they were going to create a Buddhist university in Boulder and added that he hoped Streng would come there and teach.

Cremation

Suzuki's body was returned to the funeral home. Students went there to continue sitting by his remains. Trungpa was with him there earlier that day, meditating and chanting, making special mudras with his hands.

In the morning of the following day, Suzuki's casket entered the flames of cremation as disciples and students wailed and sobbed, unrestrained by the solemnity and presence of myriad guests at the funeral. The manager of the funeral home said he'd never seen so many people paying so much respect to a departed loved one.

I went back to bed after morning service and came downstairs to learn the cremation was over. I was miffed I hadn't been told about it. I was mad at myself for not being alert enough to know.

I would have been sad anyway, but now, I was both sad and disappointed. So was Dianne.

We went to the courtyard and sat quietly on a bench by a rock garden niche in a corner. "Suzuki Roshi did this," she said after a while. "He wanted to work on it more but ... I guess he'd always have wanted to work on it more. Like he said, 'A garden is never finished.'"

Once again, to be continued ...

NOTES

From *Monterey Temple* in chapter 1—MacDonough was John's teacher before John went to the Bishop's lair at Zenshuji in LA and was given the seductive Diamond Koan.—refers to a story from the first Tassajara Stories book.

The quotes from Barry's journal in Mind Trouble, chapter 3, are excerpted from *Deep Fool* by Barry Eisenberg.

For names of people in Group photo made after Mel Weitsman's shuso ceremony, chapter 5, Seven Days, go to cuke.com/ts/images. All images will be presented larger and in better resolution there.

ACKNOWLEDGMENTS

All three *Tassajara Stories* books were written and gone over with others as one long work. Thus, I borrow heavily from the acknowledgments in the first book.

Nine bows to my Cuke Archives colleagues Peter Ford and Wendy Pirsig for all the time and effort spent in meticulously going over the text of Tassajara Stories with me for I forget how many months and going over it again for errata right before I sent it in to Monkfish. Thanks to Rick Levine and Neil Rubenking for their errata searches. Bows to Peter Ford for managing Cuke Archives so industriously which has freed me up to concentrate on getting Tassajara Stories out the door and for assisting tirelessly in various tasks that had to be done to bring the book to completion. Bows to my retired agent and co-conspirator Michael Katz for his on-going advice, support, and encouragement without which there would likely never have been any books or websites, audiobooks, or podcasts. Endless gratitude to my wife Katrinka McKay for her constant support and feedback and for the more than twenty years of love, stability, and sobriety she has brought into my life. Thanks to John Liles for excellent proofreading.

Tassajara Stories reflects material and memories derived from my own experience, and countless interviews, podcasts, conversations, letters, emails, outside sources such as books and articles, social media exchanges, work that has been going on since the 1980s.

The Wind Bell publications of the San Francisco Zen Center going back to 1961 were a great help (they're all on cuke.com).

Thanks to Jeanne DiPrima for sending the two poems by her late mother, Diane di Prima, to include in this book.

A special thanks to Paul Cohen and Jon Sweeney of Monkfish for publishing Tassajara Stories and to Jon Sweeney, the book's editor, for his excellent suggestions and guidance.

A deep bow to all those who have hit the donate button on cuke.com and shunryusuzuki.com and supported Cuke Archives of which Tassajara Stories is a major project. Great thanks to the Pacific Zen Institute and The Institute for Historical Study for being our fiscal sponsors. Without our generous contributors, this book would still be just an idea.

Shunryu Suzuki with Tassajara's one time rice harvest.

David Chadwick died in early 2026, just after finishing this book in manuscript. At the age of 21, in 1966, he first rang the bell of Sokoji, a Soto Zen temple and the original home of the San Francisco Zen Center. Thus began his serious study under Shunryu Suzuki Roshi. Ordained a Zen priest in 1971, he later wrote Suzuki's biography, *Crooked Cucumber*, as well as *Thank You and OK!: An American Zen Failure in Japan*, and *Tassajara Stories*, the first book in this series. Chadwick was the primary preserver of the legacy of Shunryu Suzuki and those whose paths crossed his. See cuke.com and shunryusuzuki.com for more information.

www.ingramcontent.com/pod-product-compliance
Lightning Source LLC
Jackson TN
JSHW031153160726
104925JS00002BA/2
* 9 7 8 1 9 6 6 6 0 8 4 5 5 *